PERFORMANCE, THEATRICALITY, AND THE US PRESIDENCY

'Men are not led by being told what they don't know. Persuasion is a force, but not information; and persuasion is accomplished by creeping into the confidence of those you would lead. Their confidence is gained by qualities which they can recognize, by arguments which they can assimilate: by the things which find easy entrance into their minds and are easily transmitted to the palms of their hands or to the ends of their walking-sticks in the shape of applause. Burke's thoughts penetrate the mind and possess the heart of the quiet student; his style of saying things fills the attention as if it were finest music; but they are not thoughts to be shouted over; it is not a style to ravish the ear of the voter at the hustings. If you would be a leader of men, you must lead your own generation, not the next. Your playing must be good now, while the play is on the boards and the audience in the seats: it will not get you the repute of a great actor to have excellences discovered in you afterwards.'

Woodrow Wilson, 'Leaders of Men', commencement address at the University of Tennessee, 1890

PERFORMANCE, THEATRICALITY, AND THE US PRESIDENCY

THE CURRENCY OF DISTRUST

Julia Peetz

EDINBURGH
University Press

Edinburgh University Press is one of the leading university presses in the UK. We publish academic books and journals in our selected subject areas across the humanities and social sciences, combining cutting-edge scholarship with high editorial and production values to produce academic works of lasting importance. For more information visit our website: edinburghuniversitypress.com

Edinburgh University Press Ltd,
13 Infirmary Street, Edinburgh, EH1 1LT

First published in hardback by Edinburgh University Press 2023

Typeset in 10/12.5 Adobe Sabon by IDSUK
(DataConnection) Ltd

A CIP record for this book is available from the British Library

ISBN 978 1 3995 0998 5 (hardback)
ISBN 978 1 3995 0999 2 (paperback)
ISBN 978 1 3995 1000 4 (webready PDF)
ISBN 978 1 3995 1001 1 (epub)

CONTENTS

ACKNOWLEDGEMENTS

More than a few times during the process of preparing this book for publication I recalled that Adam Alston told me he didn't need a print-out of my PhD thesis and that he'd wait for a copy of the book. For this reason and for his unwavering support as my PhD supervisor he is at least partially to blame for this, though all mistakes and shortcomings are my own. This book would not be what it is without ongoing advice, at various stages, from Simon Usherwood, Silvija Jestrovic, and Patrick Duggan. Thank you to Ersev Ersoy and Sarah Foyle at Edinburgh University Press for supporting this book as well as to the anonymous reviewer for their detailed and thoughtful feedback.

I am grateful for the financial support of the University of Surrey, the University of Warwick, and the Leverhulme Trust, who made this project financially viable, as well as to the Standing Conference of University Drama Departments' Glynne Wickham Scholarship and a travel grant from the Northeast Modern Language Association, which supported the research conducted in the United States.

This book has also benefited from the generosity of my colleagues at the University of Warwick. I am grateful to all of them and especially want to thank Nadine Holdsworth and Yvette Hutchison for their advice on the book publication process and Michael Saward for his encouragement and support.

Thank you to everyone who offered their input and support during the early stages of this work at the University of Surrey, particularly Rachel Hann, Andy Lavender, Laura Cull, Matthew Wagner, Dawn Duke, Christian Gilliam, Alex Harden, Sam Chase, Will Mace, David Southgate, and Jing Wang. Special thanks to Amelia Hadfield for reviving the Department of Politics' Asako Okukubo Prize for Excellence in PhD Research and awarding it to this work. Nicholas Ridout and Rachel Brooks offered invaluable feedback on my PhD thesis, which has helped me to turn it into this book. I am indebted to a number of colleagues, editors, and working groups for engaging with this work and making it better, especially the Theatre and Performance Research Association's Performance, Identity, and Community working group and the Political Studies Association's Media & Politics and Rhetoric, Discourse & Politics groups as well as Shirin M. Rai, Milija Gluhovic, Alan Read, Tony Fisher, Chris Megson, Sophie Nield,

Pedro de Senna, James Hudson, Maggie Inchley, Philippa Burt, James Martin, Andrew Quick, Richard Rushton, Annemie Halsema, Katja Kwastek, and Roel van den Oever.

I wish to express my gratitude to all of the speechwriters I interviewed for this book for their time, insight, and generosity, though they must remain anonymous. Heartfelt thanks also to the students of my Politics and Performance module at Warwick, whose keen interest in the subject always rekindles my enthusiasm and challenges me to see things from new and different angles. On a personal note, thank you to David, who shares his life with me.

INTRODUCTION: OBAMA'S TEARS

On 6 January 2021, the United States Capitol was stormed by groups of far-right protestors contesting the legitimacy of Joe Biden's 2020 presidential election victory. Among the rioting groups were anti-government militias, white supremacists, and followers of QAnon, who believed that members of the Democratic Party were satanists engaged in the sex-trafficking of children. The storming of the Capitol forced lawmakers, who had been in the process of certifying the election results, to be evacuated from the House and Senate Chambers and to hide for hours in offices and safe rooms. The riot resulted in five deaths. Though the Capitol was eventually cleared of protestors, and Biden's victory confirmed later that evening, this was the first time that the seat of the legislative branch of the US federal government had been overtaken since the British invasion and the 'Burning of Washington' in 1814, which had also been the only time in US history that a foreign power occupied the nation's capital. President Donald Trump had for months insisted that the election held on 3 November 2020 had been stolen from him. Despite the decisive result that ultimately pitted 306 electoral votes for Biden against Trump's 232, at the time of writing, Trump has acknowledged only the need for an orderly transition of power, not his loss of the election. Encouraged by Trump's performances of anger and indignation at the supposedly stolen election, the rioters at the Capitol were convinced of the righteousness of their actions and seemingly unshakeable in the belief that American democracy had been fatally compromised and that their legislature could not be trusted. As such, the events of 6 January epitomise and brought to a dramatic climax the politics of distrust with which this book is concerned.

Though the chasm between different political views was made powerfully evident in the images of rampaging protestors carrying the lectern of the Speaker of the House of Representatives and waving the Confederate flag in the Capitol, distrust is a familiar and frequently recurring theme in US politics. The historian Richard Hofstadter's classic essay 'The Paranoid Style in American Politics' ([1964] 2008) diagnosed distrust of the political establishment as a strong recurring tendency in American political life. Others have gone so far as to view antipolitical individualism as an innately American founding ideal, linked to the initial – and wildly inaccurate – perception of America as an 'empty' continent with such bountiful resources ripe for exploitation by European settlers that the need for structured political intervention in people's lives is obviated (Jaffe 1997). The popular appeal of the trope of the valiant and beleaguered outsider fighting against the powerful and corrupt political establishment had also been evident far earlier than the presidency of Donald Trump. It is the theme of Frank Capra's 1939 Hollywood classic *Mr. Smith Goes to Washington*, starring Jimmy Stewart as the eponymous Mr. Smith. In 1992, the businessman Ross Perot, a notable predecessor to Trumpism,[1] seemed for a time to be leading the three-way presidential race against Bill Clinton and President George H. W. Bush that would end with Clinton, who as Governor of Arkansas was himself something of a Washington outsider, being elected president. But whereas a generalised and diffuse suspicion of authority may be a perennial human and/or American tendency, conspiracy culture in the United States, as a 'default suspicion towards the authorities', gained particular, widespread currency over the course of the second half of the twentieth century, stimulated by the rise of the security state after the Second World War (the CIA was established in 1947) and by landmark events in twentieth-century political history like the Kennedy assassination and the Watergate scandal (Knight 2000). As the main theme of hit TV shows like Fox's *The X-Files* (1993–2002, revivals in 2008, 2016, and 2018), conspiracy thinking and distrust of the government morphed from the niche preoccupation described in Hofstadter's 'Paranoid Style' essay to become a more pervasive part of US culture during the 1990s.

According to the Pew Research Center, trust in the government has been at historic lows since Watergate (2015; see also 'Congress and the Public', n.d.). Trust can be defined as 'an individual's judgment that another person, whether acting as an individual, a member of a group, or within an institutional role, is both motivated and competent to act in the individual's interests and will do so without overseeing or monitoring' (Warren 2018, 75), and political trust more specifically as 'confidence in institutions such as the executive, the legislature, the judiciary, the bureaucracy, and the police' (Uslaner 2018, 4). Responding to declining levels of political trust internationally and in the United States in particular, there has been significant growth of research into political trust as an area of the larger field of political behaviour in recent years (Listhaug and

Jakobsen 2018, 573). Political trust is generally seen to be higher in the civil service and other supposedly 'neutral' institutions like the courts (though in the United States appointments to the Supreme Court and to a lesser extent other judgeships are increasingly politicised and thus struggle to be perceived as legitimate based on their supposed neutrality) than in elected institutions like parliaments, cabinets, and parties (Newton, Stolle, and Zmerli 2018, 40). Political trust is positively associated with voter turnout. Political distrust or a lack of trust is seen to depress turnout as well as to drive anti-incumbent and populist voting (Hooghe 2018, 617–18). In the United States, low levels of political trust are complicated by the fact that 'the American public is currently experiencing a state of affective polarisation in which Republicans and Democrats dislike each other to an unprecedented degree' (Hetherington and Rudolph 2018, 579), such that political trust and distrust are polarised along partisan lines. The *World Happiness Report* for 2018 identifies perceptions of the rise of corruption in government and business and waning trust in government as among the causes of falling happiness in the United States, despite rising GDP per capita (Sachs 2018, 147–8), whilst Marc J. Hetherington (2005) and Hetherington and Thomas J. Rudolph (2015) link polarised political trust to the increasingly sluggish American legislature and the decline of compromise in Washington politics.

The emphasis on the lack of political trust as a particular problem plaguing US democracy within the above literature suggests not only that there is *not enough* trust in the government but that there is a particular currency of *dis*trust in US politics. While a vast literature on trust and its centrality in sustaining democratic institutions exists, distrust has received comparatively less attention. Though there is a great deal of conceptual overlap between political trust or the lack thereof and political distrust, distrust is more than just the absence of trust. If political trust anticipates positive outcomes and a lack of trust indicates neutrality or uncertainty about the trustworthiness of government institutions and/or particular politicians, then distrust is distinguishable from both in that it evaluates the political system and/or its functionaries in distinctly negative ways and anticipates 'harmful outcomes' (Bertsou 2019, 220). In line with this thinking, Eri Bertsou defines political distrust as 'a relational attitude that reflects perceptions of untrustworthiness specific to the political system in its entirety or its components' and distinguishes between 'liberal distrust', which is reasonable and necessary as it justifies the establishment of institutional checks and balances on power, and political distrust, which indicates that existing institutions are 'inadequate and malfunctioning' or are at least perceived as such (220, 216). Political distrust is particularly pervasive where electorates are polarised and where communities are divided over particular social issues, and it is self-reinforcing but, unlike political trust, not self-disconfirming because distrust itself impedes cooperation, positive interactions, and ultimately the political process itself (224).

The 'currency of distrust' in this book's title should be understood both in the sense that distrust is currently a defining feature of the relationship between US politicians and their constituents and in the sense that distrust is being explicitly negotiated, mobilised, and used in politicians' public performances as they appeal to diverse audiences. This book asks how trust and distrust are linked to performance, not just in the case of Trump's populism but as structural features inherent in a representative system that relies on politicians' public performances and audiences' suspension of disbelief – a term I will engage with in depth in Chapter 1. This question ties in to more general ones about what role performance plays and what function it has in US presidential politics and in representative democracy more broadly conceived. What capacity do politicians' public performances have to mould people's perceptions of the legitimacy of politicians and government institutions, and how are those perceptions changed as the theatre of politics comes to increasingly revolve around distrust itself? In engaging with these questions, this book considers performance as a constellation of different factors: scripts, embodiment, ideas of selfhood, and historical norms and ideals. The book is interested in what performance does in politics generally and in US presidential politics in particular, but its focus is more on overarching questions about what performance is and how it works than on analysing specific, individual performances, though there are, of course, extended examples of this as well.

Performance, Theatricality, and the US Presidency is a product of theatre and performance studies as much as it is a product of political studies: the research for it was conceived of within a department of theatre and performance studies, and it was undertaken in collaboration with and is therefore deeply indebted to the perspectives of both scholars of politics and scholars of performance. Part of this research is empirical, engaging with the expert perspectives of political speechwriters and speech coaches, whose work it is not only to script but to envision, craft, and in many cases rehearse the public performances of US presidents. Speechwriters are usually not performers themselves; they do, however, have a unique position among politicians' staffers. They are often generalists rather than policy experts, and it is their job not simply to write the words their principals say but to pay attention to the politician as a person and the audiences they are addressing. As such, they are concerned with what makes their principal sound like themselves and with how to convey those of their personal traits deemed most advantageous. Speechwriters also need to think about the hooks that might engage different audiences and they have to consider the setting, tone, and style in which a speech will be delivered. Some speechwriters also function as speech coaches and/or attend and contribute to rehearsal or speech delivery preparation sessions, in which they direct their principal towards more effective delivery. For all of these reasons, the inclusion of interviews with speechwriters in this book should not be interpreted as an argument for the primary of text over performance. Portions of Chapters 2 and 4 in particular draw on these interviews.

Other parts of the book, and most especially Chapters 1 and 3, are much more conceptual and engage with debates around concepts of acting and performance, populism, embodiment, and authenticity. Integrating ideas and concepts from two different disciplines is often significantly harder to do than it is to pay lip service to, and I hope that this book offers useful impulses towards how we might think of performance and politics in a way that goes beyond citing robustly from one discipline whilst paying tribute to the other through engagement with one notable undergraduate textbook. But back to the currency of distrust as it applies to this book . . .

In US presidential politics, with which this book is primarily concerned, the currency of distrust of the contemporary moment has been traced to the candidacy of Jimmy Carter in 1976 (Cannon 1991, 101; Glad 1980, 366; Hess 2002; Strong, n.d.). By January 1975, in the aftermath of the Watergate scandal, trust in government had fallen to just 36 per cent, half the level at which it had been a decade earlier (Pew Research Center 2015, 18). This was a setting in which Carter ran as an outsider to the Washington elite, asking for 'an unusual kind' of trust, one that 'necessitated a leap of faith, a giving of the heart to an unknown stranger' (Glad 1980, 367). Despite Carter's election as an outsider, however, lack of trust in the federal government again rose sharply during his presidency, capping at 70 per cent in March 1980. And despite the fact that trust rose again during the Reagan presidency (as it would to a more limited extent in the later years of the Clinton presidency), public trust in government has never again even come close to a pre-Nixon level and has surpassed the 50 per cent mark only once: in the immediate aftermath of the events of 11 September 2001.

Alongside and to grapple with the persistent low level of public trust in the government, politicians' public performances, particularly in presidential politics, have increasingly come to centre on distrust itself, with politicians presenting themselves as outsiders and infiltrators rather than functionaries of the political establishment. In both the 2008 and the 2016 US presidential elections – the last two presidential elections not to feature an incumbent candidate – a self-styled outsider was elected president. The performances of outsiderness in 2016 (by Trump and, in the Democratic primary, by Sanders) had a notably sharper, more controversial bent to them than those by Barack Obama, John McCain, and even Sarah Palin in 2008. Nevertheless, the trope of resisting against a corrupt political establishment, of being one of the good and rational people working against self-interested Beltway insiders, is pervasive. Note that while such performances take place within an environment of documented low levels of trust in government, they are more performances of distrust than performances of low-level or lacking trust: they are not ambivalent or neutral towards political insiders, instead portraying them as definitely untrustworthy and harmful to those they purport to serve. The pervasiveness of this kind of speech is symptomatic of the extent to which populist rhetoric, which pits the good, rational people against the corrupt and manipulative establishment whilst evoking a sense of crisis and employing eye-catching, media-savvy tactics sometimes described as 'bad manners' (Moffitt 2016), has become a feature of mainstream politics. Its influence can be felt not just in the public appearances of notable populists like Trump, Sanders, and Palin but, as the next section illuminates in more detail, even in politicians known for their unemotional performance styles. As a mainstreamed style of performance, a particular 'zeitgeist' (Mudde 2004), populism complicates how politicians appear in public since its reliance on anti-establishment tropes seeks to shift perceptions of legitimacy by positing performing politicians as authentic and incorruptible outsiders, whilst maligning established institutions and their functionaries. As such, mainstreamed populism offers a way in to one of the key questions this book seeks to address: what is it that politicians' public performances actually do in representative politics and what makes for an effective political performance?

Mainstreamed Populism

Almost exactly five years to the day before protestors stormed the Capitol, on 5 January 2016, then-President Barack Obama gave a speech outlining a series of new executive actions on gun control at the White House. Obama stood at a lectern in the White House's East Room, speaking to an assembled group composed of journalists, survivors of gun violence, and relatives of shooting victims. At the time of this speech, he was entering the last year of his presidency, throughout which his intention to enact stricter gun control legislation had been foiled by the gun lobby. The stated purpose of the 5 January speech was to announce four executive actions, aimed at extending background checks on those purchasing guns, ensuring that mental health records are included in these checks, enforcing existing gun safety laws, and preventing accidental shootings through gun safety technology. Unlike executive orders, however, executive actions are legally non-binding and constitute presidential statements of intent, a detail that was largely ignored in the media coverage of Obama's speech (Farley 2016; Murse 2016). Even more than to outline new legal measures, the speech was designed to make an impassioned plea for the American public to hold gun lobbyists accountable. 'So the gun lobby may be holding Congress hostage right now', Obama said, evoking a corrupt political establishment, 'but they cannot hold America hostage'. As Obama made reference to Congress in his January speech, he left no doubt that though, as president, he might be expected to be able to exert influence on the US legislature even in spite of the fact that it had been controlled by the Republican Party intent on blocking Democratic legislation for much of his presidency, this was not actually the case. Instead, he stressed that Congress as a whole was out of line with the thinking of 'the majority of Americans' and that this was the case because 'the gun lobby may be holding Congress hostage right now'. As a consequence, Obama exhorted that 'all of us [that is, the majority of Americans] need to demand a Congress brave enough to stand up to the gun lobby's lies', thus positioning himself as a concerned outsider who sides with 'the vast majority of Americans' against a corrupt political system in need of reform.

Obama's outsider positioning in this speech exemplifies the pervasiveness of certain aspects of the populist style in US politicians' public performances. However, the speech was memorable not just as one of many examples of anti-establishment discourse emanating from the centre of political power. In the media coverage this speech attracted, the fact that Obama, whose rhetorical style more typically tended towards the professorial and matter-of-fact, shed tears as he discussed the shooting of first-graders at Sandy Hook Elementary in Newtown, Connecticut on 14 December 2012 took centre stage. How pundits interpreted Obama's tears in their coverage of the speech was largely indicative of where on the political spectrum they were situated, with left-leaning and centre-left commentators praising the speech's emotional openness (Blake 2016; Cillizza 2016; Rhodan 2016), while right-wing pundits sought to debunk the speech as 'bad political theatre' and the tears as part of a planned performance, possibly even the result of Obama having rubbed raw onion on his face before taking the stage ('Andrea Tantaros' 2016). But aside from being an obvious indicator of the level of political polarisation in American political news coverage, the extent to which the tears – and by extension Obama's emotional state, his level of sincerity, and his entire public persona – were open to interpretation highlights with particular clarity the issues of trust, distrust, and the suspension of disbelief involved in the theatre of politics more broadly. Since this book is concerned not just with (dis)trust and populism as contemporary phenomena but with theorising and evidencing the extent to which representative politics relies on public performance, the next section will focus quite literally on Obama's tears to outline how we might think of performance and theatricality in the realm of politics and why the potential for distrust is ever-present in, and ineradicable from, a representative system that works through performance and its reception.

On the basis of a long, professionalised tradition of how US presidents perform in public, we assume that what is required of a politician's public performances shifts once they are elected to the highest office. For the political sociologist Jeffrey Alexander, for instance, political candidates' '[s]uccess in a campaign depends on making the civil sphere's binary language walk and talk' such that, through the successful deployment of a reductively binary discourse that vilifies opponents whilst exalting the candidate's own side, and in spite of attempts by political opponents and the media to destabilise a politician's performed persona, the winning presidential candidate is elevated into 'a collective representation – a symbolic vessel filled with what citizens hold most dear' (2010, 11, 18). Upon being elected president, however, a former candidate has to do the reconciliatory work of disavowing their own partisanship even whilst continuing to make the binaries work for themselves, in effect appearing 'to wash partisanship from [their] body' (270). In Alexander's view, this was accomplished in Obama's case when, '[a]fter a bruising and heated electoral struggle, Obama called for the restoration of solidarity' in his victory speech at Grant Park in Chicago on 4 November 2008 (268), where the president-elect famously spoke of 'Americans who sent a message to the world that we have never been a collection of Red States and Blue States: we are, and always will be, the United States of America' (qtd in Alexander 2010, 268). In other words, winning a presidential election is seen to shift the emphasis of a newly elected president's public performances away from stressing partisan differences and towards the evocation of a sense of unity.

The notion of different 'grammars', or sets of structural features, of politics and performance, as introduced by Shirin M. Rai and Janelle Reinelt (2015b), is a helpful one here. In the most general of terms, we might distinguish between sovereign and critical grammars of politics and performance (Saward 2015). Critical grammars emphasise the personal authenticity of the speaker, the particularity of them and their causes as well as their dissension from the reigning authority or at least the opposing party. Dissidents, protestors, but also candidates hoping to get elected make use of critical grammars in their public performances. Sovereign grammars, on the other hand, aim to create a generalising sense of unity out of diversity and to speak to a broad mass of citizens in order to 'constitute an audience out of citizen subjects-objects' (Saward 2015, 219). If Alexander's argument were applied to this distinction, then one might say presidential candidates attempt to distinguish themselves in performances that make use of critical grammars even whilst they attempt to speak to a broad subsection of Americans. Performances by US presidents, particularly those that follow election campaigns which themselves emphasise and exacerbate society divisions, are paradigmatic examples of sovereign grammars, as the US president is the only person elected to represent the entirety of the American people.

The rhetoric of Obama's 2016 White House speech on gun control, however, mobilises critical grammars much more than sovereign ones, demonstrating the usefulness of performing binary divisions outside of election campaigns. Likewise, the image of the president shedding tears in front of a group of journalists and television cameras presents a startling contrast to the soaring rhetoric of the Grant Park victory speech. Obama's speech not only does not emphasise the president's 'heroic might' (Alexander 2010, 272); it makes explicit his powerlessness in the face of Washington's powerful gun lobbyists, who, Obama claims, 'hold America hostage'. Far from offering a straightforward message of unity, the 5 January speech constructs a binary division between the 'majority of the American people', including the president, and the Washington establishment, composed of Congress and the gun lobby. This division is strikingly underscored by Obama's tears, emphasising the speech's evocation of a sense of crisis that speaks to the corruptness and ineffectiveness of Beltway politics.

At first glance, Obama's expression of powerlessness simply matches the mood of the moment at which this speech was performed, late in the second term of his presidency, and might be seen as broadly reflective of Obama's perceived effectiveness as president: Gallup's continuous Obama Job Approval Poll shows that Obama started his presidential career with 69 per cent of Americans approving of him versus only 12 per cent who disapproved. In January 2016, the figures had roughly equalised, with 47 per cent of Americans approving of Obama's job performance on 4 January 2016, and 48 per cent disapproving ('Gallup Daily', n.d.). A LexisNexis News search for the phrase 'Obama is a failed president' performed on 29 September 2016 returned 262 results, including one for a debate on whether Obama is a failed president organised by the London-based debating forum Intelligence Squared for 20 June 2016 that was also scheduled to be broadcast on BBC World (Intelligence Squared 2016). These figures reflect Obama's fall in the public perception from an inspiring election victory to a more ambiguous record of accomplishments during a presidency whose agenda was hindered by an almost perpetually deadlocked Congress.[2]

However, the speech functions more shrewdly as an attempt to garner legitimacy through a demonstration of resistance in the face of corruption. Obama's reference to partisan battles within the political class characterises Congress as unable to adequately represent the American people by asserting that politicians are much more polarised on the issue of gun control than the electorate, among whom he asserts there exists a 'general consensus'. The binary here set up further pits the majority of the American people against the political establishment by asserting that its partisan squabbles ignore and run counter to the people's interests. In the picture Obama paints, the 'vast majority of Americans' are right to be suspicious of political functionaries who are supposed to represent them but are preoccupied with their own partisan battles, in which they are influenced by lobbyists who make an illegitimate oligarchy out of a system that is meant to be democratic. Flattery is a classic tool of political rhetoric, painting audiences as 'rational, honest, independent, and capable of decisions that are wise' (Alexander 2010, 91), as Obama does here. Appealing to the audience's wisdom also saves the speech from sounding too pessimistic. As Robert Lehrman, a former speechwriter for Vice President Al Gore, observes in his *Political Speechwriter's Companion*, in the United States audiences' sense of what makes for an acceptable political speech has traditionally imposed 'sharp limits on the complexity of political debate'; among the most stringent limits Lehrman identifies are the need to project a sense of upbeat optimism and an outlook towards an eventual happy ending even in the midst of crisis (2010, 11). Here, the flattering address to the audience underscores the central binary division on which the speech relies, that between 'the people' and the political establishment. By asserting that he is one of these virtuous and wise people, and therefore not part of the corrupt, polarised, irrational establishment, Obama turns his confession of powerlessness into a subtle show of strength that consists in resisting the pull of the broken system and siding with the supposedly rational majority instead.

The speech's use of anti-establishment sentiment also serves to construct the president as an authentic and trustworthy leader not swayed by illegitimate exertions of power. His remark 'I'm not on the ballot again. I'm not looking to score some points' stresses the relative freedom of expression provided by this late stage of Obama's presidency and thus recuperates, or at least approximates, something of the outsider status Obama claimed for himself in his first election campaign. In the launch announcement for that campaign he had memorably proclaimed, 'I know that I haven't spent a lot of time learning the ways of Washington. But I've been there long enough to know that the ways of Washington must change' (2007). That announcement was made after Obama was pointedly advised by both Harry Reid, then Senate Majority Leader, and former Senate Minority Leader Tom Daschle that, as a first-term senator, he could still run for president as something of an outsider to the Washington establishment (Heilemann and Halperin 2010, 33–4, 70).

Obama's reliance on binary anti-establishment rhetoric, and the 5 January speech's evocation of a sense of crisis, and even, to a lesser degree, the uncharacteristic emotionality displayed are elements of the populist style of political performance (Moffitt 2016).[3] That a sitting president other than Donald Trump was deploying elements of this style in 2016 illustrates the degree to which this style has become a feature of mainstream politics in the United States,[4] such that the style has not only lost a lot of its transgressiveness but has become an unremarkable, even expected, element of politicians' performances and their attempts to garner legitimacy. It is important to note here that considering populism as a style of performance makes it possible to discuss how different public speakers incorporate some populist elements into their public performances but not others or not to the same degree or intensity as another speaker. That is, populism regarded as a performance style is gradational rather than binary (Moffitt 2020, 26). The point in mentioning Obama and Trump in a single paragraph is not to suggest that Obama was 'just as much' of a populist as Trump, nor that Obama's populism had the same effects as Trump's – to assert this would be absurd. The aim here is to use a less than immediately obvious example of a speech incorporating elements of the populist style to suggest how commonplace elements of this style have become in American political discourse. This book builds on a wealth of populism scholarship (Arditi 2007; Laclau 2005a, 2005b; Moffitt 2016; Mudde 2004; Sorensen 2021) that has established populist discourse as a feature of the mainstream politics in Western democracies. The following paragraphs explain how performances that make use of elements of the populist style function in US presidential politics by looking at the connection between political distrust and the elevation of politicians who style themselves, paradoxically, as outsiders to the institutional and governmental system within which they work and to which they seek election.

Michael Saward's theory of the representative claim posits that representation is both performed (as in a speech given for an audience) and performative, in that a claim to represent someone constitutes, or evokes, the represented 'in the sense of portraying them or framing them in particular, contestable ways' (2006, 301–2). Having assigned certain characteristics to their constituents, representative claim-makers then 'argue or imply that they are the best representatives of the constituency so *understood*' (302, emphasis in original). Audiences who are at the receiving end of a representative claim are then in a position to accept the claim or reject it. Acceptance implies that the audience give credence to both the image of themselves and the image of the claim-maker evoked through the representative claim. Of fundamental importance here is that the claim to represent does not merely describe or reflect an existing audience's or constituency's character and the persona of the claim-maker; instead, the claim is involved in the construction of a shared, but contestable, social reality through which both audience and claim-maker come to be defined in specific ways.

In Obama's case, the audience is framed, fairly conventionally, as rational, level-headed, and capable of reasoned consensus. Secondly, and more intriguingly, the audience Obama's speech evokes is one which is rightly sceptical of its political leaders, fed up with the power struggles at the centre of American politics that do not concern it, and cognisant of the undemocratic and conspiratorial influence of the gun lobby. Obama then presents himself as an outsider to this corrupt sphere of influence and, by implication, an ideal representative of the people as he has evoked them – all this despite the fact that, as president, Obama would quite naturally be perceived as standing at the top of the very political system outside of which he claims to stand. In other words, Obama is mobilising distrust of politicians and political institutions among the electorate and making use of it in his speech on gun control. Insofar as Obama is presenting himself as someone who, however paradoxically, can present an alternative to the norm in US politics, his speech appeals to audiences by evoking a sense of authenticity, which, here, consists of the at least partial disavowal of being an institutional functionary and the presentation of himself as a frustrated outsider.

Obama's self-presentation, his characterisation of the audience, and the particular sense of authenticity which the speech seeks to evoke all relate to the speech's generation of legitimacy. While legitimacy might elsewhere be seen simply as a matter of normative or legal definition, this book considers legitimacy, or legitimation, as a complex process to explore tensions that exist between its objective and subjective dimensions. Though legitimacy might be most readily thought of as a set of established democratic norms and formal legal procedures that authorise the use of state power, Max Weber stressed that compliance with these norms and procedures nevertheless rests on the widespread 'belief in legality', meaning that those who are part of a social order accept its legal norms as binding and regard the enforcement of those norms as acceptable (1978, 37). Weber's ideas have been developed further by numerous scholars; Michael Saward's (2010) thinking around democratic legitimacy and especially Elisabeth Anker's (2014) concept of felt legitimacy and Judith Butler's (1997) theorisation of shifting legitimacy will be particularly central to this book.

Focusing on the performative generation of perceptions of legitimacy, as all of these scholars do, highlights the importance of the processual, subjective, and continually contested aspects of legitimacy. For instance, Anker argues that, despite the fact that they were never subjected to established legitimation procedures, many of the George W. Bush administration's War on Terror actions were able to garner 'vast popular legitimacy' because the War on Terror rhetoric used by Bush administration officials exerted a significant affective impact on a large part of the American electorate (2014, 110–11). Here, legitimation procedures were absent and norms of legitimacy broken, thus objectively these policies might be seen not to be legitimate at all; nevertheless, they were framed and communicated in ways that meant they were widely perceived to be legitimate, which shows the capacity of the subjective perception of legitimacy to override more objective evaluations.

Performances of mainstreamed populism, like Obama's 5 January speech, similarly disturb the association of authority and institutionality with legitimacy. Obama's speech seeks to harness legitimacy primarily not by relying on Obama's authority as the President of the United States but by disavowing Obama's entanglement with distrusted institutions and the corrupt political establishment. Legitimacy is linked to the authenticity and clear-sightedness ascribed to the critical outside infiltrator and not, or not just and not primarily, the authority conferred by holding elected office or the experience of working inside institutions. The speech relies more on the speaker's personal authenticity than on their authority. In this, it is indicative of a more broadly perceived, 'almost plangent', and certainly nostalgic hunger for authenticity that has developed in recent decades, despite, or perhaps because of, the fact that reality in the twenty-first century 'incurs not as reality but as it is *performed* (presented) and *perceived*' (Lavender 2016, 22, 24, emphasis in original). Authenticity in politics can be seen as a process that is highly contested rather than a fact (Parry-Giles 2001;

2014, 11) or as dependent on an actor's ability to 'sew the disparate elements of performance back into a seamless and convincing whole' (Alexander 2006, 55). Like much of the contemporary experience of social and political life, politicians' public performances are usually experienced in mediated and mediatised ways. Audiences who receive such performances are likely to at least suspect that, even if they accept a political representative as authentic, this representative's appearance in public life is nevertheless consciously staged and performed. What is seen as authentic in this context is not simply the opposite of the staged and performed but stands in a complex relationship to it.

In the early 2000s, the novelist David Foster Wallace detailed his own desire to believe in then-Republican presidential primary candidate John McCain's authenticity as 'something old and maybe corny but with a weird achy pull to it like a smell from childhood or a name on the tip of your tongue' (2006, 166), suggesting that associations of authenticity have a particularly strong pull in politics. If a politician can convince their audience to perceive them as authentic, then this personal authenticity might become an antidote to the increasingly pervasive lack of trust in and distrust of politicians and political institutions. But, despite professing his own desire to believe in McCain's authenticity, particularly because of McCain's war hero credentials, Wallace never quite managed to do so even after following McCain for a week on the campaign trail. He attests to a 'very modern and American type of ambivalence, a sort of interior war between your deep need to believe and your deep belief that the need to believe is bullshit, that there's nothing left anywhere but sales and salesmen' (226, 229). This ambivalence pinpoints the dilemma that haunts twenty-first-century political culture, where the desire to give in to the 'weird achy pull' to move beyond postmodern nihilism is continually ambushed by a creeping doubt that to believe ultimately results in being exploited for one's naivety. In addition to this, despite all its plangent, nostalgic relevance, a hunger for authenticity in the face of a reality that includes not just the unmediated but also 'the replicated, the staged, the reconstructed, and also, sometimes, the simulated' (Martin 2013, 15) might indeed be indicative of a 'bullshit', misguided search for an absent essence.

While it is a truism in politics and performance scholarship that the evocation of a sense of authenticity plays an important part in a performance's success (see Alexander 2006, 54–7; Alexander 2010, xii, 32; Bleeker 2009, 249, 253; Kugler and Kurt 2000, 154–5; Parry-Giles and Parry-Giles 2002, 11–12; Saward 2015, 223), focusing on authenticity has also been judged to be something of a fool's errand. In his influential lecture series *Sincerity and Authenticity* the literary critic Lionel Trilling argued that, unlike sincerity, the concept of authenticity is built around the illusory essentialist idea that an individual's innermost self can be found beyond 'all the cultural superstructures' imposed on it (1972, 2, 12, 104). More trenchantly, Richard Sennett observes in

The Fall of Public Man, his study of the decline of people's involvement in political life, that the search for the pre-cultured inner essence of a person's character is not just futile but can be dangerous insofar as it erodes people's ability to focus on questions of ideology by replacing a focus on policy issues with a valuing of authenticity through which 'self-disclosure becomes a universal measure of believability and truth' ([1977] 1986, 29–30). At the very least, the evocation in politicians' public performances of a sense of personal authenticity based on professed, if not actual, outsider status chimes with the sense that Western democracies have moved away from voters' strong affiliation with political parties to become 'audience democracies', primarily defined by increasingly personalised and image-based election campaigns and by 'reactive' voting behaviour, wherein voters respond to the terms of electoral choice as defined by candidates rather than actively expressing their identities through the act of voting (Manin 1997, 218–34). In audience democracy, a candidate's personal authenticity is a highly prized and protected commodity.

Performative success rooted in appeals to the performer's own outsiderness, and thus their (assertion of) lack of previous authority rather than their pre-existing authority, is paradoxical insofar as legitimate and institutionally conferred authority is seen to be indispensable in making performative utterances 'felicitous' (Austin 1962; Bourdieu 1991). Yet, as historically low levels of political trust persist, assertions of outsider status and disavowals of previous institutional affiliation are increasingly connected to performances of personal authenticity and to the cultivation of legitimacy. More and more presidents and presidential candidates have deployed elements of the populist style in their public performances in recent years and have done so alongside developments in the media landscape that incentivise more controversial, media-savvy, and less risk-averse performance styles. Since widespread distrust already calls the legitimacy of established institutions into question, this mainstreamed populism works through the performative enactment of a further anti-establishmentarian shift of legitimacy away from the institutions and onto the politician who presents themself as a representative of the people. It threatens to turn legitimacy into a zero-sum game. By discouraging the perception of the political system as a unified whole and by pitting different institutions and political actors against each other, populist-style performances by mainstream politicians ultimately undermine institutional legitimacy even whilst they bolster the perceived authenticity and legitimacy of individuals.

The Theatre of Politics

Whilst populism has been a nearly all-consuming focus in US politics and in politics research during the last few years, and whilst political distrust and populism reached fever pitch in US politics with the election of Donald Trump as president in 2016, the focus of this book is not limited to the contemporary moment. One of the book's central aims is to show that, even though the theatre of politics has come increasingly to revolve around distrust of politicians and political institutions, the potential for distrust inheres ineradicably within a political system that is, at its core, performance-based. If political representation happens through performance, then its functioning relies on the suspension of disbelief of political audiences rather than their more straightforwardly given belief. Suspension of disbelief is quite different from an open-ended investment of belief (Davis 2005; Tomko 2016); it is a term usually applied to fiction: audiences of fictional worlds on stage and screen are generally aware that these worlds do not actually exist, but temporarily proceed as if they did. Suspension of disbelief, then, is a fleeting, willed pause in questioning that allows an audience member to let themself be absorbed, to follow along, and give themself away for a moment, before they resume their sceptical questioning.

Why is suspension of disbelief a more appropriate concept to apply to politicians' public performances than the more straightforward belief in or acceptance of a representative claim? Politicians at the national and, especially, presidential level of politics are usually far removed from their audiences. Personal acquaintance with one's political representatives at these levels is rare, and audiences are often consciously, but at the very least subliminally, aware that politicians' performances are hardly ever unplanned or spontaneous. These performances are carefully curated and present aspects of a politician's persona that they and their team judge to be advantageous. As such, while the public personas of politicians are not exactly fictional, they are quasi-fictional constructions insofar as they are the product of the selective abstraction of characteristics from the real person of the politician for public performance with a particular goal, a kind of ideal self-presentation, in mind. Politicians' performances also strive to constitute social 'realities', rather than reflecting them.

Michael Tomko, in a study about the purpose of literature in human life, observes that people engaging in the willing suspension of disbelief cease 'striving to determine whether the[] sensations [presented to their minds] correspond to external reality' and accept them 'as if they were representative of reality, without, crucially, the concession that they are' (2016, 8). In politics, of course, the stakes for people's real lives are such that they might seek to conclude that some politicians' performances are truly representative of who the politician really is and how the world actually is, and some might hold the passionate conviction that they are, but the point here is that the distance between politicians and audiences and the mediated and goal-oriented nature of their performances means that the door is always open for doubt to creep back in. Politicians' performances, similar to fictions, might thus create a 'split between a part of the self that "believes something which another part of him [sic] disbelieves"' (Tomko 2016, 4, citing Walton 1980, 7). Tomko also argues that to engage in the willing suspension of disbelief in the case of works of art, people need not only to find them plausible but to be excited by them (2016, 4). Kendall L. Walton similarly describes suspension of disbelief as a perceived 'decrease of distance' (1980, 15). The equivalence to this in politics is that it is all too easy for political audiences to dismiss politicians' performances as fake and dissembling; it is much harder, and arguable rarer, for politicians to generate excitement.

Obama's speech on gun control from 5 January 2016, and particularly the tears he shed during this speech, serves to highlight the tensions involved in the reception of politicians' public performances. Towards the end of this speech, about 29 minutes and 30 seconds into its 35 minutes, Obama paused. He blinked repeatedly and wiped the corner of his eye with a finger. His eyes cast down, he continued to pause before he looked up and said, 'Every time I think about those kids, it gets me mad', as tears rolled down his cheeks. 'Those kids' was a reference to the twenty primary school students killed in the mass shooting at Sandy Hook Elementary in Newtown, Connecticut on 14 December 2012. Sandy Hook was one of several examples the president had given during the speech of what the media had dubbed 'an epidemic' of mass shootings in the United States. Obama wiped one of his tears away and said, 'And by the way, it happens on the streets of Chicago every day.' This rhetorical gesture served to connect the Newtown shooting to the city (known for gun violence)[5] in which the president cut his political teeth as a community organiser. Obama wiped a tear from his other cheek. In the video footage of the speech, while the camera remains focused on the president, people in the audience can be heard applauding at this moment. Shortly after this, Obama appears to recover emotionally, though when he ends the speech by forcefully stressing the need for voters to be passionate about the reform of gun laws because 'all of us need to demand a Congress brave enough to stand up to the gun lobby's lies', the footage still shows the president's cheeks glistening with tears.

As noted above, reactions to Obama's tearful speech and answers to the question of whether Obama's tears were real or fake were often indicative of where on the political spectrum a commentator was situated. While this question was thus one of partisanship, on a conceptual level it is a question of believability and of the willingness of a spectator to suspend their disbelief in a performance. In other words, it is because we have to make a judgement call on the believability of Obama's performance in the first place that judgements can diverge widely and along partisan lines.

In discounting a performance, one of the simplest, most well-worn arguments to make is that it is 'only' a performance or 'mere' theatre. This argument is contained, for instance, in Meghan McCain's dismissal of Obama's speech as 'bad political theatre' ('Andrea Tantaros' 2016). As part of a Fox News panel discussion that accused Obama of rubbing raw onion on his eyes, McCain made the argument that Obama's was a 'bad' performance. In McCain's framing of it, Obama's performance was so bad that it revealed its own constructedness, its manipulative reality, its status as mere 'political theatre'. As theatre scholar Sophie Nield observes, this kind of framing 'assumes two discrete spheres – the "real" and the "symbolic", or "theatrical"' (2010, 4). Performance and theatricality are relegated to the side of the symbolic, the assumption being that they are at best artificial and substanceless and at worst manipulative and corrupting. In its entirety, this argument is buttressed by the antitheatrical prejudice – this is the widespread hostility to theatre, manifested, for instance, in the fact that expressions borrowed from the theatre ('putting on an act', for example, or 'making a scene') generally have negative connotations. Jonas Barish's (1981) seminal study of the hostility to theatre in the Western philosophical tradition traces the roots of antitheatricality to Plato's *Republic* ([c. 380 BCE] 1968).

While it is relatively easy to call out 'bad' performances for being constructed and fake, the antitheatrical prejudice is not, of course, restricted to performances easily unmasked as insincere. If we were to concede that Obama's speech, tears and all, was performed *well*, then this raises further questions about the nature of acting and performance. Does a performance reveal an actor's inner life or does it merely represent the outward signs of one, without being bound by an inner substance? Denis Diderot's *Paradox of Acting*, written in 1773 and first published (in French) in 1830, famously argued that an actor's successful performance depends not on feeling the emotions performed but 'upon rendering so exactly the outward signs of feeling, that you fall into the trap' (1883, 16). 'The player's tears', if skilfully performed on cue, therefore, 'come from his brain', not his heart – and for the French philosopher this was true '[i]n tribunals, in assemblies', in the political sphere, as much as on the theatre stage (17, 108). For theatre historian Joseph Roach, Diderot's acting theory is not just historically the most persuasive theory of acting (1993, 226); it also goes some way towards explaining the distrust and marginalisation of professions like 'begging, seduction, prostitution, and apostasy' whose practitioners, like the actor, were historically considered to be 'professional illusionists' (138). Among political thinkers, Jean-Jacques Rousseau was so suspicious of the idea of representation that he argued in his *Social Contract* that '[s]overeignty ... cannot be represented; it lies essentially in the general will, and does not admit representation: it is either the same, or other; there is no intermediate possibility' ([1762] 1923, 83). For Rousseau, the gap between political representatives and those they purport to represent was so wide that it was altogether impossible to bridge.

Tears crystallise the tenuous and contentious connection between acting and authenticity, between the need to suspend disbelief in a performance and the nagging doubt that it is not 'real'. Unlike, for instance, anger or laughter, tears are difficult to fake and therefore pose a problem for someone intent on disavowing the validity of another's emotional investment. Insofar as tears are the emotional expression of an intense feeling of sadness, they may be a visible result of uncontrollable affect. However, tears are also more complicated than affects that result in the autonomic responses of a person breaking a sweat or blushing, because tears *can* be faked, even if it does require considerable acting skill to convincingly cry on cue. As such, tears are usually a trustworthy sign of someone genuinely feeling deeply upset, but not always. Tears are suspect because they can be faked, but only under certain circumstances and only by certain people. As literary critic Tom Lutz observes in *Crying: The Natural and Cultural History of Tears*, 'the meaning of tears is rarely pure and never simple' because the sincerity of tears remains 'in the moist eye of the beholder' (1999, 23, 60). If we do not believe that Obama's tears were spontaneous and unwilled but we credit his performance with making it look as though they were, we then have to allow that Obama is a good actor and come to the uncomfortable conclusion that he might be capable of manipulating his audience. I asked an Obama White House speechwriter about the 5 January speech and in response the speechwriter closed off precisely this uncomfortable possibility: 'he's not that good of an actor, where I could write, you know, brackets, cry here, and he'd do it'. While Obama is often recognised as a skilled orator, it was apparently important to note that he is not so good at performing that he could emotionally manipulate his audience.

In the absence of personal knowledge of the president, the tears and what prompted them become a matter of intense speculation and controversy that, in Obama's case, plays itself out along predictable party-political lines. In the context of Obama's tears, what then is at stake in asking if Obama was acting authentically? Suppose the president had felt the sincere desire to weep, but could have stopped the tears from falling in this public setting and chose not to, then to what extent could Obama still be said to be acting authentically? For audience members, whether the tears were spontaneous or planned, heartfelt or fabricated is not finally determinable. The salient question here is ultimately not about the status of Obama's tears, but about the willingness of the audience to suspend disbelief in his performance.

The historian Paul Friedland argues in his study of the French Revolution that, as soon as a system of representative democracy was established, contemporary commentators were troubled by the incongruous leap of faith required of voters in a system that lacked 'links of actual acquaintance between the representative and the represented' (1995, 207). Political audiences, then as now, had to rely on their own 'political suspension of disbelief which made abstract, representative government possible' (222). In other words, as political representatives, politicians are supposed to represent their constituents' interests and views. However, constituents, as political audiences, have to judge on the basis of politicians' public performances (as well as their previous records, achievements, and party platforms, of course) whether or not a particular politician will represent them well or is likely to do so. Because acting and performance are inextricably linked with suspicions of duplicitousness, distrust of politicians' performances is likewise an inherent feature of a representative system that relies on performance. In other words, one might assume that efforts to dismiss the authenticity of Obama's tears are instances of the antitheatrical prejudice in action, because they paint Obama's performance as merely 'bad political theatre', for instance. The pervasiveness in Western culture of antitheatrical thought that associates acting and performance with artificiality, corruption, and manipulation adds to the persuasiveness of such dismissals.

However, this book argues that, by moving beyond the antitheatrical prejudice, it becomes possible to identify a real, ineradicable tension in the representative relationship between performing politicians and their audiences. Studies of social performance that use theatre and performance as metaphors go back more than half a century – Erving Goffman's *The Presentation of Self in Everyday Life* ([1956] 1990) being the most well-known example – but the way in which this field of research now conceives of performance can be nuanced and refined through engagement with concepts like theatricality and the suspension of disbelief. This book builds on conceptualisations of theatricality emerging from theatre and performance research which locate the nature of the theatrical in a cleft (Féral 2002), breach (Davis 2003), or doubling (Nield 2006, 2014) between the real and its fictionalised representation; it uses the concept of theatricality to argue that, precisely because trust and the suspension of disbelief are asked of political audiences, the possibility of audiences failing or being unwilling to suspend disbelief and vest their trust in politicians inheres within the system as an inevitable consequence of the required investment of belief. In a system built on the suspension of disbelief, it is not possible to eradicate the possibility that audiences might not (be willing to) suspend their disbelief and might, instead, come to view the entire system with increasing suspicion and distrust. In showing that, to the contrary, distrust is an ineradicable potential within a democratic system built on theatrical performance and therefore reliant on the suspension of disbelief of receptive audiences, this books further develops theories of the performative nature of political representation and makes the case for a more nuanced understanding of how politicians' performances function within representative democracy.

Methods, Scope, Structure

Each of this book's chapters discusses different aspects of the theatre of politics and each is introduced by a salient example of US presidential performance – Hillary Clinton's apparent mismatch between uninspiring performances and inspiring potential during the 2016 presidential campaign in Chapter 1, Bill Clinton's 1993 inaugural address in Chapter 2, Donald Trump's hyperbolic performances of his own health and physicality in Chapter 3, and Woodrow Wilson's 1913 in-person address to a joint session of Congress in Chapter 4.

These chapter-opening case studies are accompanied by analyses of other presidential performances throughout the book. However, because each chapter comes at the subject of US presidential performance from a slightly different angle to explore aspects of the constellation of factors involved in politics and performance, the book does not endeavour to analyse the performances or performance style of every president mentioned systematically or chronologically. Chapters 1 and 3 are more broadly conceptual, investigating how and why we should concern ourselves with performance in politics at all (Chapter 1) and how performances cultivate legitimacy through embodiment and rhetoric (Chapter 3). Chapters 2 and 4 are more empirical, exploring early US presidential performances as well as what I call the conventional theatricality of the US presidency – the ways in which presidential speeches have constituted presidents and their audiences in the public imagination – (Chapter 2) and the ways in which changes in media ecology affect this conventional theatricality and how they incentivise a theatre of politics that revolves increasingly around distrust (Chapter 4). Chapter 2 can be thought of roughly as an empirical counterpart to Chapter 1, and Chapter 4 as an empirical counterpart to Chapter 2; however, while these chapters build on each other to develop a fuller picture of US presidential performance, to the reader more interested in some of the ideas in this book than others, each chapter should still make sense in isolation.

Chapter 1 draws on contemporary political theory and historical studies that connect the emergence of representative democracy to Jean-Jacques Rousseau's antitheatrical thought (Barish 1981; Fliegelman 1993; Friedland 2002). This chapter shows how historical concerns influence political science's persistent tendency to dismiss performance as by definition antithetical to an ideal of rational and deliberative politics. In contradistinction to the idea that 'proper' democratic politics is (or ought to be) devoid of the affective and aesthetic element of performance, the chapter situates performance at the very core of representative democracy. The chapter modifies existing theories of performative representation through a more complex conceptualisation of performance, using theatre/performance theory to show why representative democracy's reliance on performance, theatricality, and suspended disbelief makes the potential for distrust an ineradicable part of representative politics.

Through engagement with historical patterns of presidential performance and with insights gleaned from twenty interviews with political speechwriters, Chapter 2 demonstrates that political representation is a complex process in which performance, theatricality, and distrust interlink. Focusing initially on early norms limiting presidential oratory (set down in *The Federalist Papers* and other sources), the erosion of these norms over time, and technological developments that ensured that the public's relationship to the chief executive became increasingly personality focused, the chapter situates current speechwriters' work in historical perspective. The chapter goes on to demonstrate that presidential speechwriting must be understood as a professional theatrical practice, through which speechwriters from Reagan to Obama simultaneously constructed the president's persona for public performance and an idealised cohesive and receptive national audience.

Focusing on what might be called the 'establishment view' of effective presidential performance, Chapter 2 explores how speechwriters saw the rules governing performances of the presidency, largely before anti-establishmentarianism morphed from a background feature to a dominant characteristic of presidential performance. Reflecting on interviews with the people directly involved, the chapter illuminates the speech preparation processes of Ronald Reagan, George H. W. Bush, Bill Clinton, George W. Bush, and Barack Obama, focusing on each president's individual style but also on the common values and conventions that cut across the different presidential administrations.

The majority of speechwriters I interviewed were former White House and/or presidential campaign speechwriters spanning administrations and campaigns from Ronald Reagan to Barack Obama. Twenty interviews were conducted in 2017 and 2018, a majority in-person in Washington, DC, and London, UK, and some over the phone.[6] The interviews give insight into how political speechwriters work and think and thus explore politicians' public performances from the production side. Of course, the meaning of speeches and of politicians' performances more broadly cannot be reduced to the intentions behind their creation or the processes through which they are produced. Political audiences are diverse and multiple, and they are exposed to politicians' performances in many different ways. Speeches, like any cultural output, are 'not a line of text releasing a single "theological" meaning (the message of the "Author-God") but a multi-dimensional space in which a variety of writings . . . blend and clash', and their audiences are, like Roland Barthes's reader, the 'one place where this multiplicity is focused' (Barthes 1977, 146, 148). Nevertheless, the most basic ontological premise for the empirical research that contributes to this book was that 'people's views are meaningful properties of the social reality [the] research questions are designed to explore' (Mason 2002, 63), which in this case meant that speechwriters' views contribute to constituting the social reality in which both the content and the form of political speeches are produced. More specifically, the rationale for conducting interviews with speechwriters was, firstly, that speechwriters would be able to provide background knowledge on how US presidential speeches are created; this includes detailed information on collaborations between writers and politicians and on ways in which performance techniques like improvisation and performance rehearsal are used in and adapted to the political realm.

The second rationale for drawing on a corpus of interviews with speechwriters is that these give insight into how political speeches and speechwriting have changed in recent years, as well as how mainstreamed populism and changes in the media landscape affect speechwriters' work. Speechwriters' views substantiate some of the arguments presented in this book. Although the findings from qualitative interviews cannot be generalised to make assumptions about how the views represented might be distributed across a population of US political speechwriters, the data included in this book does identify distinct lines of thinking that were pervasive across the interviews conducted, which themselves span the last five pre-Trump presidential administrations.

Chapter 3 examines in detail how politicians' performances cultivate legitimacy through a variety of metalingual, rhetorical, affective, and gestural repertoires of engagement. The chapter begins by discussing the question of what it means to say a politician 'embodies' a constituency, a nation, or a set of values. Engaging with the ahistorical tendencies of some populism theory, the chapter argues for an understanding of political representation that is distinct from premodern ideas of political embodiment (like the idea of the king's two bodies) and posits that ideas about performance, and about the importance of the body in performance, can only be meaningfully applied to political performances following the development of modern political thought around representation. Acknowledging that presidential rhetoric has since Watergate increasingly called the legitimacy of political institutions into question, Chapter 3 then draws on theories of performativity and legitimacy (Anker 2014; Austin 1962; Bourdieu 1991; Butler 1997) to explore how anti-establishment performances break with accepted norms of discourse to restructure the terms of legitimacy through which institutions of the federal government are perceived. It questions whether presidential anti-establishment rhetoric raises the risk that legitimacy increasingly is becoming legible only if claims to it are accompanied by the disavowal of affiliation with democratic institutions. In doing so, the chapter brings together theorisations of legitimacy as a performative process with discursive-performative theories of populism, with the aim of thinking through the implications of presidential performances that make use of (elements of) the populist style.

Using interview data and a series of case studies of presidential speeches from Carter to Trump, Chapter 4 makes the empirical case for the currency of distrust since the Nixon era – understood both as a medium of exchange through which the representative relationship between politicians and political audiences is negotiated and as the contemporary prevalence of political distrust in US presidential performances. The chapter explores speechwriters' views of political speeches within the media ecology of the early twenty-first century and their views on how political speeches have changed and are changing. It interrogates how anti-establishment rhetoric and mainstreamed populism have become increasingly incentivised, while the conventional theatricality of US presidential performance, which relied on presidential restraint and the performative construction of national unity, is subverted.

The Afterword reflects on the dangers and inherent absurdity of a system that sustains itself through representative connections created in politicians' public performances and political audiences' suspension of belief when the performances given increasingly purport to undermine the very system they work to sustain. Although the potential for distrust is always present in representative politics, for a long time presidential performances followed a conventional pattern that emphasised contrasts to presidential predecessors but also national unity and the integrity of government institutions (the pendulum). In the contemporary moment, presidential performances increasingly follow the trajectory of a slope towards ever more entertainment-like, controversial, and anti-establishmentarian performances that erode trust in the integrity of government institutions. Insofar as presidential populism in the contemporary moment is a reaction to the de-democratisation of US politics in the era of neoconservative neoliberalism and especially to the increasing securitisation and circumscription of expressions of dissent following the terrorist attacks of 11 September 2001, it might be seen to reintroduce an element of agonism that threatened to be lost in a political environment that tended towards postpolitical consensus and moralising discourse. Nevertheless, we must ask what effects performances that purport to attack the very system that they ultimately sustain have not just on the functioning of that system but on the possibility of imagining other modes of political organisation and on expressions of dissent both within the representative system and outside of it.

Notes

1. Trumpism refers to the political ideology of Donald Trump; relevant characteristics include a business-centred, entrepreneurial approach to politics, and a populist, anti-establishment attitude that elevates the self-styled outsider (Tabachnick 2016).
2. For a detailed record of the campaign promises Obama kept, broke, and compromised on, see PolitiFact (n.d.).
3. Moffitt counts 'bad manners' as constitutive of the populist style but allows that 'bad manners' might extend to simply 'presenting oneself in more "colourful" ways than we usually expect from politicians' (2016, 60). As will be discussed later on, a definition of the populist style that includes 'bad manners' like swearing, over-the-top claims, and political incorrectness as essential features more accurately describes forms of right-wing populism than it does populism's left-wing, or, as in Obama's case, centre-left, expressions. 'Bad manners' might be amended to include media-savvy displays that catch the public's attention through a variety of techniques – including displays of emotion, solidarity, and controversial rhetoric – to describe different inflections of the populist style more accurately.
4. Bart Bonikowski and Noam Gidron show that 'populism is predominantly used by political challengers rather than incumbents and that it is more prevalent among candidates who can credibly position themselves as political outsiders' but also that

'populism is a significant feature of American presidential politics among both parties' (2016, 1595).

5. By some distance the highest number of homicides and non-fatal shootings committed in any major US city were committed in Chicago, both in 2016 and in 2017.
The Chicago Police recorded 650 homicides in 2017, for instance, whereas the next
highest number of homicides in a major city was 318, recorded by Baltimore Police
(Major Cities Chiefs Association 2018). However, as *The Trace* points out, Chicago's homicide rate per capita was only the ninth highest in a major US city in 2017;
moreover, in 2015, Chicago's non-fatal shooting rate per capita was the eleventh
highest in a major US city (Mirabile and Nass 2018; Mirabile 2016). Nevertheless,
The Trace observes that there is a higher prevalence of fatal shootings (as opposed
to other types of homicides) in Chicago than in many other cities: while the difference between the rate of other types of homicide in Chicago and New York was less
than 1 percentage point in 2015, 'the fatal shooting rate in Chicago was five times
as high as it was in New York' (Givens 2017).

6. For an in-depth look at my methods of interviewee selection and interview analysis,
see Peetz (2019).

CHAPTER 1

PERFORMANCE AT THE CORE OF REPRESENTATIVE DEMOCRACY

The question of a politician's skill as a performer is a frequently debated one. Some politicians – among US presidents and presidential candidates notably Ronald Reagan, Bill Clinton, and Barack Obama – have been lauded as naturally gifted orators. Others, Hillary Clinton, George W. Bush, and John McCain for instance, have been maligned for their lacklustre acting ability or, conversely, it is asserted in their defence that politicians should not have to be good performers in the first place. This argument is easily inverted, too: Bill Clinton's long-time nickname 'slick willie', for instance, was coined by Arkansas journalist Paul Greenberg in 1980, who explains that 'slick willie' does not mean lying so much as dissembling, the telling of 'a very lawyerly, sophisticated, elastic lie', and the tendency to get away with waffling and obfuscating rather than holding fast to one's core principles (Merida 1998). 'Slick willie' refers to what people perceived to be Clinton's duplicitous ability to weasel himself out of any disadvantageous situation. It implicitly casts Clinton's virtuosic improvisation skills as a negative (Ryan 2013). David Foster Wallace's essay (2006) on John McCain's 2000 presidential campaign implies a similar kind of distrust associated with politicians' ability to give suave and seamless performances. Wallace details how, in contrast to other politicians, he welcomed McCain's obvious discomfort with prepared speeches and his strong preference for conversational townhall formats of audience engagement, both of which inclined the novelist to trust McCain more than other politicians. While public performance is understood to be an essential skill for contemporary politicians, at the same time it is one that is viewed with a great deal of suspicion.

This long-standing suspicion of politicians' performances has been interpreted as an expression of the antitheatrical prejudice – the ambivalence towards acting, performance, and the theatre and association of the same with duplicity, manipulation, and moral breakdown, which reaches all the way back to Plato's *Republic* ([c. 380 BCE] 1968). For Plato, the theatre was liable to corrupt actors, since he supposed imitating less than virtuous characters would lead actors themselves to take on these characters' less than virtuous characteristics; mimesis corrupts because 'those who imitate tend to become what they imitate' (Barish 1981, 21). In his book-length study *The Antitheatrical Prejudice* Jonas Barish explains that Plato also rejected the theatre for being detrimental to societal cohesion at large, rather than just individual actors' virtue, since 'whatever tends to widen the individual's range tends to undermine the fixity of his role, and imperils the stability of the social order' (1981, 26). Theatre and acting have always been seen as 'being radically founded in multiplication of roles and transgression of boundaries', which is why, more than any of the other arts, the theatre 'may be said to embody what Plato fears and distrusts' (26). In the *Laws*, Barish adds, Plato expanded his objection to the theatre by focusing on theatrical innovations, such as 'mixtures of genres, new instrumental timbres, and licentious words' (27). In Plato's eyes, innovations like these made the theatre less like a classroom in which audiences were taught how to behave and feel and more like an anarchical, 'evil sort of theatrocracy' that brings about disobedience and the disrespect of social rules (2008, Book 3).

Among Enlightenment thinkers, Jean-Jacques Rousseau was the most infamously antitheatrical, decrying the hypocrisy and the hatefulness of the theatre, in a way that Barish characterises as adding little but a particularly fiery passion to Plato's thoughts on the same subject (1981, 261). Rousseau conceived of the theatre as epitomising the societal corruption to which all humans, having broken away from what he thought of as the simpler, nobler, and more virtuous state of nature, are subject. Strikingly, Rousseau's distaste for theatre is linked to his objection to representation in general. Rousseau does not object to all of the spectacles we might call 'theatrical'; he allows for 'athletic contests, gymnastic games, naval tournaments, and chaperoned balls', all of which, Barish contends, are united by the key feature of enabling 'total participation, the breaking down of the arbitrary barrier between stage and audience' (289, 290). The crucial point is that in all of the spectacles Rousseau supports '[n]o one any longer *represents* anyone other than himself' (Barish 1981, 290, emphasis in original). Consistent with his rejection of representation in the theatre, Rousseau also strongly objected to political representation as a principle enabling legitimate government, arguing that '[s]overeignty . . . cannot be represented; it lies essentially in the general will, and does not admit representation: it is either the same, or other; there is no intermediate possibility' ([1762] 1923, 83). This objection, in turn, provided a model and springboard for resistance to the new system of representative democracy that emerged following the French Revolution.

Representation, both in the theatre and in politics, was suspect from the very moment that it arrived. Moreover, theatre and performance are associated with the realm of the nonrational, with the force of affect, emotion, and aesthetics, as well as with the frivolous, playful, and inconsequential. For this reason, it has been argued that performance has no legitimate place in the study of politics, that it detracts from the serious business of enacting government policy and merely focuses the minds of political audiences on the wrong things. In the academic discipline of politics, 'central concepts – interests, preferences, policies, and so on – are approached as serious and *real* as opposed to superficial *performances*', the editors of *The Oxford Handbook of Politics and Performance* establish at the beginning of their over 750-page volume (Gluhovic et al. 2021, 9, emphasis in original). The philosopher Chiara Bottici similarly begins her *Philosophy of Political Myth* by noting the impact of the insistence on rationality within politics, observing that in the major works of political theory of the last half century, John Rawls's *A Theory of Justice* (1999) and Jürgen Habermas's *Between Facts and Norms* ([1992] 1996), human life is conceptualised as a sphere of activity in which 'one can count on the rationality of the actors involved' (2007, 1). Indeed, Rawls defines goodness as rationality, arguing, for instance, that 'life plans' chosen according to the principle of deliberative rationality 'are superior' to all other life plans (1999, 409), where deliberative rationality is defined by 'care for reflection in which the agent reviewed, in light of all the relevant facts, what it would be like to carry out these plans and thereby ascertained the course of action that would realize his [*sic*] more fundamental desires' (417). Habermas likewise defines his most influential concept of the public sphere as facilitating 'people's public use of their reason' (1989, 27) and stresses the importance of rational argument and consensus in ways that, as Janelle Reinelt points out, are exclusionary of affective or emotive communication and any form of argumentation that is not 'linear or deductive' (2011, 18). Though acknowledging that both Rawls and Habermas propose models for rather than descriptions of everyday politics, Bottici counters that the risk these models nevertheless pose is that 'a purely rational model of society risks being a model for a world that does not exist', since humans beings frequently act irrationally and are influenced by 'powerful symbols and images of the world' (2007, 1).

While the mainstream of politics research has historically tended to view affect, aesthetics, and performance as extraneous and insubstantial, there exists a growing body of work arguing that, though these elements do not neatly fit into a political system normatively conceived to be deliberative and governed by the rational choices of voters and their representatives, any attempt to understand politics – either in its narrow conception as the art and science of government or more broadly conceived as the continuous struggle in human societies for power and resources – that does not take into account the force of performance and emotion is incomplete. This body of scholarship includes work aimed at facilitating the interdisciplinary study of politics and performance, such as Shirin M. Rai and Janelle Reinelt's 2015 volume *The Grammar of Politics and Performance* and the aforementioned *Oxford Handbook of Politics and Performance* (Rai et al. 2021) as well as a collection of scholarship emerging over the course of long-standing collaborations between the Department of Political Studies and the Department of Theatre and Performance Studies at the University of Warwick, UK, such as Michael Saward's work on representative claim-making (2006, 2010, 2014) and Rai's work on ritual and ceremony in parliament (Rai 2014; Rai and Spary 2019). It extends further to research that focuses on examining affective and performative phenomena within politics, including Bottici's research on political myth (2007; Bottici and Challand 2013), Karin Wahl-Jorgensen's *Emotions, Media and Politics* (2018a), Stephen Coleman's *How Voters Feel* (2013), Jeffrey Alexander's numerous publications (2006, 2010, 2011, 2016; Alexander and Jaworsky 2014), a special issue on electoral theatre of the journal *Contemporary Theatre Review* (Bottoms and Hollweg 2015), the volume *International Politics and Performance* (Edkins and Kear 2013), and work by Shawn Parry-Giles (2001, 2014) and by Shawn and Trevor Parry-Giles (2002).

Most readers of this book will no doubt tend to agree with the premise behind this body of work that performance is central to democratic politics. This chapter seeks to extend and partially revise politics and performance research's important insights into how performance operates in politics by considering representative democracy as by nature both performative and theatrical and by focusing particularly on how we might see performance as inextricably linked to distrust. Recognising the dilemma posed by the requirement for politicians to perform in public and the public's tendency to dismiss performance as suspect and manipulative, scholars frequently refer back to the pervasiveness of the antitheatrical prejudice in Western culture generally and in politics in particular (Inchley 2015; Levin and Freeman 2016). As mentioned above, *The Oxford Handbook of Politics and Performance* (Rai et al. 2021) notes that antitheatricality has contributed to the dismissal of performance in mainstream political science. However, although the antitheatrical prejudice, as a default, culturally conditioned antipathy for theatre and performance, does influence people's perceptions of performance in politics, my goal here is to look beyond people's prejudiced judgements of politicians' public performances. This book considers anxiety about the true nature of politicians an ineradicable feature of a political system that bridges the gap between representatives and represented through performance.

The case of Hillary Clinton during the 2016 presidential campaign helps to illustrate this. When Clinton became the Democratic nominee for president, she had been in the public eye for three decades, initially as the First Lady of Arkansas and then as FLOTUS, but later, in her capacity as Senator from New York and Secretary of State under Obama, as a politician in her own right. Clinton had always had a troubled relationship with the press, and, perhaps as a result, was perceived to have changed her stance and personality several times, in ways that invited the public's suspicion of the seemingly unknowable candidate.[1] During the 2016 campaign, there were some commentators sympathetic to Hillary Clinton who made a familiar and well-reasoned, but also somewhat antitheatrical, argument in support of her. They claimed that most people were unable to see the true, much more likeable and less aloof Hillary Clinton because Clinton's approachable true self was obscured by her public awkwardness and by the fraught relationship she had always had with the media. Rebecca Traister's *New York Magazine* article 'Hillary Clinton vs. Herself' (2016) and the film *Michael Moore in Trumpland* (2016) both explicitly make this point, positing that Clinton is more gregarious and sociable in person and that she would have made a more progressive, more hands-on, and altogether better president than the guarded public self she exhibited during the campaign had led many people to believe. While acknowledging that Clinton is 'uneasy with the press and ungainly on the stump', Traister wrote, for instance, that it is 'hard for people who know [Clinton] to comprehend why the rest of America can't see what they do'. Traister posited that 'there is something about the candidate that is getting lost in translation', and that, while reporting on the Clinton campaign, she herself felt that '[t]o be near her is to feel like the campaign is in steady hands; to be at any distance is to fear for the fate of the republic'. In short, the distance, bridged imperfectly through mediatisation, between Hillary Clinton and the American electorate was framed as the problem with the candidate. Clinton's public performances did not sufficiently create the illusion of giving audiences access to her private self. If only the electorate could have seen Clinton as Traister had had the privilege to, then people might have been more strongly drawn to her. Traister's article, which explored Clinton's personal and professional history in some detail, comes across as a would-be antidote to Clinton's perceived remoteness.

Michael Moore in Trumpland was a stage performance given by the documentary maker Michael Moore in Wilmington, Clinton County, Ohio, for an audience with ostensibly mixed political views on 7 October 2016 and released as a film eleven days later. Moore performs in front of a wall of larger-than-life projections showing Hillary Clinton as a young woman, and, in the last fifteen minutes of the hour-long show, comes around to his central point: that Hillary Clinton has been biding her time and therefore letting herself be pressed into choices she would not otherwise have made. Among these, Moore suggests, was the choice to give up her maiden name when Bill Clinton was running for a second term as Governor of Arkansas in 1982 after having lost his re-election campaign in 1980. Clinton's re-election loss had been at least partly attributed to the fact that his wife had been known as Hillary Rodham all throughout his first term, a nonconformist act perceived as 'alien, and even subversive' in conservative Arkansas (Bruck 1994). Hillary Clinton furthermore made a comment during Bill Clinton's presidential run in 1992 that was widely used to characterise her as a radical feminist in the national imagination, a characterisation that has been so persistent that it has been seen to have provided the baseline frame for any future evaluations of Clinton's authenticity (Parry-Giles 2014, 24–53). Pressed to comment about potential conflicts between her role as potential future First Lady and her role as a practising attorney, Clinton summarily dismissed such concerns by asserting that she 'could have stayed home and baked cookies and had teas, but what I decided to do was to fulfill my profession which I entered before my husband was in public life' (1992a). Clinton's comment about cookies and tea is part of a duo of statements made during the 1992 presidential campaign that seemed to reveal her distaste for traditional female roles. The other statement was made in light of accusations that Bill Clinton had an extramarital affair with the former model Gennifer Flowers. Seated next to her husband, Clinton commented on the television news programme *60 Minutes* that her continued support of her husband should not be construed as being indicative of her 'sitting here as some little woman standing by my man like Tammy Wynette' (1992b). Moore opines that the more radical-feminist version of Clinton who voiced her disdain for staying at home to bake cookies 'sounds pretty good to me' and proposes that Clinton might have ultimately made the compromise to start 'baking the cookies and hosting the teas' as First Lady only because she could have been playing the 'long game'. He asks, 'what if Hillary becomes our Pope Francis?', by which he means, what if Clinton turned out to be a surprisingly progressive figure once elected?, and then plays a recording from the college graduation speech Clinton gave at age twenty-two, noting that 'it reads like Bernie wrote it', before imagining a string of remarkably progressive executive orders President Hillary Clinton might sign during her first 100 days in office. Much like Traister's article, *Michael Moore in Trumpland* posits that the public has hardly ever known the woman behind the mask, the 'authentic' Hillary Clinton, at all. Moore also reinforces the presumed authenticity of the image of Hillary Clinton as a radical feminist and the dismissal of any deviation from it as politically calculated and inauthentic, even though he positions himself as sympathetic to or at least understanding of the necessity for political calculation. The film argues tantalisingly that, far from being lost, the authentic version of Clinton is just waiting to reveal herself and in the process revert to the progressivism of her early twenties, if only she is given the public support to do so by being elected president.

While explicit in their support of Clinton and her assumed hidden virtues, more implicitly the argument put forth by both Traister and Moore is that audiences are too easily led by charming and skilled public performers and miss out on political leaders whose strengths are less showy but more valuable. A useful corrective, these commentators seem to suggest, would be for these audiences to look beyond politicians' public performances in the moment. Audiences should instead look to the promise of their policy proposals and appreciate their past accomplishments. Frustrated with heavily mediatised and personalised politics, these commentators rely on the antitheatrical prejudice to strengthen their arguments. By suggesting that politicians' performances are inherently false, manipulative, and calculated, and by pitting them against an imagined pure and genuine reality that is free from the mask of performance, they rehearse the often unconsidered equation of theatre and performance 'with some kind of rhetorical emptiness' as well as 'inauthenticity' and 'artificiality' (Nield 2014, 549). In other words, Clinton's public 'ungainliness' is preferable to her husband's 'slick willie' smoothness, because it does not, indeed cannot, pretend that the performance is the real thing. This sort of argument implies that the fault lies with political audiences rather than with the political system itself. The assumption is that audiences focus on the obvious but wrong and superficial thing (performance) at the expense of the important and substantive thing (policy) – they are too easily taken in by the shiny distraction and miss what can affect their lives in consequential ways. And because Hillary Clinton's public appearances were less than mesmerising, they could potentially help to refocus the public's attention away from the superficiality of performance.

In the end, Clinton failed to get elected president, though she won the popular vote by almost three million votes. It is difficult to parse to what extent Clinton's inability to charm and galvanise audiences in a way similar to Barack Obama in 2008 was responsible for her loss of the election, which, in the end, came down to fewer than 50,000 votes in Wisconsin, Pennsylvania, and Michigan – swing states that the Democratic Party had deemed relatively secure as part of the 'blue wall' that the Democratic candidates had won in every presidential election since 1992. Despite commentators' objections to the influence of performance on politics, however, the imperative for politicians to give public performances is unlikely to dissipate in this media-saturated age. Moreover, politicians have to be seen to perform as themselves, rather than performing fictional characters, and to address a variety of different audiences. Their performances must therefore accomplish two distinct tasks: they must simultaneously move crowds of people, in effect doing an actor's job, and convince these crowds that they really are the public personas they perform, which is a far thornier proposition in a culture that has historically associated theatre and performance with artifice and inauthenticity. The problem is seen to lie in the perception of a 'mimetic gap' between the persona performed and the performing politician (Bleeker 2009, 253). Jeffrey Alexander posits that it is the 'complexity' of a society itself that gives rise to such gaps, as performances can attain the status of socially effective rituals only when those involved have a 'mutual belief in the descriptive and prescriptive validity of the communication's symbolic contents and accept the authenticity of one another's intentions' – something that is difficult to achieve in divided and polarised political environments (2006, 29). Even though Traister and Moore seem to advocate for looking at a candidate's more progressive youth or accounts by sympathetic journalists with personal knowledge of the candidate as an antidote to the distrust resulting from the perception of the mimetic gap, observing a politician's publicly performed persona is as close as the vast majority of audience members will ever come to knowing the candidate. The problem of distance thus remains. It is particularly acute in national and presidential politics, where the distance between voters and representatives is greatest. In effect, if we focus on the antitheatrical prejudice's pervasiveness in politics, we are applying to institutional politics Erika Fischer-Lichte's contention that some performance settings require staging strategies that are effective only if what has been staged appears not to have been staged at all (1998, 87).

What remains underexplored in defaulting to the antitheatrical prejudice as an explanation for the hostility engendered by the public performances of politicians is why the delicate interplay between performance and public trust, and the always looming threat of public disbelief, should matter so much in the first place. This is, above all, a question about the role and function of politicians' public performances in democratic politics. If these performances were not essential and merely distracting or obviously and always manipulative, then why should it be so hard to look away? We need to look beyond casting politicians as disingenuous poseurs and their audiences as easily distracted by political spectacle to address how the reception of politicians' performances affects the way the system of representative democracy functions. Audiences do not distrust politicians merely because they have been culturally conditioned to look at performance with antitheatrical suspicion, but also because, in representative democracy, a primary means of forming representative relationships between politicians and their constituents is through public performance and its reception. While a politician's job as a representative has potentially real, material consequences for constituents, a connection forged through public performance is tenuous insofar as it invites the audience's suspension of disbelief, rather than their more straightforwardly given belief or acceptance of a representative. The tenuousness of this connection means that insufficient trust and distrust are always inherent potentials within the system of representative democracy.

This chapter links historical contextualisation with theoretical argument to make the point that representative democracies are performative and theatrical political systems, the legitimacy of whose political representatives depends on the system's performance-based core. This also means that the importance of performance in politics is not wholly reducible to today's mediatised politics. Performance is central to democratic politics not exclusively because of the highly mediatised political environment of the late twentieth and early twenty-first centuries. In other words, it is not just because, for instance, Bill Clinton's saxophone performance of 'Heartbreak Hotel' on *The Arsenio Hall Show* in 1992 was widely televised that performance should be seen as an important analytical category in US presidential politics. Certainly, mediatisation incentivises specific kinds of personalised and controversial performance, as Chapters 3 and 4 explore in detail. However, performance, and politicians' public performances in particular, also plays a more foundational role in representative democracy.

Leading scholars in both political science and performance studies have increasingly recognised the performative nature of institutional politics in recent years; nevertheless, this chapter's historico-theoretical orientation aims to provide a unique theorisation of the link between performance and democratic legitimacy. Social science scholarship on politics and performance in particular underestimates the analytical value of the concept of theatricality, which complicates the matter of performative representation. Politicians' performances are performative in that they interpellate the constituent-audience, the politician-speaker, and the representative relationship between the two. But these performances are also theatrical, which means that their success rests on the tenuous matter of the audience's suspension of disbelief in the politician's performance, rather than their more straightforwardly given belief. Performance should not be reduced to performativity, and performance research needs to account for the theatrical nature of politicians' public performances if a fuller analysis of how political representation works as performance practice is to emerge.

PERFORMANCE AND POLITICAL LOGIC

It is worth dwelling on the strong objections some politics scholars have voiced to the influence of performance in politics. Continuing Rousseau's wholesale objection to political and theatrical representation, some have argued that performance only functions as an antipolitical corruption within politics. This view entails a sharpening of the argument against the supposedly excessive degree to which politicians' performances are able to influence voters beyond the metaphorical equation of performance with falsity. In a volume entitled *The End of Politics?* published in the late 1990s the political scientist Andreas Schedler argues that an emphasis on politicians' performances is pernicious because the logic of performance and theatricality is antithetical to the logic of politics. In Schedler's definition, politics is determined by Habermasian 'communicative rationality' and political logic is defined as rational deliberation in language-based arguments (1997b, 12). This definitional tie of politics to rational argument-building allows Schedler to identify a number of antipolitical logics: instrumental, moral, amoral, and aesthetic. Aesthetic antipolitics is defined as 'the intrusion and foreign occupation [of the political realm] by the logic of theatre and drama, rock and roll, sports and entertainment, design and advertising, the fine arts, television, religious confession, psychotherapy and intimacy' (13).

One may object that Schedler's long list of aesthetic antipolitical logics threatens to overwhelm his meaning – in what sense can psychotherapy really be said to be exerting an influence on politics similar to that of sports and design? But Schedler is quite clear that in the consequences he envisions aesthetic antipolitics brings about the corruption of a more pure, deliberative, rational – and, hence, political – discourse above all through the privileging of performance and theatricality. Schedler claims that aesthetic antipolitics 'downgrades political deliberation and decision making to mere acts of backstage performance and as a countermove pushes theatrical forms of action to the centre stage of politics', so that what prevails are 'the expressive codes of short-distance relations over the moral codes of the public sphere' and 'the credible expression of emotion over the plausible lining up of arguments' (13–14). I bring up this argument here not because I assume readers will agree with Schedler's position, but because it crystallises some of the central issues that performance raises within democratic politics. The point Schedler is making here goes beyond rehearsing the antitheatrical prejudice – that is, beyond the equation of performance with artifice. Rather, for Schedler, there may be a realm for the expressiveness of emotion and for 'theatrical' (however conceived) forms of action, but the sphere of democratic politics, with which Schedler concerns himself, is not that realm. Aesthetic expressivity – and specifically the aesthetics of theatre and performance – is thus thought of here not merely as responsible for what is perceived as an irritatingly superficial focus within contemporary political discourse but as by definition incompatible with the logic of politics. Any role performance might play within politics is then dismissed as purely negative and corrupting. Performance and theatricality might be ever-present, but only as something that detracts and distracts from, and has the status of a contaminant within, what would otherwise be a more wholesomely deliberative political realm. Ideally, if one could think of a way, one would eradicate performance and theatricality from democratic politics altogether.

One could respond to Schedler with Jacques Rancière's argument that aesthetics is inherently political and politics inherently aesthetic since, for Rancière, aesthetics structures what can be perceived in the first place (the 'distribution of the sensible') and politics refers to an intervention that restructures what can appear and be perceived ([2004] 2013). This chapter, however, seeks to respond to Schedler's argumentation in a way that is closer to the terms Schedler himself sets out and does not require recourse to Rancière's 'very particular and original definitions of aesthetics and politics' (Alston 2016, 190). It makes the case for why the system of representative democracy is, at its core, performance-based – by which I mean that the system functions through politicians' public performances that should be seen as both performative and theatrical in specific ways this chapter will seek to elucidate. The chapter thus provides a rebuttal to Schedler's point that performance and theatricality, and an attendant emphasis of emotional expressivity, are necessarily antipolitical and destructive to institutional politics. To the contrary, performance – and politicians' public performances in particular – fulfils a central and irreplaceable function within the system of representative democracy.

This chapter builds on previous scholarship on performance and politics, most particularly Saward's theory of the representative claim. The strength of Saward's theory, as I see it, lies in the way it emphasises the centrality of the interaction between politicians and their citizen audiences. By focusing on the performative evocation of audiences through politicians' claim-making and by distinguishing between different articulations of claims, different makers of claims, and the constraints under which claim-makers exist in different empirical scenarios and according to which they are more or less free to position themselves in various ways to different audiences in order to persuasively make their representative claims, Saward provides a model for thinking through the process by which audiences come to accept or reject claims to representation (2006, 306–9; 2014, 727–33). I argue that introducing the concepts of theatricality and suspension of disbelief into the theory of performative representation allows us to better account for the always ambiguous nature of performance and thus to develop a theory that explains why representative democracy will always be fraught with doubt and distrust. Well over half a century after Erving Goffman wrote about the 'natural movement back and forth between cynicism and sincerity' in the (self-)perception of people's public presentation ([1956] 1990, 12), performance is still often assumed to work more straightforwardly and less complexly than it actually does, and this chapter endeavours to remedy this misapprehension.

Contrary to Schedler, and with Saward, I argue that representative democracy works with and through performance, and this chapter theorises the role and function of performance in representative democracy. I build on Paul Friedland's historical scholarship (1995, 2002), which examines concerns around performance and politics that arose in the transition from an estate-based representative model to the system of representative democracy during the French Revolution. By putting Friedland's historical insights into dialogue with arguments about the performative nature of political representation put forward most notably by Saward and with Sophie Nield's conceptualisation of theatricality as an analytical category that is applicable to the objects of social science research, this chapter makes an argument for why politicians' public performances should be regarded as functionally important elements of representative democracy. Taking a theory-driven, historically anchored approach, I argue that the representative relationship between politicians and constituents on which representative democracy is built is constructed through politicians' performances and their audiences' suspension of disbelief.

In addition to demonstrating that 'politics cannot be analysed seriously without a sophisticated understanding of its performances' (Rai and Reinelt 2015b, 2), the deeper point made is that some of the concerns Schedler raises about the influence of performance in politics ought to be taken seriously rather than simply written off as being antitheatrical and therefore indicative of prejudicial judgement. Insofar as he posits that performance and theatricality introduce emotion, distrust, and irrationality into democratic politics, Schedler's argument is sound. Focusing on concepts of theatricality serves to elaborate why the reliance on performance necessarily brings with it the potential for distrust. But it does not do to dismiss nonrationality, distrust, and emotion as antipolitical corruptions that ought to be excised. Representative democracy cannot do away with these consequences, troubling though they can be, any more than humans really are the ideal rational agents envisioned in the models of politics put forth by Rawls and Habermas. To insist not just that political audiences are potentially manipulated and certainly distracted by politicians' performances but that such performances are altogether antipolitical is to mischaracterise democratic politics and to reduce it to an unreachable ideal. Instead, it is necessary to account precisely for how and why representation works through performance and what consequences this has for political distrust.

The Performance-Based Core of Representative Democracy

Politicians' performances, their consciously considered and stage-managed appearances and self-presentations in public space, fulfil a specific function in representative democracy and should not be regarded as either a superficial ornament or an antipolitical contaminant. To show this, I draw on historical and theoretical insights into political representation: Paul Friedland's historical focus on the transition to representative democracy sheds light on concerns about the system that were raised during and just after the French Revolution. Jay Fliegelman's work on oratorical ideals that were influential at the time of the American Revolution suggests that similar concerns became pertinent in America during the eighteenth century. In contrast to Friedland's and Fliegelman's work, Saward's theorisation of the performativity of political representation tends towards ahistorical abstraction. However, by bringing historical and theory-focused sources into a dialogue with one another, a case for the broad applicability of the link between politics and performance emerges.

It is worth noting here the difference between Friedland's work on different historical concepts of performance, their ties to political events, rituals, and conceptions of absolutist and democratic leadership, and Jeffrey Alexander's sociological work on performance and ritual. Alexander argues that successful performances in complex ('de-fused') societies struggle harder to approach social efficacy (or a 'ritual-like' character or a state of 're-fusion') than performances in societies that are supposed to have 'simpler', less differentiated social organisations (which are 'fused') (2006, 32). Alexander sets up this dichotomy between 'simpler' and more 'complex' societies to produce a 'universal' theory of social development (2006, 49). In doing so, he directly engages with some of the ideas around people's lack of trust in and questioning of politicians that are central to this book. However, my work does not endeavour to produce a universal theory, and I believe work that aspires to universality and locates the advent of social complexity in ancient Athens (whilst acknowledging that ancient Egypt had a sort of pre-complex social organisation) should be engaged with and nuanced from indigenous and 'non-Western' perspectives (Alexander 2006, 44ff.). The research in this book is concerned firstly with the US presidency and secondly with 'Western' representative democracies, and thus cannot engage with Alexander's work from those perspectives.

To be clear, I consider Alexander's work that deals with the US presidency directly to be highly illuminating (which is why I engage with it throughout this book) and I appreciate his acknowledgement that in attempting to produce a universal theory of social development he makes 'broad historical generalizations' (Alexander 2006, 52). Nevertheless, while the idea that successful political performances manage to temporarily 're-fuse' previously 'de-fused' societies (or at least audiences and performers) makes a compelling metaphysical point, it does not capture everything necessary about how performance operates in politics. The mental image of fusion and de-fusion more readily serves to visualise the success of certain performances in politics: Obama's election (Alexander 2010), for instance, or Bill Clinton's surviving his impeachment over his affair with his intern Monica Lewinsky with high approval ratings (Mast 2012). The idea of social de-fusion assumes that suspicion is the default state in contemporary 'complex' societies because of social differentiation, media fragmentation, and so on. The concept itself does not delve into the very good reasons why performance should be viewed with suspicion, instead positing a pre-complex societal arrangement where performance could be equated to ritual. In contrast to this, I draw on the work of Friedland and others to distinguish between premodern and modern performances of representation (or, as a shorthand, between rituals and performances) in order to account for different historical understandings of performance, acting, and so on.

Before the middle of the eighteenth century, political representation was understood to be a fairly straightforward, literal concept. Friedland meticulously details the contrast between the nature of political representation in representative democracy as it arose in the wake of the French Revolution and the earlier, estate-based form of representation that it supplanted. Prior to the Revolution, Friedland argues, political representation was conceived of literally insofar as it was seen to entail 'a metamorphosis of the body of the representative into the body of the represented', in a material and concrete way that resembled the Catholic doctrine of transubstantiation (1995, 61, 105). Friedland thus expands Ernst Kantorowicz's (1957) seminal insights into the connection between theology and political theory from monarchical to democratic politics (1995, 62). Over the course of the second half of the eighteenth century, and particularly with the establishment of the National Assembly as a representative body following the Revolution, a shift in the concept took hold that saw representation taking on a symbolic rather than literal meaning. Before the conceptual shift, and by those who were eager to preserve this idea of representation in the wake of the Revolution, 'the political representation performed by the Estates General', which represented the clergy, the nobility, and the common people, 'was based upon the literal perception of France as a living organism' (102). Early modern commentators, such as the legal scholars Guy Coquille and Charles Loyseau, described the composition of France variously as a 'body with several heads' or as a body where 'the King is the head and the people of the three orders are members', but always as a symbiotic arrangement, in which 'each political body depended on the others for verification of its legitimacy' (103, 107, 114). Crucially, in this premodern context, public spectacles such as royal processions were 'not primarily intended to manufacture symbols for the benefit of others; these spectacles were first and foremost about the metamorphosis of political actors' (Friedland 2002, 41); in other words, spectacles did not primarily address audiences of spectators but produced meaning for their immediate participants. The idea was for the king himself to assume his national role with conviction, rather than to address an external audience.

In contrast to the premodern literal and organismic conception, the newly established representative body, the National Assembly, was no longer seen to literally re-present (in terms of manifesting the essential component parts of) the social body. Instead, the National Assembly was based upon a conception of representation that Friedland describes as 'analogic and aggregate', in that it conceived of the social body 'as the sum of individuals within the nation', which could be represented by a body that, as an abstracted aggregate entity 'bore a certain *resemblance* to an organism' (1995, 124, emphasis in original). Theorists of the Revolution, such as the Count of Mirabeau and the Abbé Sieyès, argued that an assembly composed of members only from the Third Estate (that is, the common people), which made up 96 per cent of the population, was positioned to adequately represent the nation, because, in Sieyès's words, the resemblance was '*good enough* for them to confer upon themselves the title of national Assembly' and thus stand as an abstraction of the nation as a whole (Friedland 1995, 128, emphasis in original). The consequence of the conceptual shift from a literal to a more abstracted view of representation was that legitimacy became less straightforward and more debatable, as it now 'depended upon the willingness of political spectators to find the performance of its representatives *vraisemblable*' – that is, convincing and sufficiently true-seeming (63). By adopting this new, symbolic meaning, representation had become abstract rather than physical and demanded a level of trust rather than being seen to provide concrete, tangible evidence in itself. Political representatives who made up the National Assembly had to be trusted to give voice to those they represented. In Friedland's view, this was so because, having been 'formed by abstraction', the new representative body 'could base its legitimacy only on a tautology': it was legitimate because, and as long as, it was seen to be legitimate (131). Having moved away from their inward, and quasi-magically transformative, character, public spectacles and politicians' performances had thus turned decidedly towards the address of political audiences. According to Friedland, this new configuration required the audience's 'suspension of disbelief', taken here to imply that 'no boundaries [were drawn] between political and theatrical representation' following the French Revolution (9). Friedland's use of the term 'suspension of disbelief' is significant, and I will return to its implications later in this chapter.

Focusing on the American Revolutionary context, Jay Fliegelman's *Declaring Independence* (1993) details a development roughly analogous to that described by Friedland. Fliegelman's argument revolves around his case that the Declaration of Independence was written to be performed aloud, with Jefferson including marks for pauses during spoken delivery in his draft text that were omitted in its first printing but remain traceable through additional white spaces left in the printed text. According to Fliegelman, Jefferson's preoccupation with the oral delivery of the Declaration is, whether or not he actually ended up performing it aloud (a question which remains unresolved), indicative of his enmeshment in a revolution of rhetorical culture that was under way during the eighteenth century and particularly influential in America to the extent that its adherents conceived of Americans as part of a new 'society of common feeling' from which both Loyalists and British people were excluded (191–2). In the course of what Fliegelman calls the 'elocutionary revolution', the public were given 'new franchise to be critical' and much greater emphasis was placed on making public speaking an occasion for the 'revelation of a private self' (2, 20, 24). Moving away from the reliance on classical tropes and tightly circumscribed, ceremonial conceptions of public speaking, revolutionary America was influenced instead by rhetoricians such as James Burgh, Thomas Reid, and John Witherspoon, who proposed a view of rhetoric that emphasised tonal and gestural delivery – public performance, in other words – aimed at influencing the passions of listeners and revealing the full self of the speaker in the 'nakedness of truth' and in the throes of the 'fullness of his natural feelings' (32).

Fliegelman's thesis in *Declaring Independence* stands in complex tension with Michael Warner's argument that print culture in revolutionary America 'played an active role in the constitution of power' such that print exerted an ideological force which 'valorized the general above the personal and construed the opposition between the two in the republican terms of virtue and interest' (1990, 76). Warner suggests that the emphasis on rationality in Benjamin Franklin's writing, for instance, 'should be seen as part of a project of supplanting speech and immediacy with writing and generality' (1986, 115), such that authority came to be associated with a kind of impersonal writing 'based in a negative relation to one's own person' (1990, 81). As Suzette Hemberger notes (1994, 472), Fliegelman does not do enough to resolve the apparent discrepancy between his argument and Warner's, but he does insist that there was in the period a 'dialectical relation between the authority of impersonality rooted in the discourse of descriptive science and the authority of sincerity rooted in the discourse of affective experience' (Fliegelman 1993, 128). Indeed, throughout *Declaring Independence*, Fliegelman details a series of tensions manifested in and through eighteenth-century rhetorical culture, including tensions between 'self-effacement and self-assertion', between 'sincerity and hypocrisy', and between 'rational persuasion and affective appeal', between which the oratorical ideal that prevailed in America in 1776 attempted to mediate (190). Building on Habermas's work on the public sphere (1989, [1992] 1996), Warner likewise sees the rise of print culture as part of a move 'from a world in which power embodied in special persons is represented before the people to one in which power is constituted by a discourse in which the people are represented' (1990, 39). The gulf between their arguments belies that both Fliegelman and Warner are concerned with unearthing struggles for new sources of legitimacy that emerged in eighteenth-century America alongside the people's right to represent themselves.

Warner contends that the Constitution's printedness allowed it 'to emanate from no-one in particular', to appear to rise above its authors and at the same time interpellate 'the people', who paradoxically in the Constitution 'are always coming across themselves in the act of consenting to their own coercion' (1990, 112). Fliegelman likewise argues for the need to transcend that which is perceived to be contestable, arguing that rhetoric was supposed to alleviate what he characterises as a growing distrust of reason and rational persuasion in eighteenth-century America; public performance thus came to be invested with the 'wishful faith' that oratory was capable of giving audiences direct access to an 'irresistible discourse of feelings' which made both the orator's sincerity and the truth of his speech entirely plain and self-evident (1993, 96). For present purposes, and in a way that is does not seem as opposed to Warner's argument as the speech-vs-print focus of the two works initially suggests, it is particularly pertinent to note that Fliegelman's sees the elocutionary revolution he outlines as part of a larger development which established consensus as a cultural ideal, one whose pursuit performative persuasion enabled by 'proposing sincerity as a new form of social and political legitimacy' (189). Fliegelman's emphasis on a public culture of performance, and particularly the stress placed on what was conceived of as the obvious and incontrovertible sincerity of the performer, strongly resonates with Friedland's argument that it was the performer's quality of being sufficiently true-seeming that came to be seen as a central marker of legitimacy following the French Revolution. Mladen Dolar's (2006, 109) argument that an ideal linking 'the living voice' to the democratisation of justice emerged during the French Revolution also echoes both Fliegelman's and Friedland's focus on a new culture of public performance that emerged at the advent of representative democracy.

Representative democracy as a political system should be seen as based in performance, which means that politicians' public performances play a crucial role in establishing and maintaining legitimacy. A key aspect of the connection between representative politics and performance is contained in Friedland's description of legitimacy-through-tautology. Since he is concerned with historical specificity rather than theoretical thrust, however, Friedland eschews analysis of this new system of political representation through theories of performativity. To make the connection between performativity and the idea of legitimacy-through-tautology, it is necessary to take into account the theorisation of political representation as performative. In political studies, the incorporation of ideas of performativity into the study of political representation forms part of a 'constructivist turn', which explores the relevance of ideas of performativity as developed by J. L. Austin (1962), Jacques Derrida (1988), and Judith Butler ([1993] 2011, 1997) to the study of political structures and institutions and champions the interdisciplinary engagement between political science and performance studies scholarship (Brito Vieira 2020; de Wilde 2013; Disch 2011, 2015; Moffitt 2016; Montanaro 2012; Severs 2012). Michael Saward's work on the representative claim (2006, 2010, 2014) has proved particularly influential. Saward argues that political representation should be understood as the creative, performative, and aesthetic process of making representative claims. Politicians, or other claim-makers, give performances (in the form of speeches, for example), which interpellate their audiences by presenting them as a more or less homogeneous body of people sharing certain features. Having assigned certain characteristics to their audiences, representative claim-makers then 'argue or imply that they are the best representatives of the constituency *so understood*' (Saward 2006, 301–2, emphasis in original), thereby constituting themselves as the ideal representatives of a particular constituent-audience. As in Friedland's contention that, in abstract representation, it is ultimately the spectators' suspension of disbelief that turns a politician into a representative, the audience at the receiving end of Saward's representative claim may either accept or reject the claim, in effect rendering it felicitous or infelicitous.

Significantly, Saward envisions legitimacy not as a formal kind of authorisation, but as depending on the acceptance of a politician's performed representative claim by relevant political audiences, arguing that legitimacy is best thought of in terms of 'provisionally acceptable claims to democratic legitimacy across society . . . for which there is evidence of sufficient acceptance by appropriate constituencies under reasonable conditions of judgment' (2010, 145). Emphasis is thus placed on both the performance and its reception, as both are important in establishing the representative relationship between politician and constituent. 'Sufficient acceptance' might be thought of as a fuzzy, imprecise measure in a similar way to how, in Friedland's terms, the goal of a politician's performance is to achieve the status of being 'true-seeming', rather than being actually 'true'. Nevertheless, for the system to work, a relationship between politician and audience must be established through the politician's public performance and the political audience's acceptance – or, rather, their suspension of disbelief. In other words, the endurance and proper functioning of representative democracy is ultimately not grounded in anything more firm or reliable than the politician's ability to perform and the political audience's willingness to buy into this performance. This is legitimacy-through-tautology. The distinction between the more straightforward idea of 'acceptance' and the more tenuous connection forged through 'suspension of disbelief' is an important one, however, and will be explored immediately below.

Theatricality and the Suspension of Disbelief

Controversies about representative democracy and the role performance plays in it, which arose with the transition to this representative system and persist to this day, stem from the fuzzy and subjective way in which the legitimacy of a political performer is judged. The potential for distrust of politicians should be regarded as the unavoidable complement to, or flipside of, an increased dependence on trust and make-believe that inheres within the representative system. The tendency towards distrust is amplified not just on account of the long history of antitheatrical thought in Western culture but also due to the expressly theatrical nature of politicians' public performances. It may seem opportune simply to conclude that the suspiciousness with which political performers are viewed is antitheatrical, and certainly antitheatricality heightens the potential for distrust rather than just the absence or insufficiency of necessary trust since antitheatricality is not at all neutral but specifically antipathetic towards theatre and performance. However, even beyond the prejudice with which performance is viewed, anxiety about the true nature of politicians is an inevitable feature of a political system that bridges the gap between representatives and represented through theatrical performance.

From the way in which Saward elucidates the difference between legitimate and illegitimate representative claims, one might assume that such claims can, in general, fairly straightforwardly be judged to be either 'provisionally acceptable' or not. Reading Saward, one gets the impression that representative claims are performed and then succeed in being performatively felicitous or fail to be felicitous at all – in either case, the judgement seems definitive. To borrow from J. L. Austin's (1962) seminal phrasing about the nature of performativity, politicians claiming to represent constituencies will either succeed in doing things with words or they will not. Of course, this may be different for different groups of constituents, but nevertheless, in Saward's theorisation of performative politics, the matter appears, while 'provisional', still relatively clear-cut in that the performative utterances under scrutiny are assumed to be constitutive of the shared social reality people experience. (Similarly, while Alexander posits 'fusion' as a necessary condition for a performance to attain ritual-like character and as something that it is difficult to achieve, it is assumed that performers can and do in practice achieve fusion in connecting with audiences.)

Friedland's contention that the newly and abstractly conceived representative relationship required the suspension of disbelief of political audiences makes the matter seem more fraught with tension. The term 'willing suspension of disbelief' originates in Samuel Taylor Coleridge's *Biographia Literaria*, where suspension of disbelief is taken to constitute 'poetic faith' (1834, 174). In theatre studies, the phrase has frequently been applied to an audience's willingness to enter into the fictional world of a theatre play, such that Tracy Davis refers to it as the 'necessary condition for dramatic reception' (2005, 59). Suspension of disbelief is not the same as belief; it is a temporary, willed pause in questioning that allows an audience member to let themself be absorbed, to follow along, and give themself away for a moment, before, inevitably, resuming their sceptical questioning. Suspension of disbelief, then, is quite different from an open-ended investment of belief. Importantly, it is a term usually applied to fictional worlds: audiences of fictional worlds on stage and screen are generally aware that these worlds do not actually exist, but temporarily proceed as if they did. Friedland's use of the term 'suspension of disbelief' is an implicit recognition of the fact that an audience's willingness to buy into a politician's performance is similar to, though – since real-world consequences are at stake – frequently perceived as more fraught than, the suspension of disbelief when seeing a fictional text performed. This also implies that, while politicians performatively constitute their own personas and performatively conjure their audiences and the issues they propose to tackle as features of the social reality their audiences experience, such performative evocations retain the status of the quasi-fictional – regardless of the actual truth-content of their statements. This means that the willingness to suspend disbelief itself could be suspended.

In sum, while we rely solely on a conceptualisation of performativity derived from Austin (1962) and Butler (1997), we might assume to be on firm ground insofar as performative utterances are seen as constitutive of collectively shared social reality. If we begin to think in terms of suspension of disbelief, however, things become unmoored. Suspension of disbelief implies that what we see, hear, and experience might actually belong to the realm of fiction, and that, despite this being a conventionally accepted form of fiction that constitutes a part of human social reality, there is nothing but each audience member's temporary suspension of disbelief that holds it together. Representative claim-makers thus would seem to have to contend with the possibility of the audience failing, or being unwilling, to suspend disbelief and have to perform for audiences in ways that will hopefully not disrupt their suspension of disbelief. For US presidents, this is an enormously difficult task given the highly polarised and mediatised politics of the late twentieth and early twenty-first centuries.

To elucidate further how the performativity of politicians' performed representative claims is rendered more complex, it is helpful to introduce the concept of 'theatricality'. Among theatre and performance scholars there is broad agreement that what defines theatricality as a concept is that theatrical performance, whether in the theatre or in social and political life, entails a doubling, split, or breach in perception that opens up a perspective that fictionalises what is seen (Carlson 2002; Davis 2003; Féral 2002; Fischer-Lichte 2009; Nield 2014; see also earlier influential explorations in Burns 1972 and Fried [1967] 1998). Sophie Nield's work on theatricality is particularly useful here, since it explicitly intends to account for how theatricality operates beyond and outside of theatre settings. Nield argues that theatrical appearance entails the 'uncoupling of presence and representation' (2014, 553). This theatrical uncoupling has the effect that people (or objects) 'appear both as themselves and as what they represent. They imitate, or pretend to be, the things that they already are, articulated through the deployment of symbolic language, otherwise they will simply not be visible' (553). Being made to pretend to be, or play, oneself implies that someone is watching or at least the possibility of being watched; as a consequence, for Nield, 'a "theatrical" space could be one in which the gaze (or its possibility) is embedded; in which visuality is at work; in which things are available to be seen – and which is conditioned by the awareness of that possibility' (553). In other words, being watched by political audiences means being made to play to the expectations of those audiences, not merely in the sense of appealing to their political views and concerns and figuring oneself as a credible representative based on those views (as the theory of the representative claim has it), but in terms of playing oneself in a way that has to convince audiences to suspend their disbelief in that performance. As Nield puts it, in a theatrical situation, 'you "play" yourself, and hope you are convincing' (2006, 65), and this playing to a real or imagined audience entails abstraction and fictionalisation, in the sense of a self-conscious 'imagining [of] the self from the outside – placing oneself in space and time in the abstract – not here, but there: on a map, in a country, in a public square or other situation' (2014, 554). What is at stake is not merely the appeal to the audience's political sensibilities and aspirations but the personal authenticity of the speaker, which is in question precisely because the theatrical situation in which the performance takes place has introduced a cleft/split/breach that has uncoupled the speaker's presence from their abstracted, fictionalised representation.

The performative elevation of a representative claim-maker into the representative of a political audience thus has to be seen to be rendered more complex by the theatrical situation in which representative claims are performed. This is a situation which entails the abstraction and the fictionalisation of oneself in order to then represent oneself in accordance with the expectations of the real or implied audience whose presence makes the situation theatrical in the first place. Because the performance is theatrical in the sense that one is seen to be playing oneself in a self-conscious way that is understood to encompass a degree of fictionalisation, it is indeed the audience's suspension of disbelief that is at stake here,[2] rather than the audience's more straightforwardly configured belief or, in Saward's language, their 'acceptance' of a representative. Suspension of disbelief is always tenuous; it entails the possibility of disbelief failing to be suspended either fully or partially, precisely because the theatricality of the situation has introduced a cleft/split/breach between the person present and their representation. Importantly, the theatrical doubling of presence and representation here needs to be seen as personalised; that is, its success does not depend entirely on the political views or policy positions expressed, though alignment with these undoubtedly makes audience members more willing to suspend disbelief in the first place. However, the success of a theatrical performance depends on the believability of the performance of the person professing to hold certain views and the degree to which that performance allows or enables the audience to suspend their disbelief that the representation of the person they are seeing in fact corresponds to the person present. Finally (and in spite of Nield's astute observation that, conceptually, theatricality should not be reduced to being seen simply as a marker of artifice and falseness), because the theatrical has in Western culture so often been perceived in antitheatrical terms, a performance that is understood to be theatrical in the sense just described is liable to be dismissed as fake and manipulative. Indeed, this possibility is made explicit in Davis's etymological tracing of the meaning of theatricality, as Davis stresses that theatricality entails 'a sympathetic breach . . . effecting a critical stance towards an episode in the public sphere' (2003, 145). Where the theatricality of the performance entails the need for suspension of disbelief, antitheatrical dismissals are much more likely to be successful than in more strictly and simply performative (that is, less 'theatrical') moments: Austin's paradigmatic example of saying 'I do' at one's wedding, for example, is a much more straightforwardly performative act than the representative claims made by politicians' public performances in representative democracy.

Friedland's historical scholarship captures something of the theatrical character of politicians' performances I have just described, using historical sources to show that both Jacobin and counter-revolutionary commentators expressed an acute and widespread anxiety over the new concept of political representation and explicitly linked this to the idea that it was impossible to definitively determine a politician's credibility (1995, 146–224). Jean-Jacques Rousseau's strongly voiced rejection of abstract representation provided a model and springboard for objections to the new representative system, since Rousseau saw representation as incompatible with the expression of the *volonté générale*, the will of the people as a whole. As mentioned above, Rousseau's *Social Contract* famously argues that it is impossible to bridge the gap between political representatives and those they purport to represent, because '[s]overeignty . . . cannot be represented' and 'does not admit representation' ([1762] 1923, 83). Although scholars disagree over whether Rousseau's objection to representation was in fact as principled as it appears in the *Social Contract*'s most vociferous passages (cf. Douglass 2013; Fralin 1978), it undoubtedly had far-reaching influence on contemporary political thought. As Friedland shows, in the wake of the French Revolution elections were perceived as lacking transparency: the infamous revolutionary Maximilien Robespierre, for instance, raised the issue that the represented had insufficient personal acquaintance with their representatives. To guarantee a politics 'free of corruption and distortion', Robespierre advocated for 'a closer geographical bond between representative and represented' as well as 'eternal vigilance and the incessant unveiling of fraudulence and monstrosity' (Friedland 1995, 207–8).

In a way that illuminates the reach and significance of expressions of distrust such as Robespierre's, Davis shows that the term 'theatricality' was coined by the English philosopher Thomas Carlyle in 1837 to describe the ability of spectators to denounce the falsity of certain machinations of the state–theatre complex that came into operation during the French Revolution (2003, 132–6). Joseph Roach similarly makes the point that a level of distrust in the sincerity of actors is bound to extend to what were historically considered to be other 'professional illusionists', like '[t]he beggar, the seducer, the prostitute and the unbelieving priest' (1993, 138) – and, one might add, the politician operating in a system based on abstract representation. Fliegelman's work might appear to contrast with these arguments, in that it details attempts to strip public performance in eighteenth-century America of what were perceived to be artificial and antiquated rhetorical devices, thus purportedly giving access to the naked and unambiguous sincerity of the speaker. What emerges most clearly from Fliegelman's study, however, is not the straightforward association of natural language performances with sincerity at all, but the persistent cultural tensions this emerging ideal of performance managed only imperfectly to mediate between: Jefferson, for instance, remained 'deeply and revealingly conflicted' about the superior orator Patrick Henry (1993, 94). Friedland's, Davis's, Roach's, and to some extent Fliegelman's historical research showcases the unease brought about by the new reliance on politicians' performances. As it replaced the old organismic concept of representation in which legitimacy had been considered self-evident, abstraction served to highlight the constructedness, the theatricality, and therefore, ultimately, the fragility of the political order.

Anxiety over the trustworthiness of politicians, their capacity and volition to adequately represent constituencies, persists. It is clearly in evidence when Rebecca Traister (2016) writes of the 'dichotomy between [Hillary Clinton's] public and private presentation', the 'wall between the two' that Clinton has apparently built, and the fact that Clinton, in her unknowability, 'can seem a fictional character'. In that audiences had to suspend their disbelief in her, Clinton during the 2016 campaign was indeed like a fictional character. But the suspension of disbelief demanded of Clinton's audiences was by no means a straightforward matter, partly because questions of trust and distrust are built into a representative politics that is both performative and theatrical. The potential for distrust was aggravated, as Traister notes, because as well as being 'ungainly on the stump' (as a live performer), Clinton was also 'uneasy with the press'. As Saward observes, a politician typically tries to make representative claims that will be accepted 'by shaping . . . strategically his persona and policy positions for certain constituencies and audiences', although '[c]ontemporary normative frames stress singular and consistent roles for political actors', which means that 'shape-shifting' politicians are painted as 'deceitful or manipulative' (2014, 723–4, 735). In Clinton's case, this extended to her opponents' exploitation of widespread distrust through its conflation with criminality, as indicated by rallying cries to 'lock her up' throughout the 2016 presidential campaign (Stevenson 2016). The tenuous nature of the theatrically enacted representative connection makes shape-shifting problematic. Friedland alludes to this when he argues that, in the newly established French representative democracy, '[e]xactly as in theatrical representation, the political actor succeeds in encouraging the audience to partake in the illusion not by drawing attention to the process of acting, but by acting the role to perfection' (1995, 137). In other words, while politicians are performing, and to be persuasive have to perform differently for different audiences, there is pressure for them to be seen to successfully downplay the theatrical nature of their performances: they have to be seen not to be acting and not to be moulding themselves to appeal to their listeners. Clinton, however, was 'ungainly' and 'uneasy' as a performer, and this exacerbated the suspicion with which political performers are inevitably viewed. Her failure to find a form of theatricality that was sufficiently true-seeming impeded the performative success of her public self-presentation, in that Clinton did not appear knowable and thus was unable to establish solid representative connections with her audiences. In addition to this, over the course of a long public career in a male-dominated field, Clinton had been pressured into performing many different versions of herself, a circumstance that further undermined her capacity to project consistency. Non-male, non-cis, and non-white politicians also struggle more to evoke a sense of legitimacy because they do not conform to the white, male, able-bodied, cisgender model of political authority that is entrenched in American culture (see Chapter 3).

Political scientists increasingly acknowledge that politicians' performances are an important part of politics, thus turning their backs on positions like Schedler's (1997a), which seek to conceptualise politics as foreign to and corruptible by performance. Bernard Manin has argued influentially that Western democracies have become 'audience democracies', marked by people's tendency to vote for individual politicians rather than broad party platforms and an emphasis on 'the personal nature of the representative relationship', for instance (1997, 219). Benjamin Moffitt's more recent work on populism likewise recognises that 'contemporary politics are intensely mediatised and "stylised"', and argues that therefore 'the "aesthetic" and "performative" features of politics are particularly (and increasingly) important' (2016, 39). Often, in this work, performance is emphasised as a feature of heavily mediatised twenty-first-century politics, although Moffitt's argument that performativity is 'particularly' and 'increasingly' important now implies that representative politics must always have had a performative dimension.

This chapter's focus on historically distinct conceptualisations of performance emphasises aspects of performance, performativity, and theatricality that are not exclusive to the mediatised age. In fact, it is striking how immediately concerns about the impossibility of ever truly knowing politicians' inner selves and motivations through their public performances arose, and were obsessed about, after the advent of abstract representation in the context of post-revolutionary France. Performance functions as the linchpin of the system of representative democracy, establishing democratic legitimation as a dynamic, performative, and theatrical process that depends on the interaction and the tenuous connection between politician-performers and political audiences. Concerns around the credibility of politicians' public personas are likewise an inherent feature of the system of representative democracy, not merely the result of its degradation. If a 'natural' and 'healthy' lack of trust results in democratic safeguards like checks and balances on institutional power, distrust, on the other hand, can arise despite institutional safeguards (Bertsou 2019). Reliance on performance in representative democracy itself is liable to give rise to distrust – both as a side effect of culturally ingrained antitheatricality and because of the suspension of disbelief required when audiences are asked to accept planned and rehearsed theatrical performances as the natural (and, often, spontaneous) truth.

NOTES

1. For a thorough account of Clinton's relationship to the US media, see Parry-Giles (2001, 2014).
2. Hence also Nield's contention that 'the theatre's production of space demands a kind of *suspension of disbelief* which . . . remains constant to it, despite its taking on different aspects and configurations that change with the particular historical context' (2006, 64, my emphasis).

CHAPTER 2

PERFORMING THE US PRESIDENCY

'My fellow citizens: Today we celebrate the mystery of American renewal', the newly inaugurated President Bill Clinton declared on 20 January 1993 (Clinton 1993). With lyrical flourish, Clinton connected the wintery day – many in his audience were wearing hats and gloves despite the sunny weather – to his inauguration speech's theme of rejuvenation and restoration: 'This ceremony is held in the depth of winter. But, by the words we speak and the faces we show the world, we force the spring. A spring reborn in the world's oldest democracy, that brings forth the vision and courage to reinvent America.' Clinton went on to speak of core American ideals – life, liberty, the pursuit of happiness; he thanked his predecessor, President George H. W. Bush; he referred to great historical challenges that have faced the United States in the Great Depression, in fascism, communism, and the Cold War; he dropped the name of George Washington and outlined how much the United States had changed since the country's founding. As an inaugural address, the speech was uncontroversial, even unremarkable. It was a speech on renewal that anticipated the turn of the millennium while touching on key moments and figures from American history. Clinton conveyed some sense of the enormity of the challenges facing the United States in a globally connected world, but on the whole this was an optimistic speech. There was a hint of broadly anti-establishmentarian manoeuvring as Clinton asserted the need to ensure 'that power and privilege no longer shout down the voice of the people' and promised 'to give this capital back to the people to whom it belongs', but there was no anger in the newly inaugurated president's voice. At the same time as calling for the restoration of civic-minded public service in Washington, DC, Clinton also reminded the crowd that 'in this city today, there are people who want to do better'. Although Clinton speechwriter Michael Waldman writes of Clinton's 'surprising vehemence' in his 'rapid-fire' dictation of his dig at the Washington elite during speech preparation (2000, 33), the crowd's applause to these lines as delivered was enthusiastic but not fervent. This was clearly an audience whose political sensibilities had been pleasingly tickled, not one moved to either tears or red-faced anger.

While fairly unremarkable as a political speech, Clinton's inaugural address is more revealing if one looks at it for what it lacks. Clinton implored the assembled, 'Let us put aside personal advantage so that we can feel the pain and see the promise of America'. This self-referentially cites Clinton's much-vaunted ability to feel other people's pain (see Herbert 2016, 138), an ability not otherwise demonstrated by this inauguration speech, which gave no insight into the empathetic self Clinton had projected throughout his campaign. The speech was devoid of personal anecdotes or individual stories, and decidedly not conversational in tone. In part, this can be ascribed to the formal setting in front of the United States Capitol and the occasion of taking office. More intriguingly, this speech accompanied the moment at which, through the performative act of taking the oath of office, Bill Clinton the candidate became Bill Clinton, President of the United States. One of Clinton's White House speechwriters explained this transformation, and its impact as they saw it on the inaugural address, to me:

> If you look at the very early speeches . . . there's an awkwardness, they don't sound like themselves to me. . . . I feel like what's happening in those early speeches is that they're trying to figure out how to make themselves sound like a president. For Clinton the role model is very obviously JFK and so some of those early speeches have this Sorensenian,[1] . . . JFK-kind-of construction to them. And it doesn't work for him. . . . He was great during the campaign because he was just being . . . his best self, and then all of a sudden: My gosh, here I am, I'm in the White House, I'm standing at the presidential podium, I need to sound presidential in a way that I didn't quite during the campaign. And so what does that sound like, me being president? And he and his speechwriters were grappling with . . . how do we find an authentic Bill Clinton that's also the President of the United States?

In some ways, the thought that Bill Clinton the presidential candidate is not the same as Bill Clinton the US president is confounding. Of course, there was only one Bill Clinton present at this inauguration, and this was the same person before and after taking the oath of office. Given Michael Saward's work (2006, 2010, 2014) on the representative claim and Jeffrey Alexander's (2006, 2010,

2011, 2016) contention that electoral success elevates a candidate into a collective representation, one might assume that Clinton's status after having been elected was a relatively straightforward one. All Clinton would seem to need to do is reaffirm his status as the nation's representative, a status that had just been established by his clear win of the election. But this moment was actually more complex, precisely because Clinton, performing his inaugural address, was being perceived theatrically and therefore had to perform as such, which entailed turning himself into a theatrical character for the public to spectate. We can think of a theatrical moment as one in which objects or people perform 'through a sort of "doubling" of themselves, as they appear both as what they are and as what they represent', so that a judge, for instance, will theatrically 'appear' in court 'in his or her formal role in costume, and according to routine or ritual tropes of behaviour within time-limited requirements' (Nield 2014, 553). In other words, a judge without their robes is just a person, invisible insofar as they cannot be perceived as inhabiting the specific role they are required to play in a particular, theatrical, moment.

The US president does not, of course, wear any kind of instantly recognisable attire, nor does he verify his status through a particular document. Taking the oath of office at the inauguration is a ritualised performative act, which, by the convention of presidential legitimacy, casts Clinton in this particular role. In his physical presence, Clinton remains constant on this occasion, but what he represents changes profoundly. In one moment, Clinton is the president-elect, a successful presidential candidate; in the next, he is President of the United States, charged with leading the nation. According to theatre scholar Sophie Nield, the experience of being in theatrical space can have the effect of leaving people feeling 'alienated from [them]selves' as they are 'externally "framed" and "directed"' and as a result begin to 'imagin[e] the self from the outside' (2014, 554). We can only guess whether Clinton felt alienated, as if he were standing beside and watching himself, as he stepped up to the podium to deliver the inaugural address, but something approaching this possibility is captured in the speechwriter's quote above. If theatrical space is space 'in which the gaze (or its possibility) is *embedded*' and 'which is conditioned by the awareness of that possibility' (Nield 2014, 553, emphasis in original), then the presidential inauguration is a theatrical occasion par excellence. Clinton is, after all, surrounded by thousands of people, politicians and dignitaries as well as ordinary citizens, all of them looking to him to rise to the task of representing the nation to itself. As the White House speechwriter above opines, the need to sound presidential comes with what Clinton is now tasked with representing. To sharpen this point: in his role as US president Clinton does not represent himself through the wearing of a particular costume or by producing the right document, but through the public performance of himself as the US president. As the previous chapter argued, the theatrical performance of oneself requires a degree of abstraction and self-fictionalisation, which is why theatrical doubling opens up the possibility of not appearing to be that which one already is.

On this occasion, Clinton's most memorable line, coming roughly midway through the inauguration speech, was, 'There is nothing wrong with America that cannot be cured by what is right with America'. Written by Clinton's first Chief Speechwriter, David Kusnet, the line survived the many drafts the speech went through. In its parallelism, it is distinctly reminiscent of the famous line 'ask not what your country can do for you – ask what you can do for your country' from John F. Kennedy's inauguration speech (1961), given thirty-two years earlier (see also Waldman 2000, 32). If Clinton was attempting to be convincing in playing himself as the US president, then he here reached for Kennedy as a presidential model, not to sound exactly like or 'play' Kennedy but to imbue himself with the presidentiality he was newly tasked to exude. This emphasis on presidentiality came, at least following the above speechwriter's line of thought, at the expense of being able to convey personal specificity, as Clinton had not yet found a way of representing himself as 'an authentic Bill Clinton that's also the President of the United States'.

This chapter investigates performances of the US presidency and the representative task they seek to accomplish in detail. Initially, the focus is the broad strokes of the earliest performances by US presidents alongside Jeffrey K. Tulis's landmark work *The Rhetorical Presidency* (1987), which, insofar as it is concerned with constraints and limits placed on presidential oratory, needs to be examined in light of the argument presented in Chapter 1 that performance is a core feature of representative democracy. In discussing the US context it is immediately apparent that the much-venerated framers of the Constitution – or, as they are also commonly referred to, Founding Fathers[2] – of the United States sought to circumscribe the power of the president by imposing norms that sharply limited the kinds of public performances presidents were expected to give. Alexander Hamilton's Federalist Paper No. 1, for instance, speaks directly to the framers' concerns about the connection between a leader's public appeal and the degradation of the constitutional order they sought to construct: 'Of those men who have overturned the liberties of republics, the greatest number have begun their career by paying an obsequious court to the people; commencing demagogues, and ending tyrants', Hamilton asserts here (Hamilton, Madison, and Jay [1788] 2003, 29). This begs the question of whether, and how, presidential leadership can be divorced from the idea of appealing to the people through public performance. This chapter argues that the framers' carefully placed constraints on presidential oratory in fact allow for the link between performance and democratic legitimacy to be carved out in greater detail. Rather than necessarily being motivated by the view that performance had no place in politics, early efforts to rein in presidential oratory should be understood as attempts to circumscribe the immense power performance has due to its inherent link with democratic legitimacy.

The chapter goes on to explore the loosening of the norms for presidential performance the framers had established and in this way opens up the exploration of how presidents in the late twentieth and early twenty-first centuries perform for and seek to establish a relationship with the public. A definitive shift away from prior norms can be located in the presidencies of Theodore Roosevelt (1901–9) and Woodrow Wilson (1913–21), though some scholars argue that the shift should be seen as gradual and that elements of it can be traced to the much earlier nineteenth-century examples of popular presidential leadership by James Monroe (1817–25) and Andrew Jackson (1829–37) (cf. Bimes 2007; Ellis 1998; Ellis and Walker 2007; Tulis 1987, 2007). What is certain is that developments towards greater engagement with the national public by the president were enhanced as technological advancements like radio and, later, television became widely available and ensured that the public's relationship to the chief executive became increasingly more personality-driven – a circumstance that raised the question of the president's personal and professional 'authenticity'. In conjunction with these changes, the creation of presidential speeches became increasingly professionalised: Warren Harding's 'literary clerk' Judson Welliver was the first presidential speechwriter. This chapter's second half focuses in detail on professionalised performances of the US presidency over the last forty years. Drawing on the specialised knowledge of speechwriters and speech coaches for presidential administrations and campaigns from Ronald Reagan to Barack Obama, the craft of preparing, rehearsing, and delivering presidential performances that aim to construct a coherent presidential persona and an idealised, unified national audience is explored. What emerges is a picture of how presidential performances in the distant past and the contemporary moment have been geared in different ways towards audiences whilst aiming to fulfil the president's task of representing the entirety of the nation but also appealing to an idealised national community in a way that belies the division, polarisation, and negative partisanship that characterise the contemporary United States.

PERFORMATIVE LEGITIMACY AND THE RHETORICAL PRESIDENCY

One of the central claims of Jeffrey K. Tulis's seminal study *The Rhetorical Presidency* is that '[n]othing could be further from the founders' intentions than for presidential power to depend upon the interplay of orator and crowd' (1987, 89). Tulis argues that the founders of the United States, as well as almost all presidents before the twentieth century, subscribed to an informal but, with very few exceptions, effective doctrine that placed significant constraints upon the kinds of popular performance presidents were able to give. To back up this argument, Tulis notes that *The Federalist Papers*, written by Alexander

Hamilton, James Madison, and John Jay between 1787 and 1788 to promote the ratification of the United States Constitution, begin and end with the framers' concerns about the susceptibility of the United States to demagogues (27–8). Tulis therefore argues that '[f]or most federalists, "demagogue" and "popular leader" were synonyms', which is why the founders tried to subdue politicians', and particularly presidents', public performances (27).

While this line of thought might seem to controvert the argument presented in Chapter 1 for the place of performance at the heart of representative democracy, it is important to note that the framers did not proscribe all kinds of public presidential performance, only appeals they considered too frequent or partisan. The Federalist No. 49, for instance, makes the argument that 'the people are the only legitimate fountain of power', but the document nevertheless cautions against frequent popular appeals (Hamilton, Madison, and Jay [1788] 2003, 310–11). Madison, as author of The Federalist No. 49, argues

> that as every appeal to the people would carry an implication of some defect in the government, frequent appeals [to the people by political leaders] would, in a great measure, deprive the government of the veneration which time bestows on everything. (311)

The Federalist No. 49 indicates that the framers were acutely aware of the extraordinary power popular appeals might have to disturb and potentially upend the political system:

> We are to recollect that all the existing constitutions were formed in the midst of a danger which repressed the passions most unfriendly to order and concord; of an enthusiastic confidence of the people in their patriotic leaders, which stifled the ordinary diversity of opinions on great national questions; of a universal ardor for new and opposite forms, produced by a universal resentment and indignation against the ancient government; and whilst no spirit of party connected with the changes to be made, or the abuses to be reformed, could mingle its leaven in the operation. The future situations in which we must expect to be usually placed, do not present any equivalent security against the danger which is apprehended. But the greatest objection of all is, that the decisions which would probably result from such appeals would not answer the purpose of maintaining the constitutional equilibrium of the government. (312)

What Madison propounds here is that the revolutionary situation in which the United States were founded was an occasion for popular appeals, because its very monumentality served to focus the people's attention on what were the vital questions. In future, if the stability of the constitutional order is taken as a given, popular appeals would be counterproductive insofar as they produced a level of discord and upheaval disproportionate to the smaller policy questions the government would now be seeking to address. This same goal of insulating the constitutional order, and the separation of powers, from popular upheaval appears to have been at the heart of the choice to elect the president through 'an intermediary body of electors' who would be less swayed by the 'heats and ferments' of public debate than the general public (411). Terri Bimes argues that debates during the Constitutional Convention revolved around fears that the 'ignorant public' could be roused and manipulated by popular appeals made by elite factions into selecting a president of unsuitable character (2007, 242–3). It seems clear that the founders were keen to limit impassioned addresses to the public on matters of policy. Importantly, however, the argument contained in the passage cited above, that too-frequent appeals to the people would have the power to unduly raise 'the passions most unfriendly to order and concord', is qualitatively different from Andreas Schedler's (1997a), who sees performance as by definition incompatible with politics (see Chapter 1). The framers understood that national politics would inevitably involve 'nondeliberative appeals' (Tulis 1987, 37–8), but they sought to circumscribe presidential oratory in such a way that it would encourage deliberation more than anything else.

The goal in nudging political communication towards a deliberative style was to foster presidential performances that would reinforce, rather than act divisively upon, the constitutional order. Tulis explains that it became the norm for presidents to explicate and reflect on the Constitution in publicly held speeches, while commentary on specific policies was, due to its more partisan nature, made in writing and addressed to Congress, not the general public (47–51). George Washington's first inauguration speech (1789) had addressed not the general public but 'Fellow-Citizens of the Senate and of the House of Representatives'. His second inauguration speech (1793), though addressed to 'Fellow Citizens', had been all of 135 words long. John Adams's inaugural address (1797) resembled Washington's first, but it was Thomas Jefferson's first inaugural address (1801) that became the initial model for presidential oratory (Tulis 1987, 50).

Jefferson, addressing 'Friends and Fellow-Citizens', calls for unity after a contested election campaign and reflects at length on the strength and value of the American constitutional order. Indeed, Jefferson opens on a strikingly self-deprecating note:

> Called upon to undertake the duties of the first executive office of our country, I avail myself of the presence of that portion of my fellow-citizens which is here assembled to express my grateful thanks for the favor with which they have been pleased to look toward me, to declare a sincere consciousness that the task is above my talents, and that I approach

it with those anxious and awful presentiments which the greatness of the charge and the weakness of my powers so justly inspire. . . . Utterly, indeed, should I despair did not the presence of many whom I here see remind me that in the other high authorities provided by our Constitution I shall find resources of wisdom, of virtue, and of zeal on which to rely under all difficulties. To you, then, gentlemen, who are charged with the sovereign functions of legislation, and to those associated with you, I look with encouragement for that guidance and support which may enable us to steer with safety the vessel in which we are all embarked amidst the conflicting elements of a troubled world. (1801)

Most notable in the above is Jefferson's emphasis on the interdependence of the institutions of the constitutional order, particularly the president's reliance on the legislature. Following the Jeffersonian model, and the framers' belief in constitutional unity, each successive president performed his legitimacy not as a partisan trying to curry favour with the people, but as a chief interpreter of constitutional values whose effectiveness was reliant on the support he received from the other branches of government. The Constitution, the preservation of whose vigour is referred to in Jefferson's first inaugural address 'as the sheet anchor of our peace at home and safety abroad', was thus cast as a non-partisan intermediary that provided a focal point for presidential performances of democratic legitimacy. Tulis seminally argues that it was not until the turn of the twentieth century that presidential oratory broke definitively with the Jeffersonian model.

Numerous scholars have quibbled with the clear-cut breaks in presidential performance style and the conception of the presidency that Tulis identifies, arguing for more nuance and complexity in the treatment of the historical timeline. They have suggested, for instance, that '[t]he relationship between the presidency and the people was not a widely shared norm but rather one of the defining issues separating the two parties in the years leading up to the Civil War' (Ellis 1998, 5); that nineteenth-century presidents James Monroe (1817–25) and Andrew Jackson (1829–37) moved much more decisively towards popular presidential leadership than Tulis acknowledges (Bimes 2007; Ellis 2008, 36–7; Ellis and Walker 2007); that presidents in the first half of the nineteenth century did communicate directly with the public on matters of policy, but did so through newspapers rather than public oratory (Laracey 1998); that changing strategies leading to more candidate-centred presidential campaigns in the 1890s were more influential in shifting norms of presidential speech than Woodrow Wilson's conception of presidential leadership (Gamm and Smith 1998); that Teddy Roosevelt was equally if not more pivotal in bringing about the rhetorical presidency as Wilson was (Gamm and Smith 1998, 92); that Wilson was more wary of demagogues and struck more of a balance between working with his party in Congress and appealing to the public than Tulis suggests (Bimes and Skowronek 1998; Stid 1998); and that Tulis ignores the role of later presidents, particularly Franklin Delano Roosevelt, in consolidating the rhetorical presidency (Milkis 1998, 183). Jason Mast, building on Richard Neustadt ([1960] 1990) and Fred I. Greenstein (1988), considers FDR to represent 'the breakthrough that established the modern presidency' since FDR's frequent public performances 'cultivated the association of the president's persona with the office' and since FDR's presidency coincided with the widespread dissemination of presidential performances to the public via newspapers, radio, and cinema newsreels (2012, 29–30). Mast also argues for the importance of the rise of television in 'reshap[ing] the political arena' to focus more intensively on politicians' bodies, personas, and images and thus defining Kennedy's success against Nixon in the first televised presidential debate in 1960 as well as facilitating the rise of Reagan (2012, 33–4, 41–2; see also Raphael 2009). Despite all of these quibbles and disagreements, the broad strokes of Tulis's argument – that there was a particular vision of the president's relationship to the public that the founders promoted and that this was exemplified by Jefferson and continued to be influential for a time before giving way to a much more public-focused conception of the presidency around the turn of the twentieth century – remain useful. Examples of Wilson's rhetoric will be used in the following to illustrate the newer, public-focused conception.

Though presidential oratory completed a significant change at the cusp of the twentieth century, this does not mean that legitimacy became performative. Rather, following the Jeffersonian model, presidential oratory in the nineteenth century tended to perform the president's legitimacy by emphasising his position within and his understanding of the Constitution. Later presidential performances move away from this pattern. In the beginning, however, the Constitution served as a neutral, and uncontested, ground between the orator and his audience, which, precisely due to its presumed universally accepted and revered status, served to shore up the president's legitimacy. As such, political audiences' perception of the president's legitimacy was focused less on the successful theatrical appearance of his public persona as an authentic person and more on the president's conformity to a pattern that posited the explication of the Constitution as the president's central representative task. Put differently, the success of the president's theatrical appearance and the consequent public perception of his legitimacy were, following the framers' vision, less tied to the president's personal characteristics than they are today. To some extent, therefore, the norms governing early US presidential oratory decoupled legitimacy from the orator's personal qualities through the introduction of the Constitution as an intermediary focal point for the performance of legitimacy. Despite the tight constraints imposed on presidential performances, legitimacy in the early United States was still performative and performed, and no radical upheaval was required for early twentieth-century presidents to break away from the established norms governing presidential rhetoric. Indeed, one of the persistent criticisms of Tulis's work is that what he characterises as a break away from the early norms against partisan oratory was more of a fluid and gradual evolution, and even Tulis admits that the possibility for change was already 'latent in the previous constitutional order' (2007, 487).

By the twentieth century a different kind of presidential performance was established as the norm. Theodore Roosevelt is credited with coining the term the 'bully pulpit', which first appears in 1909 in a profile on the president in *The Outlook*, then a significant weekly news magazine. *The Outlook* describes Roosevelt reading out an address he was to give in his library, 'when he suddenly stopped, swung round in his swivel chair, and said: "I suppose my critics will call that preaching, but I have got such a bully pulpit!"' (Abbott 1909, 430). Tulis argues that Roosevelt represents a 'middle way' between the founding perspective that limited presidential rhetoric and the rhetorical presidency inaugurated by Woodrow Wilson in that Roosevelt used popular addresses extensively, but did so to champion moderation and tamp down demagoguery (1987, 95–116). Following Roosevelt, Wilson's first inaugural address (1913b) presents a remarkable contrast to Jefferson's. Far from shying away from matters of policy, Wilson's inaugural responded to contemporary circumstances: it addressed issues of taxation, the banking system, the industrial and agricultural economy, and infrastructure. Wilson begins on a partisan note, dwelling on Democratic electoral victories in the House of Representatives, the Senate, and the Presidency, then goes on to address the people by referring to the 'human cost' of the industrial achievements made in the United States, as well as the 'fearful physical and spiritual cost to the men and women and children' and the 'groans and agony . . . coming up out of the mines and factories', which 'the great Government' had done nothing to address. The anti-establishmentarian tone in which Wilson tackled these issues is striking. While he praised American industriousness, enterprise, and natural abundance, Wilson censured the federal government for its failure to direct these towards the public good:

> With the great Government went many deep secret things which we too long delayed to look into and scrutinize with candid, fearless eyes. The great Government we loved has too often been made use of for private and selfish purposes, and those who used it had forgotten the people. (1913b)

In Wilson's view the government's loss of integrity had caused the nation to be 'deeply stirred, stirred by a solemn passion, stirred by the knowledge of wrong, of ideals lost, of government too often debauched and made an instrument of evil' (1913b). This is a formulation surely designed to provoke rather than bracket the people's passions. Wilson's inaugural address thus reflects a decisively different idea of the relationship between president and people from the founding vision which stressed the president's role within a system of government institutions and his task of explicating the Constitution. In the way the address pits the people and (on their side) the president, who figures himself as their chief spokesman and interpreter, against the 'great Government',[3] in how it breaks with the style and tone of previous inaugural addresses and then performs a crisis of government by asserting that 'much fine gold has been corroded', Wilson's speech reads, from today's perspective, like populist diatribe. An intriguing inconsistency in Wilson's assertion about the corrosion of gold is that gold is known to be 'very inert and resistant to oxidation and corrosion' on any but cosmological timescales (Goodman 2002, 22). Wilson's is a hyperbolic statement, with which he is performatively, and to boost his own political capital, evoking a crisis in government, which may or may not have an objective basis (depending, of course, on what objectively measurable criteria one might see fit to apply to the situation in the first place). The important aspect of this strained metaphor is that it helped Wilson to paint himself as the clear-sighted saviour who sees through the system's corruption and is on the side of the people: Wilson needed the political system to be broken, the gold to be corroded, even if that entailed making his audience believe impossible things.

Gone from Wilson's speech is the Jeffersonian self-deprecation and focus on the unity and interdependence of political institutions; Wilson substitutes these with an insistence on whom and how the government has failed and, most strikingly, by making reference to the corruption with which the 'great Government' has 'for private and selfish purposes' been infested. In further contrast to the Jeffersonian model, Wilson, rather than eschewing matters of policy, boldly declares, 'We have itemized with some degree of particularity the things that ought to be altered', and proceeds to list a number of concrete economic issues, among these 'a tariff which . . . makes the Government a facile instrument in the hand of private interests'. The word 'Constitution' does not appear in Wilson's inauguration speech; instead, he ends by stressing explicitly the degree to which he sees his presidential authority as deriving directly from the people: 'I summon all honest men, all patriotic, all forward-looking men, to my side. God helping me, I will not fail them, if they will but counsel and sustain me!' Wilson's biographer John Milton Cooper, Jr. notes that a moment right before Wilson started to give the inaugural address seemed to encapsulate the change in the relationship between the president and the people that the speech itself vocalises: 'Noticing that the police had cleared a space in front of the platform [from which Wilson was to give the speech], he directed, "Let the people come forward"' (2011, 198). In short, Wilson's appeal is not to the other political institutions to help in the task of fulfilling the demands of the presidential office, but for the people to take on this task.

According to Tulis, Wilson's framing of the president's mandate fundamentally changed the nature of presidential oratory, which became more frequent, partisan, and personalised. If the president had previously performed his legitimacy by way of being seen as the chief explicator of the Constitution, he now performed his legitimacy by making reference to his ability to 'tap[] into the public's feelings' and 'translate the people's felt desires into public policy' (Tulis 1987, 135, 128). While it may be tempting to ascribe this striking change in rhetoric exclusively or mainly to the evolution of media technology, Wilson did not give his first live radio address until 1923, after he had left office. Wilson did, however, expand on his predecessor Theodore Roosevelt's conception of the bully pulpit and had long envisioned his presidency as providing forceful and persuasive oratorical leadership (Kraig 2004, 103–8). According to Wilson's biographer Robert Alexander Kraig, Wilson also showed an awareness of the increasing mediation of mass communication, drawing the conclusion that democratic leaders now had to be 'inordinately skilled rhetors' to cut through to the public (75). The impact on the performance of democratic legitimacy was decisive: the perception of legitimacy was no longer tied primarily to a supra-political set of ideals (as enshrined in the Constitution) but instead was understood to derive directly from the president's personal qualities. The president thus had to possess some combination of personal style, charisma, and empathy to be accepted by the public as a credible representative of the nation as a whole. Where the perception of legitimacy had previously depended on performances that held the president above the fray of partisan politics, it now relied on the president's ability to tackle such issues persuasively.

Tulis outlines a number of consequences brought about by these developments in presidential oratory: the erasure of the difference between campaigning and governing; the establishment of speechwriting as a profession and the institutionalisation of speechwriting in the White House; the increased autonomy of the press; and the rise of presidential anti-Congress rhetoric (1987, 181–8). To observers of early twenty-first-century politics, the persistence of presidents positioning themselves against Congress will be readily apparent, not just in Donald's Trump's populism but also, for instance, in the way in which Barack Obama still positioned himself as an outsider in 2016, when he was most of the way through his second term of office (see Introduction). Such performances' resemblance, however subtle, to Wilson's inaugural is significant because it clearly illustrates the shift from presidential performances of legitimacy that tended to bolster the institutional structure to performances that seem to undermine it. The erosion of the early pattern of presidential rhetoric, which stressed the president's interdependence with other institutions, and all of these institutions' respect for the Constitution, would have left presidential performances in a vacuum, where, without the Constitution as a focal point, the president would have no intermediary bulwark to guarantee public support. In this circumstance, an obvious strategy, and one of which presidents have made widespread use, is to rail against the ineffectiveness and corruption of other institutions so as to make the president stand out as a contrast to them.

It is important not to overstate the case, however. While it is tempting to see Wilson as a precursor to contemporary political rhetoric that knocks Congress, Terri Bimes and Stephen Skowronek point out that, for all the bluster of his inaugural address, Wilson remained wary of demagogues, sceptical of presidential campaigning, and, in contrast to Teddy Roosevelt, favourable to popular appeals on 'matters of war and peace [rather than domestic issues] where the president presumably had the strongest constitutional claim to leadership', such that, in their view, Wilson was actually 'barely keeping pace with' the course of development of presidential leadership as opposed to piloting a striking new vision (1998, 160). Daniel Stid similarly argues that, in governing, Wilson 'believed that appealing to public opinion was not a viable method when the president was trying to overcome opposition in the Senate' and looks to Theodore Roosevelt as the main culprit for establishing the rhetorical presidency (1998, 167). It is also noteworthy that, despite no longer featuring as the central focus in presidential oratory, much like the so-called Founding Fathers, the Constitution has remained an object of reverence. In 2017, news outlets suggested that Donald Trump had committed the outrage of calling the Constitution 'archaic' and 'a really bad thing for the country', an argument that was quickly countered by others, who clarified that even that least presidential and reverential of presidents had been talking about Senate rules, not the Constitution (Volokh 2017).

The Conventional Theatricality of the US Presidency

The rhetorical presidency brought about the professionalised mediation between president and public through speechwriters and communications staff and elevated the president to the status of a celebrity. The remainder of this chapter focuses on what I call the conventional theatricality of the US presidency, the professionalised production of presidents' public appearances that enables presidents in the contemporary moment (that is, in the late twentieth and early twenty-first centuries) to perform for and to the public. The term does not imply that different presidents conform to a single process of how speeches are written, prepared, and rehearsed, nor does it imply that the outsourcing of speechwriting and speech preparation tasks to a team of professional speechwriters is necessarily incompatible with communicating the president's own voice and intent. The process of speech preparation is typically tailored to each president. For instance, a George W. Bush White House speechwriter explained in our interview that 'the way it worked for Bush' was that 'the person who had his voice the best was the one who ended up informally having final say on how something should sound'. This speechwriter described the ability to write speeches for a principal as 'sometimes it's not even something you can articulate', as 'an instinct', akin to knowing 'what your mom would think about something'. Most of the speech-writers I interviewed stressed the importance of spending time with the politician they were writing for and getting to talk to the politician informally about top-ics they would later write about in speeches. A second George W. Bush White House speechwriter explained that they learned from a colleague how to do this effectively by informally questioning the president about the topic they had been assigned to write about:

> [My colleague] asked the president in a meeting of a group of speechwrit-ers what he envisioned, what the president envisioned the Middle East looking like in, I think it was either 15 or 20 years . . . from when this conversation was happening. And . . . the president proceeded to give a very detailed sort of country by country outline of what he thought that might be. At the moment, I thought it was sort of an interesting ques-tion. I wasn't really sure where it came from. And then I subsequently learned that [my colleague] was writing a major foreign policy address that dealt with this topic, and he knew he had it coming up, so . . . he was very cleverly getting the president to sort of write some of the speech for him. You know, . . . getting . . . the readout in a closed, sort of relaxed setting, knowing of course that . . . you polish it, tweak some of it, but . . . that's a very effective way of doing that.

The Obama White House speechwriters I interviewed similarly emphasised the degree of Obama's involvement in the speechwriting process. One of them told me, 'if you just google, like, [White House photographer] "Pete Souza Obama edits", you'll see all these photos of all the times Obama worked on a speech. And wrote a speech by hand. He was . . . intimately involved with it'. This speechwriter characterised Obama's involvement in the speechwriting process as follows: 'Obama is so passionate about his speeches in the sense of, you know, this is what I wanna say, I wanna make sure it's exactly what I wanna say'. They noted that Obama gave edits that went beyond the level of the speech's content and instead concerned its rhythm and flow, likening the speech to performing jazz:

> I remember giving him [the draft of a big speech], it was the first draft I gave him, about a week before the speech. And I give it to him, I think on a Monday night, went home to sleep, came back the next day, wait-ing to hear from him. I hadn't heard from him, I was surprised. He called me and asked me to come up to have lunch with him, so I go up and I'm thinking, 'oh shit'. You know, . . . if he just calls to say, 'let's talk about this', it's usually a bad thing. He goes, . . . 'so, I think it's all

here, man'. Like, 'everything I wanna say is in here'. I say, 'that's great'. He goes, 'it is, but the problem is, everything I wanna say is in here. The entire speech is up at a nine or ten and every sentence has meaning, every sentence is packed with something, there are no moments of quiet'. And I said, 'I know, you're right, . . . I just wanted to get everything in there'. He's like, 'right, I mean, I can't deliver the speech when it's all up at this level, so I do need some filler sentences. I need some pauses and some quiet moments'. And he said, 'do you ever listen to jazz?' And I was like, 'I mean, sure, sometimes, you know, got some Miles Davis on my iPod'. He says, 'good, go home, go home tonight, don't work on the speech, it's in good enough shape, you can take the night off. And listen to some Miles Davis'. . . . And he said, 'it's the notes you don't play. It's the silences [that] really make a jazz song cool'. And I went home and listened and he was right. It's the quiet moments.

Whilst being closely involved with crafting the language of a speech, Obama apparently did not rehearse speeches very often. For a major speech like the State of the Union address, one of his speechwriters told me, Obama 'would do one run-through', about four hours before giving the speech itself. The sense conveyed by this speechwriter that at least some politicians at the presidential level are remarkably gifted and able to perform speeches with minimal rehearsal was echoed in interviews with Bill Clinton's, Ronald Reagan's, and Sarah Palin's speechwriters, indicating the importance of performance skills or at least the apparent desirability of appearing (or having the reputation) to be so gifted at performing that rehearsal is hardly necessary.

One of Bill Clinton's White House speechwriters told me:

> Very few people can do what Bill Clinton does, which is to sound natural and unrehearsed having never looked at the draft before he needs to do it on the spot; it's like sight-reading of music, almost no one can do that.

Another of Bill Clinton's speechwriters echoed this, saying:

> he's such a gifted speaker, . . . not only does he not need someone else to prepare remarks, he doesn't even need to prepare remarks himself. He can just extemporise, you know, perfect sentences, perfect paragraphs, a perfect narrative, a little maybe . . . meandering in parts, but a perfect narrative.

This speechwriter specified that Clinton either tended to deliver speeches of which only one draft had been written for him, or, for major speeches, 'he would sweat over every little detail'. Clinton's speech development process was, however, remarkably different from Obama's, as the Clinton speechwriter explained:

> the process would be something that used to appear on his formal schedule as 'speech preparation' . . . which reflected the fact that it was a cross between rehearsing the speech and me writing the speech. Rather than sit, you know, he would sit at his desk sometimes and make little notes on the speech. He would not do formal line edits. And what would happen was we would then have a rehearsal session and he would get up and give the speech and, as he gave the speech, he would edit it by speaking it differently than the text. And we would have tape recorders and our notepads and we would take down his revisions. And then, or else if he added like, a particularly good and different turn of phrase we would interrupt him and say to him, you know, . . . 'Mr. President, is that the way you want to say it?' . . . He would not sit at his desk and edit something and then give us back the edits.

The examples above showcase a couple of different ways in which presidents and their speechwriters, who also frequently take on the role of speech coaches when they help prepare for delivery, collaborate in preparing speeches. A Republican speechwriter who had worked on several presidential campaigns told me that 'the best speechwriting process is always going to be one where you're . . . sitting physically side by side, working on it. It's a collaboration'. However, another Republican speechwriter noted that, for Ronald Reagan, the process worked differently, with speechwriters working from a 'long catalogue of speeches that [Reagan] had given' as well as his radio addresses, rather than collaborating closely with Reagan himself. A speechwriter for both President Reagan and Vice President George H. W. Bush confirmed that direct access was less important to Reagan's speechwriters, asserting that, despite this, 'I never had a problem with Reagan's voice and I never had a problem with Bush's voice. I just sort of knew'. Both Reagan and George H. W. Bush also used speech doctors, who contributed lines to speeches remotely, especially humorous ones, rather than working in the White House itself. One speech doctor explained that they usually did not do research that was specific to a speech assignment. They said, 'as I'm writing, I'm hearing in my head how it should sound when they say it'. Reagan's speechwriters tended to emphasise, and perhaps idealise, the importance of Reagan's acting career to the ease of working with him as a performer. A speech doctor elaborated that, despite not writing or rehearsing speeches in direct collaboration with Reagan, 'only in Reagan's case did [what I had written] come out exactly the way I heard it in my head. He . . . knew which word to emphasise, he knew where to pause – all of that, I'm sure, is because he was an actor'.

Despite arriving at the content and desired delivery of a speech through different processes, there are, as the remainder of this chapter will explore, a lot of commonalities in how presidential speeches address the public and frame the relationship between the president and the American electorate. Presidents, moreover, are pressed to give more and more speeches: Clinton apparently spoke 550 times in a 'typical year' of his presidency, while Ronald Reagan spoke 320 times, and Harry Truman only 88 times (Waldman 2000, 16). All of this public exposure and the professionally tailored processes through which speeches are created do not mean, however, that the connection between president and public is now a straightforward matter. Indeed, even though presidents address the public all the time on all manner of questions, performances of the US presidency have to strike a number of balances, between professionalism and personality, between contrast and continuity, and between distance and closeness. A striking feature of the late twentieth-century presidency is the way in which presidential travel, which ostensibly aims at bringing the public and president closer together by enabling live, in-person encounters, instead reinforces the image of a 'regal' presidency, since presidents of necessity travel with their staffs and under tight security (Ellis 2008, 13). While on the one hand appearing in highly personalised ways in the mass media, the president tends to remain at a mediated distance from the day-to-day experience of most people's lives. 'The distant motorcades of presidential display' are among the most familiar tropes of symbolic power, serving 'to summarise ideological and political positions in order that they be easily legible as the vocabularies of power' while existing at a remove from ordinary life and exemplifying the president's ultimate unknowability (Nield 2015, 125). Images of the president are now ubiquitous, and presidents are almost universally recognised, but they appear, paradoxically, much more distant and less approachable than nineteenth-century presidents, who could still travel without bodyguards and be approached directly by the people they came across on their travels. As such, the need to strike a balance between the elevated office and the idea of being one of the people remains a central concern in how presidential performances address the public.

In the contemporary moment, the connection between president and electorate is both amplified and complicated by the complexly mediated political landscape within which US presidents operate. On the one hand, as Bernard Manin (1997) observes, there is an intensified focus on personalised politics in contemporary 'audience democracies', where election results are no longer determinable by the social and economic characteristics of voters but are influenced significantly by the individual qualities of candidates. In audience democracy, successful candidates tend to be 'media figures' (220), a tendency exemplified by Bill Clinton playing 'Heartbreak Hotel' on the saxophone on *The Arsenio Hall Show* during his 1992 presidential campaign as well as more recently by Barack Obama's many talk show appearances, including seven on *The Daily Show* alone during his presidency, and, of course, by the election of Donald Trump, the former host of the reality television show *The Apprentice*.

Issues of representation, distrust, and performance are fundamental to representative democracy, but, even so, the US presidency is in many ways singular. The president is the only representative elected to represent the entirety of the American people and commands an unprecedented level of national and international visibility. One consequence is that, even when presidents address relatively small and local audiences, their performances always have the potential to extend to multiple national and even international audiences. Speechwriters thus have to navigate addressing multiple audiences at once. In our interview, one former Democratic White House speechwriter described this awareness as follows:

> Everybody else is listening. Or at least this is going to get played on the news or people will tweet about it. So you're never talking about policies that will only benefit Cleveland. You are talking to the wider world. And especially when it comes to a speech about national security and foreign policy. We knew the rest of the world would listen carefully.

A second Democratic speechwriter noted the president's temporal rather than geographic reach, referring to the importance of 'speaking to history, which is something that presidents get to do'. A former Republican White House speechwriter characterised the president as someone 'who sort of lives in people's living room, right? I mean, you see him on the news every night'. Because the president is so omnipresent that he practically 'lives in people's living room', this speechwriter observed, the president has to be somebody that the people 'feel comfortable with entrusting the country to and somebody that they feel comfortable with being sort of a ubiquitous presence in American life for . . . four or eight years'. The idea of feeling 'comfortable' with a particular president and 'entrusting' the country to that person implies a vision of national consensus. The president is, necessarily, presumed to be someone invested with trust by the country's sovereign people, who are, likewise, idealised as a unified national audience that can agree on and conceivably be represented by a single national representative. I will return to the question of how presidential performances constitute audiences later in the chapter.

Presidential ubiquity has some disadvantages. The Republican speechwriter who described the president as 'somebody who sort of lives in people's living room', for instance, went on to discuss how the president's ubiquity 'on the news every night' means that 'you can wear out your welcome quickly', so that the public gets fatigued and, at a certain point, 'public opinion sort of calcifies and they're . . . tired of you'. A Democratic speechwriter likewise noted that a consequence of presidents' constant presence on the national stage is that presidents are 'rhetorically spreading [themselves] thin', which means that 'there are too many speeches that presidents give that are just not worth hearing. They don't say anything, they feel rote, there's no energy in them'. Speechwriters also linked the scope of presidential speeches and the wide variety of subject matter about which presidents speak in public to the demands on presidents' communicative abilities as well as to what they perceived as the mistaken assumption that anything presidential was essentially a done deal in policy terms. 'A president has to be able to talk about anything. Anything that happens, anything that could happen', one Republican speechwriter observed, while a second Republican speechwriter stated their view that 'there's a requirement for the job in a lot of ways to be a good communicator' but also cautioned that 'the rhetorical presidency was a little overblown' if it raised the expectation that 'well, if it's in a speech, it's going to happen'. Given the immense power inherent in the office of the presidency, audiences might be forgiven for expecting presidential speeches to be more literally performative – in the sense of unifying words and actions – than they often are. But both Democratic and Republican speechwriters stressed the weight of responsibility that they felt comes with representing the nation. A Democratic speechwriter explained:

> If you're President of the United States . . . you're speaking on behalf of the country . . . so the words that a president or a secretary of state says [are] attributed to the nation. That's very different than 'vote for me', that is, 'this is what America believes and stands for, these are our ideals and values that other nations and leaders will listen to and interpret'.

In a similar vein, a Republican speechwriter made the argument that presidents should not be 'thin-skinned' in their dealings with foreign leaders, but should, instead, whilst facing discord, say, 'I'm sorry we have disagreements and still, here, [I'm] holding out my hand in friendship'. The speechwriter linked this argument implicitly to the president's task of representing the nation, saying, 'he can do that [hold out his hand in friendship despite disagreement] from a position of strength because the United States is the most powerful country in the world'.

This magnanimous presidential handshake performed when meeting foreign dignitaries on the international stage is a straightforward trope of presidential performance. Donald Trump's tug-of-war-like handshake with French President Emmanuel Macron on 25 May 2017 and Trump's apparent refusal of German Chancellor Angela Merkel's offer of a handshake on 17 March 2017 made headlines because each broke with the expected performance of combined presidential magnanimity and strength (Rogers 2017). The widespread discussion of Trump's apparent self-consciousness about the smallness of his hands in major media outlets (Christensen 2016; Hopper 2016; Shapiro 2016) likewise highlights specific ideals of presidential embodiment, particularly the association of presidential hands with masculinity and even-handed strength. It is because the US president is not just a person but in an important sense a theatrical character who has to perform to specific requirements and expectations of what constitutes presidential performance that seemingly small moments – presidential handshakes, Obama's tears, Bill Clinton's inaugural transformation, and so on – are imbued with such significance.

The Theatrical Presidency

Theatricality implies a doubling of the self, a split between presence and representation that results in the imperative to play oneself. This performance of the self is necessarily circumscribed in specific ways, as it is created as a response to the potential of being spectated and as such involves a degree of self-conscious abstraction and fictionalisation of the self. It is never wholly unselfconscious. As Nield puts it, '[t]he power of abstraction is that we internalize the eye' (2014, 553). Something of the pervasiveness of the internalisation of the eye and the difficulty of masking its effects is captured in Joseph Roach's seminal examination of charisma in his monograph *It*, wherein Roach insists that charisma relies on a performer's ability to evoke a sense of public intimacy and unselfconsciousness (2007, 3–4). Charisma, for Roach, depends in part on the performer's ability to negate or downplay what might be seen as the natural, or at least most common, response to being spectated, which is self-consciousness. Though charismatic performers are able to project a sense of public intimacy and downplay their self-consciousness of being observed, however, the public performance of the self remains incompatible with the idea of wholly revealing one's 'true self'.

Theatre scholar Liz Tomlin contends that

> what used to be understood as an authentic inner self, however this might have been influenced by its social environment, is now recognised, through a postmodern and poststructuralist lens, as a construction made up of materials that can only be drawn from the common hyper-reality of which it is part. (2013, 101)

By way of extending to the present Elinor Fuchs's (1996) analysis of character in the theatre, which posits that changes in how character is represented in the theatre reflect cultural changes in the perception of the self, Tomlin argues that 'theatre at the turn of the century . . . is haunted by free-floating, mischief-making apparitions that are concomitant with the contemporary understanding of identity as made up of multiple and provisional selves' (2013, 81; see also Lehmann 2009, 31). This reflects a broader tendency in how scholars think of the self; Jonas Barish, for instance, claims that in his antitheatrical rejection of the theatre Plato was 'looking down the wrong end of the telescope', since the freedom to rethink and reconceive of one's social role should be thought of not as a threat to social cohesion but 'as a liberation and an enrichment' (1981, 25). Indeed, like Barish, thinkers on authenticity and the self tend to regard the proposition of an essential self with a great deal of scepticism. Lionel Trilling's *Sincerity and Authenticity* makes an influential critique of authenticity, which, in contrast to the more straightforward idea of sincerity (that is, 'congruence between avowal and actual feeling'), Trilling sees as built around the essentialist idea that an individual innermost self can be found beyond 'all the cultural superstructures' imposed on it (1972, 2, 12, 104). Trilling's thinking around authenticity as a relatively recent, and largely troubling, focus in moral life is echoed in Richard Sennett's *The Fall of Public Man*, as Sennett argues that '[p]olitical tyranny and the search for individual authenticity go hand in hand' ([1977] 1986, 121). For Sennett, the premium placed on authenticity erodes people's ability to focus on questions of ideology, so that 'self-disclosure becomes a universal measure of believability and truth' (29–30). Thus,

> simply being able to generate emotion in public showed that the person acting had a superior, because 'authentic' personality. In this way, the politician used personality as an anti-ideological force; to the extent that he [*sic*] could arouse interest, respect, and belief in the quality of his appearances in public, to that extent he could divert his audience from dealing with either his or their own position in the world. (230)

Building on Sennett, theatre scholar Nicholas Ridout argues that a focus on personal authenticity tends to rid politics of its essential agonistic character: 'If our sense of authentic self is always at stake in public interactions, then we will tend to behave in ways that minimize, negotiate, or manage conflict', the result being that 'social relations modeled upon the intimate relationship . . . encourage a politics of consensus' (2008, 18–19). Scholars' scepticism towards the existence of an essential, precultural self that can be revealed through public performance thus extends beyond epistemology to focus on the potentially detrimental effect an obsession with politicians' essential character and its revelation might have on democracy. For my purposes, the interest in this subject matter revolves not so much around the metaphysical question of whether we have an essential self or not as around the undeniably present expectations of both political audiences and speechwriters that we do.

While some note that personal authenticity, or at least the perception thereof, has seemed to be back in fashion in post-postmodernism (Lavender 2016, 22), recent scholarship largely follows postmodernism's discreditation of the notion of an essential authenticity of the self and defines perceived authenticity as an effect of performance and/or mediation (Adiseshiah 2016; Kalisch 2000; Parry-Giles and Parry-Giles 2002; van Alphen and Bal 2009, 3–5). In Nield's take on theatricality, for instance, the imperative to play oneself always refers to playing oneself in a particular capacity. At national borders, one ideally performs oneself as a law-abiding citizen of a particular country, one who is authorised to enter this or another country (Nield 2006). Similarly, Nield introduces the example of a judge who 'is of course a judge all the time' but appears in this capacity only in particular moments (2014, 553). While a judge having dinner with their family at home is still a judge, of course, this particular capacity comes to the fore only in the theatrical space of the courtroom, where there is the demand for the judge to appear, to be present and represent themself, in this particular professional capacity. In contrast to the paradigmatic case of the judge where costuming and the tightly scripted setting of the courtroom serve to inevitably evoke the judge as inhabiting this particular professional role, the US presidency demands that a more delicate balance be struck between the performance of its official capacity and the revelation of the president's personal self through public performance. Participants and attendants in a courtroom trial do not tend to demand to get to know the private self of the judge, but the public demand a sense of who the US president is as a person, their authentic self, and this demand shapes the practice of presidential performances. Performances of the US presidency need to strike a balance between representing the president's office and being revelatory of what is conceived of as a true self in an essentialist vein, though the speechwriters I spoke to simultaneously believed in the existence of authentic selves and understood that the president's publicly presented 'self' is a consciously constructed one.

A speechwriter who had written for multiple Republican presidential campaigns explained how they thought the performance of personality:

> [The public are] never gonna get to know the candidate I know, because I've spent time with them and this was particularly true of [this candidate], where the private interaction was so different than the public perception. . . . And so, my view of [the candidate] is really different than the public perception of [that candidate]. I know that no one is ever really going to see you know seventy-five dimensions of [the candidate]. They're just gonna see one [version] that has, like, one or two or three quality traits. And so, my philosophy about it has always been that I'm trying to write you, write with you, a script or a speech that allows you to convey the best parts of yourself. Like, you on your best day . . . and allows people to see that.

This speechwriter also made a point of stressing that a speechwriter's focus on the principal's personal characteristics and values was unique amongst the politician's staff, because 'we're paying attention to them as a person', which meant that speechwriters think about the politician's 'personal connection' to an issue, and 'not what poll-tested well'. The contention that the speechwriter's job is to bring to the public the best features of a principal (the person a speechwriter is writing for) was widely echoed throughout my interviews. Since they were aware that not all of a president's self can be known by the public, the best course of action, as they articulated it, was to focus on highlighting the observed characteristics of the principal that seemed to be most advantageous. This is a distinctly theatrical process of abstraction and fictionalisation: speechwriters aim to reduce a multiplicity of possible dimensions down to two or three features and to develop these into a coherent public persona on the basis of the resulting persona's anticipated success in public performance. This work of crafting the presidential persona responds to the theatricality of the performance situation – the awareness that this work happens in anticipation of being spectated – and should therefore be understood as a form of professional theatrical practice.

Notably, several speechwriters pushed back against the idea of creating a separate character for their principal. The speechwriter quoted above referred to the idea of inventing a character as 'the craziest, stupidest thing I ever heard'. A Democratic senatorial and vice presidential speechwriter asserted that it was a speechwriter's job to 'work hard to understand who [their principal's] unique self is and then find ways to help them express or reveal it, not to mask or shade it'. All of the writers I spoke to stressed the need to be familiar with the principal in order to draw out their personal characteristics and ways of speaking. And yet, selecting for public presentation two or three characteristics out of seventy-five observed and partly contradictory or at least incompatible dimensions of a person's character is not a neutral or objective process. The public performance of the presidency, particularly along these lines, is incompatible with the idea of wholly revealing the president's true self. Thus, speechwriters were aware, simultaneously, of the need to construct an advantageous version of their principal's self and of the need to deny this version's constructedness.

Two interviewees stressed explicitly that they thought the ability to perform in public had to already be established by the time someone became president, such that speechwriters could rely on an established basis. The presidential persona was thus often seen as already abstracted and fictionalised for public performance in a way that was helpful for the speechwriter to draw on in their work. A Democratic speechwriter mentioned that they did not have to worry about crafting the president into a character, as '[h]e was already fully formed by the time we got there'. This speechwriter also referred to the principal's voice as 'something we were very protective of' because '[i]t was an asset'. A Republican speechwriter similarly argued that 'every person alive has two versions of themselves, they got the public self and the private self', and that a career politician 'preparing to give a speech is preparing to engage with a version of himself that he for the most part established'. Speechwriters did not tend to see themselves as inventing their principals' public personas, but instead believed they were drawing on an established public 'self', and, whilst attempting to bring this 'self' out in speeches, were aware that the presidential persona was a construction that balanced the established public 'self' with the abstract quality of presidentiality. The example that introduces this chapter is particularly illustrative of the balance between presidentiality and personality that presidents need to strike. As the speechwriter I quoted there stressed, Bill Clinton at his inauguration, and likewise George W. Bush after him, needed to integrate his personality with the presidency, which meant that 'he and his speechwriters were grappling with . . ., "how do we find an authentic Bill Clinton that's also the president of the United States?"'

I asked all of the speechwriters I interviewed the question, 'To what extent is a politician giving a speech the same as an actor giving a performance?' In their responses, almost all speechwriters were careful to distinguish between actors, who play someone else, and politicians, who play themselves, despite the fact that playing yourself can involve the creation of a particular voice or persona, which, for the purposes of public perception, might be indistinguishable from acting. As one Democratic speechwriter put it:

> Most presidents and presidential nominees, you know, they've never been actors. I guess the difference . . . is that as an actor you're playing someone else and, you know, especially if you want to be authentic [as a politician] you're playing yourself, you're trying to create maybe a new voice for yourself and the best version of yourself, but you're not being someone else.

Some speechwriters, while insisting on the giftedness of their principals as orators, also emphasised that politicians were less adept at performing than trained actors. One stressed that 'almost every speaker is going to retain something of a crutch that actors don't get, which is, they're gonna have something on the page or on the teleprompter, even if it's just talking points, it's something'. This speechwriter went on to say that politicians generally 'don't have the confidence' to go without notes and 'hit it the way they want to hit it'. As I mentioned in the Introduction, an Obama speechwriter observed that Obama, though a gifted orator, was limited in the level of emotion he would be able to perform on cue: 'he's not that good of an actor, where I could write, you know, brackets, cry here, and he'd do it'. Both the idea that many politicians at the presidential level are 'naturally' gifted orators and the contention that they are nevertheless not actors serve to stress the authenticity of these politicians in performance: if they come across as polished, articulate, and charming, we are meant to believe that this is their 'natural' predilection for public speaking and not a 'falsely cultivated' habit.

One Republican speechwriter rejected the idea that the presidential candidate they were writing for might be thought of as an actor by contrasting an actor's short-term commitment to a character with the consistency with which politicians perform their public roles over the course of their career. Other speechwriters explicitly linked acting to deceitfulness to explain how politicians' performances were different from acting. A Democratic speechwriter argued, for instance, that 'the core' of acting 'is deception', whereas in politics, 'there is a fundamental truth that I . . . am speaking to you . . . in my capacity as your Senator and your Congressman or your Governor or your President', with the truth stemming from the fact that the speaker's particular capacity implied 'an obligation' or a 'relationship' to the audience that was based in a 'kernel of trust'. Another Democratic speechwriter similarly averred that there was a fundamental difference between actors and politicians:

> Actors would probably say, I'm going to be doing whatever I can do within the bounds of this character to evoke a real emotion in you. And politicians are saying, I'm doing whatever I can within the bounds of who I am as an actual human being to evoke this very real emotion in you.

Again, these explanations of how and why politicians are not actors reveal a perceived need to establish a sense of distance between performing a fictional character and performing an abstracted and fictionalised persona presumed to be a version of the politician's authentic self. In this, these comments are coloured by the antitheatrical prejudice insofar as the theatre and acting are negatively inflected and need to be contrasted with politicians' 'more real' self-presentations. Insofar as it presupposes that audiences believe politicians to be 'real' in their public performances, this stance presumes a level of trust and goodwill among audiences that is frequently not a given. Scholarship on acting and politics has taken a more nuanced view of the interplay between the two; Katherine Goktepe, focusing specifically on Sanford Meisner's Acting Technique (an offshoot of Method Acting), argues that acting, both in performances of fictional characters and in performances in the public sphere, 'draw[s] on real techniques of listening and responsiveness' and champions 'theater as a mode of citizenship training' (2018, 383, 384).

There is one clear exception to this generally pervasive line of argument in the corpus of interviews I conducted. Ronald Reagan's speechwriters were, because of Reagan's professional acting background, much more comfortable likening the president to an actor. One of Reagan's speechwriters told me, 'when Reagan was asked about acting, his answer was that, "I don't know how you could be president without being an actor"'. A second Reagan speechwriter made this even more explicit, arguing that Reagan 'put together his character, as president, as a composite of . . . Washington, Lincoln, FDR and Eisenhower', combining Washington's 'aloofness and distance', Lincoln's 'humour and humanity', FDR's 'ebullience and optimism', and Eisenhower's staged befuddlement into a consciously crafted presidential character. Because Reagan had been a professional actor and explicitly embraced acting as a tool in politics, his speechwriters appeared much more ready to accept the idea that presidential performances involved acting and they did not appear to think of acting (necessarily) in terms of making use of techniques to manipulate and deceive audiences. All the other speechwriters I interviewed, though they allowed for the fact that presidential speechgiving involved performance, nevertheless shied away from crediting the presidents they had worked for with the sort of techniques they would associate with an actor's skill. This is particularly striking in light of the fact that speechwriters were (a) aware that their principal's public self was a consciously constructed persona and (b) hired to construct or perpetuate the construction of this persona through public performance as part of the theatrical practice they were engaged in. Speechwriting very much works to facilitate presidential performances in a way that is in line with Nield's conceptualisation of theatricality, which requires that 'you "play" yourself, and hope you are convincing' (2006, 65). Given that US presidents not only play themselves in order to be received by vast local, national, and potentially global gazes but also outsource much of their theatricalising work to a team of speechwriters, presidential authenticity is at once highly prized and difficult to define and achieve.

Authenticity, Balance, and Presidential Haunting

The debate around the extent to which presidential performances constitute acting poses the question of what it means to 'act authentically', not just as an actor performing on a stage but also as a political actor in public life. All of the responses to my question, 'If you had to define authenticity, how would you define it?' follow the idea that politicians' public performances ideally convey something true about the person underneath the public role. Speechwriters referred to authenticity as 'an invitation', 'allowing someone in to . . . see, to understand, to know your true thoughts, your beliefs about anything', as 'being the guy that the observer expects you to be', as 'speaking in your own voice and being comfortable in your own skin', as being 'consistently in the same ballpark in terms of their actions and their ideas and their goals', as 'genuine and deeply felt expression', as 'being unapologetic about who are you are', 'being true to who you are', and 'having your words integrated with your conduct'. Some speechwriters noted that authenticity in the contemporary moment seemed to be frequently misinterpreted in public discourse as meaning 'unfiltered, off the cuff'. As such, the possibility existed to be 'authentic to a fault' and it was observed that it was dangerous 'if authenticity means we're gonna value someone who is sometimes in error, but never in doubt'. One Republican speechwriter, referring to Trump, summarised these concerns as follows: 'Authentic, a component of that would be, he's truthful. You would think. Not necessarily. You can be an authentic liar. . . . He's authentically untruthful, authentically a fraud. You know, authentically a grifter'. This dichotomy between a desirable, positively valued kind of authenticity and its potentially dangerous expression as purely unfiltered, improvised public presentation roughly translates to the way in which speechwriters spoke of ideas of rehearsal and authenticity. In general, and despite also stressing how gifted many presidents were at performing and how little these gifted performers actually needed to rehearse, speechwriters affirmed that rehearsing speeches was essential to 'authentic' delivery. As one Bill Clinton White House speechwriter put it:

> The argument that I make, and I really believe this, [is that rehearsal is] key to natural delivery. . . . [I]f you simply just read it out loud to yourself or your spouse, twice, even, you develop the muscle memory, and you also catch the parts that just like trip up your tongue and looked fine on the page but, you know, maybe . . . it sounds awkward and you can't get past that so you have to change that. But you understand the rhythm of the speech and . . . it's not that you have to memorise the thing word for word, as if it's a performance on Broadway, but you know it, . . . on a certain level you've absorbed it, and so when you stand up to deliver it you're more confident, you're more natural and you are liberated from reading it on the page.

This line of thought links natural, or authentic-seeming, delivery to rehearsal, in the sense that a state of appearing 'natural' can only be achieved if the material delivered is familiar to the extent that the speaker has developed the 'muscle memory' of its natural delivery. Alongside this, however, a second, and contradictory, approach to authenticity emerged. Speechwriters observed that authenticity could also be found in bad delivery, or in remarks that were delivered without any preparation whatsoever, as such delivery revealed resistance to a certain kind of smooth, standardised, politician-like public performance. While most speechwriters affirmed that they encouraged moments of improvisation from politicians who had the ability to improvise, as these were effective when connecting with audiences, they generally resisted the idea that off-the-cuff speaking should be seen as more authentic than carefully prepared speeches.

For example, the Bill Clinton White House speechwriter quoted above opined that there is 'this wrong idea that to be authentic you have to be shooting from the hip, just saying whatever comes to mind' and that having 'weighed your words' is inauthentic, characterising this as 'an overreaction to this, you know, professionalised, carefully crafted, poll-tested language'. This speechwriter acknowledged that what they characterised as an overreaction was a result of the skilful deployment of language by politicians like Clinton, who famously asserted during the Lewinsky scandal, 'I did not have sexual relations with that woman'. The speechwriter explained that this came down to a language game, of questioning what exactly is meant, for example, by 'sexual relations', and what was meant by Clinton's assertion in the present tense, that 'there is no relationship', which left open the possibility that there had been one in the past. In this example, Clinton's virtuosic ability to perform in public was seen, at least by the portion of the electorate that did not agree with him politically, to work against him. The speechwriter acknowledged that 'people were onto the game, and there was a game'. While rehearsal was thus generally regarded as essential to natural, or authentic-seeming, performance, smooth delivery itself could, much like acting technique, be interpreted to indicate inauthenticity and deceitfulness. Such suspicion of natural-seeming performance harks back to the French philosopher Denis Diderot's seminal idea that good acting is dependent not on deeply felt emotion but 'upon rendering so exactly the outward signs of feeling, that you fall into the trap' (1883, 16; see Introduction). Of course, scandals like the Lewinsky affair have confirmed the suspicions of audiences, such that it has become even harder to convince them to suspend disbelief.

An opposite example to Clinton is the late Senator from Arizona and 2008 Republican presidential candidate John McCain, who was described in my interviews as someone who 'doesn't know how [to act]. He just doesn't know. I don't think it would occur to him to . . . act a speech. But even if he did . . . it's beyond his capacity'. While speechwriters associated with the McCain–Palin presidential campaign in 2008 indicated that they wished McCain had had a more theatrical side, they contrasted McCain with Ted Cruz, who was characterised as 'like the worst ham of a Shakespearean actor you've ever [seen], you know, just . . . overacting, sing-songy', and with Obama, who was 'definitely theatrical, but much subtler' so that 'you don't see him act as much, but he definitely understood the theatrics of a speech'. While Obama was seen as a more skilled performer in a desirable way, McCain's inability to act was posited as at least more desirable than Cruz's bad acting, and therefore as something of a (limited) asset. Speechwriters described Trump's authenticity as residing in a similar inability to act, but coupled with an unwillingness to prepare, so that 'the trap we've gotten into is this false choice between, on the one hand, contrived, poll-tested sound bites and, on the other hand, just letting your id, you know, have free rein'. Two ways of thinking about authenticity in political performance exist in tension with each other: on the one hand, good performance and rehearsal tend to make for authentic delivery, at least in the eyes of relatively benevolent or at least neutral audiences. On the other hand, 'bad' performance can, in its obvious awkwardness with 'parsed' or carefully prepared language, have its own authenticity. Both of these ideas about what constitutes authenticity rest on the assumption that presidents not only have a true inner self but that this self can be revealed by, rather than being constituted through, its public performance and then recognised as true by audiences. Authenticity may ultimately be a media effect, and audiences may on some level be aware that presidential performances are carefully planned, scripted, and (sometimes) rehearsed, but neither circumstance makes it any less important for presidents to appear to transmit their authentic selves through public performance – whether that performance is polished and accomplished or bumbling and ad hoc.

While stressing the necessity of having personal knowledge of and access to the president for writing a presidential self that will convince in public performance in terms of its authenticity, presidential speechwriters also insisted that they had to strike a balance between showcasing a president's personal character and conveying presidentiality as a more abstract, official quality that communicates the dignity of the presidential office. The evocation of 'pure' or unadulterated authenticity was usually not the goal. A Republican White House speechwriter, for instance, made a point of saying:

> You don't necessarily want a president to be completely authentic. . . . What I mean by that is, you want some sense of restraint that this person has imposed on themselves because of the gravity that they perceive to be appropriate for their office.

Asked to explain how this translated into conveying a sense of trustworthiness for political audiences, the speechwriter went on:

> I think, at least in the past [before the Trump presidency], that some measure of restraint, what we're calling seeming presidential, could . . . actually garner more of a sense of trustworthiness, because people wanted to know that there was a steady hand on the wheel. And a certain . . . amount of restraint would lead your typical viewer or listener to think, 'okay, this person is self-possessed, this person has certain boundaries that they're imposing on themselves and given the tremendous responsibility that they have, that's something that I respect and am actually looking for'.

A second Republican speechwriter took this argument one step further: 'I would say that what I personally believe is that the presidential persona should always come first. That's what it means to serve your country in that way'. The first

Republican speechwriter cited above, on the other hand, seemed to weigh the balance between conveying personality and conveying presidentiality more ambiguously, arguing that 'this is a logical by-product of a democratic system . . . you wanna see a little bit more of a reflection of yourself in the . . . presidents you get', but the speechwriter also emphasised that the balance between presidentiality and conveying personal character could be skewed in different ways. Whereas the United States had had some 'famously austere presidents . . . who did not think it was their responsibility to sort of publicly empathis[e]', there seemed to be 'no market for that' in contemporary politics, where the president is 'just sort of the . . . tailend of the transmission line of what the public wants'.

These statements encapsulate much that made the conventional theatricality of the US presidency distinctive in the pre-Trump era. Given the president's visibility and his enormous task as the only elected official charged with representing the entirety of the nation, he (and they were all 'he's) was expected to strike a balance between the personal and the professional in public performance: it was judged that it was precisely the restraining of the president's personality and the perceived self-possession and respect of self-imposed boundaries while shouldering tremendous responsibility that the national audience would perceive as appropriately 'presidential'. The above statements imply the existence of a national public whom the president is tasked with representing that is far more uniform and consensual than lived reality would seem to imply. In 2015, for instance, one in five Americans in a poll conducted by CNN/ORC (Opinion Research Corporation) still believed in the 'birtherist' lie that Obama was born in a foreign country and, hence, not a legitimate president (CNN/ORC International 2015; see also Hughey 2012; Kumar 2013).[4] Likewise, there is a plethora of evidence of a substantial part of the public's non-acceptance of Donald Trump's presidency: the 'women's marches' in Washington, DC, and 466 other locations in the contiguous US on 21 January 2017, the day after Trump's inauguration, and existence of the 'Not My President' Political Action Committee (PAC) – which claims to represent 650,000 Americans, is active in all fifty states, and saw it as its mission to 'organize and resist Trump's agenda' and to 'work[] to get rid of Donald Trump, 365 days a year' – are just two obvious indicators of this ('Sister Marches', n.d.; Not My President PAC, n.d.). For the 2020 election and the Biden presidency it appears that even several months after Biden became president, well over half of all Republicans, in one poll as many as 71 per cent (PRRI 2021b), and roughly a quarter of all Americans still saw Trump as the 'true' president of the United States (Ipsos/Reuters 2021). The legitimacy of presidents remains much more widely contested throughout their time in office than the speechwriters' conception of 'the public' would seem to acknowledge.

Presidential speechwriters in the last five administrations before Trump tended to work on the basis of a configuration of the public that relies on an illusion of consensus. The pre-Trump orientation of the above reflections on their work by speechwriters is particularly evident in the following quote from a Democratic speechwriter, who conceived of the limits within which presidential performances tended to fluctuate between presidentiality and individuality as a pendulum:

> You can't act like you have Tourette's disease. You can't just say whatever comes into your head. . . . [N]o one expects someone . . . with their finger on the nuclear button to just say whatever they think and feel. On the other hand they don't want someone that seems completely scripted. So there's . . . a middle ground. It's sort of – . . . maybe the metaphor is a pendulum, you don't want it at the extreme in either direction, but it's swing[ing].

Earlier in the interview, this same speechwriter had talked about two viable templates for the negotiation of social class within which presidents can fit: one is 'the man of the people who becomes president', who has a 'down-to-earth public manner' but still needs to cultivate a sense of being presidential. Examples of this type given by the speechwriter were Andrew Jackson, Abraham Lincoln, Harry Truman, Jimmy Carter, and 'to some extent Bill Clinton and Lyndon Johnson'. The other template the speechwriter proposed is a president 'from an affluent and "aristocratic" family', as examples of which were given both Presidents Bush, as well as Franklin Delano Roosevelt and John F. Kennedy. The speechwriter stressed that presidents who fit into the second template needed to cultivate a sense of seeming down to earth and be careful not to 'talk down to people'. This was so because, in the view of this speechwriter, there were 'two things that Americans . . . want in a president', which are 'sort of at cross-purposes with each other':

> It's that, you have some kind of dignity and that you're also down to earth. Because you're the head of state, the head of state of a democracy, so you know . . . historically, we don't want someone who's crude, vulgar, undignified, but we also don't want someone who sort of puts on airs. . . . If you're Franklin Roosevelt, you have to be down to earth. If you're Harry Truman, you have to be dignified.

The presidency is configured here as a negotiation between social classes in a way that, ideally, strikes a happy medium between high and low as is seen as appropriate for American democracy, which, while not being actually classless, has nevertheless often been conceived of as such or at the very least as allowing for meritocratically earned social mobility between classes (cf. Aronowitz 1992; Kingston 2000; Olin Wright 1985). The idea that the president has to perform in a way that appears to encompass the spectrum of social classes also stresses the aspiration to the 'deep, horizontal comradeship' Benedict Anderson sees as fundamental to the imagined community ([1983] 2006, 7), a concept that will be become more central below. It is hard to escape the impression that these speechwriters, who are Washington insiders, have been outmanoeuvred and blindsided by Trump's success; whether Democrat or Republican, they all came across as disdainful of Trump's lack of professionalism while at the same time having to recognise, and lament, the effectiveness of his performances.

Speechwriters perceived the balance between personality and presidential-ity to have veered back and forth throughout history as something that had to be negotiated by each successive president and his speechwriters in terms of capturing the president's voice, representing the nation, and working within changing or fluctuating norms of whether the personal or the presidential is privileged in presidential performances. Nevertheless, the picture that emerges from these different ways of expressing ideas of balance is that speechwriters in general considered it necessary both to portray the president as a knowable, specific, and personalised 'self' and to convey the dignity of the presidential office and the president's capacity to represent the nation. The successful the-atrical appearance of the US president, then, might be seen as dependent on performing a balance between the personal and the presidential that speaks to the public at a particular historical moment. In other words, for the perfor-mative and theatrical construction of the president as a representative of the nation to be successful, the president and his speechwriters assume the neces-sity of evoking the president both as a familiar presence in American life and as capable of representing presidentiality as a more abstract, dignified quality. The individualised presidential persona figures as a counterweight to the lofti-ness of the president's office, to what Nield describes as 'the distant motorcades of presidential display' (2015, 125) and what Richard J. Ellis terms the 'regal presidency' (2008). Although the president's ubiquity in public life is largely limited to his virtual presence, it signals the president's apparent willingness to be known as well as his and his speechwriters' ability to convey something of the personal through public performance in response to the public's demand for emotional investment in their highest national representative. This perfor-mative and theatrical construction of the presidential self relies on a degree of cynicism as a sense of personal authenticity and public cohesiveness is posited that obfuscates the actual unknowability of the president and the diversity and polarisation of the public. In addition to conveying personality, the president is also tasked with representing his official capacity, his leadership, and his power. Underlying the sense of presidentiality is a performative and theatri-cal construction of the public along consensual lines that belies the increasing polarisation within the US electorate and instead posits the public as a cohesive imagined community.

While the need to balance between presidentiality and personality and the highlighting of characteristics perceived to be positive imply a degree of abstraction and fictionalisation in the public performances of US presidents, this is intensified as each president must project not just a selection of characteristics deemed to be advantageous but a selection of characteristics that present a particularly compelling contrast to the immediate predecessor. A balance between the personal and the presidential was perceived to be central to the theatrical appearance of US presidents, but the particular ways in which this balance may be struck depended on the specific historical context and especially the president's immediate predecessor with whose performance the new president had to break in compelling ways.

Theatre scholar Marvin Carlson's work on 'ghosting' is instructive here. According to Carlson's *The Haunted Stage*, theatre is a 'repository of cultural memory' but also 'subject to continual adjustment and modification as the memory is recalled in new circumstances and contexts' (2003, 2). 'Ghosting' in this context is defined as presenting to an audience 'the identical things they have encountered before, although now in a somewhat different context' (4). Carlson describes the role of Hamlet as a paradigmatic case, as this role is ghosted 'by the memories of famous Hamlets of the past' in such a way that a new actor attempting the role needs to have 'already developed a strong individual style and achieved a sufficient level of success and reputation to test himself against the role generally regarded as the hallmark of the art' (79). Carlson argues that 'the memory of the bodies, the movements, the gestures, of previous actors haunt all theatrical performance', but also observes that, unlike most cultures, modern American theatrical culture 'places relatively little value on either memory or tradition' (82). While this observation might be accurate as it applies to contemporary American theatre culture, American 'theatrical culture' – in an expanded definition of the term 'theatrical' that is inclusive of the sphere of presidential politics and performance – is suffused with both memory and tradition to a much greater degree. Each successive president must contrast with his predecessor, but such contrast is, of course, possible only in relation to and with orientation towards what came before. Presidents, in other words, are haunted by their predecessors' ghosts. Presidential ghosting plays with contrast and continuity: on the one hand, a whole series of traditional performances of the presidential role persist (the inaugural address, the State of the Union address, the turkey pardoning, the state visit, the peaceful transfer of power, and so forth) as do the norms of able-bodied masculinity typically associated with the role (see Chapter 3; see also Mast 2012, 30). On the other hand, each successive president must perform to these norms and traditions in a way that also, and especially, highlights the ways in which he departs from his predecessor.

In our interview, a Republican speechwriter expressed the imperative to perform contrast in the following terms:

in the context of the American presidency . . . there is what strikes me as a pretty clear although not ironclad rule that Americans, when it comes to the rhetorical predilections of their presidents, tend to choose contrasts. They tend to choose people who are seen as having . . . some characteristics that . . . contrast with the perceived deficiencies of their predecessor.

The speechwriter referred to George W. Bush's dignified, religious character as a contrast to Bill Clinton's perceived moral shortcomings, as evinced in the Lewinsky scandal. Clinton himself, however, could, the speechwriter explained, be seen to have been elected as a more empathetic corrective to George H. W. Bush's reputation for being out of touch, and Barack Obama could be characterised as having provided a compelling contrast to George W. Bush's 'bumbling inarticulate character'. A second Republican speechwriter characterised Donald Trump as 'almost the mirror image of Barack Obama' and then described the contrasts between successive presidents from Reagan to Trump in terms of different genres of music. A Democratic speechwriter likewise identified 'the pattern in modern American politics' as, 'when you have a two-term president, the country tends to elect their polar opposite [next]'. Several of the speechwriters I interviewed linked the need for contrast to the overexposure of contemporary presidents, with a former gubernatorial speechwriter stressing that 'when you speak as much as a . . . current US president has to speak, people get tired of listening to you'.

It is striking to observe in these quotes the emptying out of policy and ideology in favour of personality. The first Republican speechwriter quoted above, for instance, framed the need for contrast in terms of an analogy between the relationship of the electorate to the president and romantic relationships: 'when [people] fall out with somebody, the next person they date usually offers a contrast', in a way that tends to overemphasise the aspects they disliked in the first person. Speechwriters did not talk about a need to articulate policy contrasts, and policy emerges from the interview corpus as an afterthought to the requirement to perform personality contrasts. The above analogy about romantic relationships was made in the context of a follow-up question about the need to balance presidentiality and personal qualities in presidential performance; still, at no point did the speechwriters interviewed make the effort to stress that 'contrast' might be needed because policies pursued by one president might be perceived to have been unsuccessful. To some extent, speechwriters take matters of policy as a given; one speechwriter explained, 'I would not be able to write a persuasive speech for a socialist 'cause I'm a free-market conservative'. Unlike presidents themselves, speechwriters are free to focus on public appearance. They tend to be generalists and not policy specialists, and some think of speechwriting as an art, which meant that they considered their work as something that 'isn't necessarily formulaic . . . to some extent it's instinct and experience . . . and you know, not to be pretentious, but it's art', which stance implies a very different set of priorities from the goal-oriented pursuit of particular policies.

A second speechwriter averred that while they considered their job to be 'paying attention to [the principal] as a person', they aimed for 85–90 per cent agreement with the principal on matters of policy as a prerequisite for taking a speechwriting job. Nevertheless, it is clear that the president's personal qualities as performed in public are perceived to be vital to their success. This position highlights the theatrical construction of the public as homogeneous: clearly, the public are here thought of as at least homogeneous and un-ideological enough that a personally conceived, compelling contrast to a presidential predecessor can be assumed to be necessary to achieve electoral success.

The theatricality of the American presidency – defined here as the extent to which the presidency as a political role embeds the potential of being seen and entails the imperative for theatrical appearance – has expanded dramatically in recent history, as presidents are constantly observed and give many more public performances than they ever have before. In this setting, much like in the case of a play of such iconic significance as *Hamlet*, 'the density of . . . ghosting' is particularly high. If the role of Hamlet presents itself to actors as a 'formidable even daunting challenge' (Carlson 2003, 79), we might think of the US presidency in a similar vein: the US presidency is arguably not just 'the hardest job in the world' (Dickerson 2020) but also a formidably demanding role it may be increasingly impossible to inhabit and perform to broad agreement. This is due to the breadth and reach of its theatricality, because of the requirement to construct a presidential persona that balances between personality and presidentiality, and because each new political actor that takes on the presidential role has to contend with the cultural memory of those who came before, not in frank imitation but in a way that both continues the tradition of presidential performance and is uniquely the president's own.

Constructing the National Audience

Positing that presidential performances are theatrical implies that audiences will understand that politicians always exist in public in response to a particular gaze and with a particular agenda: as audiences, it is that consciously constructed agenda that they are exposed to, not any supposedly unguarded, much less pre-cultural or 'essential', presidential self. This is why theatrical reception is a matter of suspending disbelief rather than a more straightforward investment of belief. But the professionalised theatrical construction of US presidential performances is fraught with tension in an additional way: because the audience of the president is always at least potentially national, presidential performances tend to be targeted at, and tailored for, a broadly imagined national audience. This audience is constituted along the lines of Anderson's imagined community as a 'deep, horizontal comradeship' ([1983] 2006, 7), but it is also at odds with the highly polarised political landscape of the contemporary United States.

To show that, like the president's public persona, the presidential audience is a theatrical construction, this subsection investigates how, at what stages, and with what purpose and level of specificity and/or generality speechwriters think of audiences as they prepare speeches. All of the speechwriters I interviewed identified the audience as among the first things they would think of as they prepare to write a speech. One exception to this was a case mentioned by a Republican speechwriter, who observed that there could be specific presidential speeches for which the preparation process would start the other way around, with the message of the speech, rather than with the audience. This speechwriter explained that, in the White House, advisors would sometimes suggest that the president highlight a particular policy by giving a speech. In those cases, the president's speechwriters would 'kind of craft an audience around what they want the speech to say', to advance a specific message or policy. Crafted audiences like these would be thought of as 'a sort of microcosm of the grander people [*sic*] you're trying to reach'. Even though in such cases audiences are crafted to match the speech, rather than the speech, the audience, attention was still paid to creating an appropriate match between speech and audience, and the speech remained fundamentally addressed to and directed at an audience. In this sense, the audience here was a much more forthrightly theatrical construction than it was in other cases: it was crafted specifically so that it might be spectated by others in its act of spectating.

This sort of crafting of audiences appeared not to be the norm, however. All the other speechwriters I spoke to explained that they generally thought of audiences in terms of tailoring a speech to an audience rather than vice versa. Nevertheless, audiences were addressed in specific terms either only on a superficial level or in ways that catered to their presumed particular concerns and perspectives by way of folding these back into the president's agenda and, hence, a national vision. Speechwriters affirmed either that they thought of the audience first or that they thought of the goal of the speech first and the audience second. A Democratic speechwriter, for instance, explained, 'The very first step is, you have to think about: what is the goal of the speech? And then, secondly, okay, who is in the audience?', as well as what might be the most effective tone, theme, and structure to connect with the audience in a specific context to reach the goal. A second Democratic speechwriter described their thought process in nearly identical terms, as 'work[ing] backwards from what it is that you're trying to achieve'. A third Democratic speechwriter gave as an example of bad practice a speech that would fail to address its immediate audience directly, noting that while John F. Kennedy's 1963 commencement address at American University was about 'very important statements about America and the Cold War', it was nevertheless a failure as a commencement address, because it made no attempt to speak to 'a bunch of hungover college kids and their parents'. This speechwriter referred to the need to address different kinds of audiences with a single presidential speech as 'a classic tug of war', because 'it's a trap to just speak to the audience in the room, but it's a trap to just speak to the audience beyond'. Other speechwriters also made a point of saying that it could be difficult to find a balance between addressing different audiences, the immediate audience in the room versus larger and more dispersed audiences that would be exposed to the speech in mediatised form, for instance. One technique commonly mentioned for addressing the immediate audience was 'the handshake': a Democratic White House speechwriter noted, 'We . . . had, an incredible advance team that would scout locations and send us photos' as well as looking up any 'fun' stories about a specific town the president would be visiting. They explained that this research resulted in 'the handshake': references to the specific local context, which are designed to 'show people you know about their city, why you've come, you tell a couple of jokes about the local sports team, what's happening in the news – that just gains a little bit of the audience's trust'. Presidential speeches, the speechwriter noted, would then usually open out to be inclusive of wider audiences beyond the people in the room. In other words, to balance between various audiences, speeches would start with a 'handshake' but then broaden out to address larger – usually national – concerns.

In further addressing the issue of multiple audiences, a Republican speechwriter explained that 'there was a . . . point in time where you could write for the audience that the president . . . was in front of and the message would, if not be limited to them, it at least would be largely limited to them' but that, in the contemporary moment, 'you can only target your message so much because the media environment is such that it's going to get out to everybody'. However, a second Republican speechwriter denied that they thought about balancing between different audiences in this way. In response to my question, 'How do you try to balance between the audience that's going to be in the room to hear the speech and a potential larger audience that will be exposed to the speech later on through different media?', this speechwriter said, 'I don't think I do', and explained that they tended to limit their focus to 'what do we want him to say, and what's a compelling way for him to get it across'. A few other speechwriters echoed this more holistic focus on the speech and its impact as a complete piece, rather than its dissection into smaller parts. A Democratic speechwriter thought of speeches in terms of telling stories for audiences, asserting, 'if I tell you a story about a human whose life has been affected [by a policy], it's just how we're gonna remember things, how we're gonna [get] convinced of things. It's just – we work better with stories' and 'speeches are really the place where stories are told, which is how our brains work'. Another Republican speechwriter also expressed their focus on the larger arc during the speechwriting process, claiming that, while writing,

> I would feel what the audience – what I imagine the audience was feeling. And I would feel, 'okay, we're getting a little fatigued here'. . . . Gotta switch from, maybe an abstract discussion to a story, or from seriousness to humor. Here . . . at this point I want to feel this. That's how I would experience it. I would be kind of in a trance, as I was writing, and that trance involved basically living the life of the audience.

This speechwriter is imagining their ideal audience as a cohesive entity, capable of experiencing the speech in one specific, prescribed way. Their work relies on a stipulation of consensus that may very well be a false consensus, insofar as it entails seeing '[one's] own behavioral choices and judgments as relatively common and appropriate to existing circumstances while seeing the alternative as uncommon, deviant, or inappropriate' (Ross, Greene, and House 1977, 280): the speechwriter is extrapolating from their own experience to that of the projected audience. Rather than being a failure of presidents and their speechwriters to address varied audiences with precision, however, the quasi-fictional construction of the president's public persona and the similarly abstracted and fictionalised construction of the US electorate as a homogeneous entity derive from structural features of US presidential performance: the president's encompassing representative task and his ubiquitous visibility to a multiplicity of local, national, and global gazes. Here, a particular way of perceiving and responding to a speech is posited as the single appropriate response to it. This speechwriter also stated that 'sound bites, the catchy phrase, the memorable phrase' and stories were notable not so much because they could stand alone, but because these elements of a speech would ideally serve as mnemonic devices for the audience, as 'hooks' for people to 'sort of reconstruct the speech in their minds', because 'that's when they actually absorb it'. Again, this indicates the speechwriter's imagining of an ideal audience, as it is doubtful that most contemporary audience members would consume a speech in its entirety or that they would be so entranced by it that they would try to recall it in minute detail afterwards.

A second Republican White House speechwriter stated in a very similar vein that speeches were 'inviting the audience member to take this journey with me'. A third Republican speechwriter, one unaffiliated with this particular speechwriting company, affirmed a similar belief that 'speeches are important, like, the whole thing' in its extended form. A comparable imagination of the audience as one entity, albeit with a more local focus, seems to be at work in a Democratic speechwriter's attempt to get beyond the superficiality of 'the handshake' in connecting with an audience in terms of getting 'a sense of what is this town like? . . . what do they care about?' Here, too, while the audience is addressed with specificity, the focus still is on one particular experience of life, albeit one specific to a local setting. Additionally, whenever a local audience is imagined with specificity to its local setting, this is done with a view to incorporating the specific, local concerns into the president's or presidential candidate's agenda; the speechwriter noted that the goal was to translate 'indecipherable governmentalese into what a policy means in someone's life'. As such, the focus is very much on using the speech in a way that aligns with sovereign grammars of politics and performance, to craft 'an audience out of citizen subjects-objects' (Saward 2015, 219), by using the speech as a unifying device that folds particular interests back into a broader national agenda.

Imagining the president's audience of spectators engaged in a common ritual at a distance is to conceive of them as an abstract, fictionalised entity – a theatrical construct – representing an ideal of political spectatorship that sharply diverges from the political reality of the early twenty-first-century United States, which, to the contrary, is increasingly characterised by political polarisation and negative partisanship. Political scientists do not agree on whether polarisation originates among political elites, thus leading to 'a disconnect between the American people and those who purport to represent them' (Fiorina and Levendusky 2006a; see also Baldassarri and Gelman 2008; DiMaggio, Evans, and Bryson 1996; Fiorina 2017; Fiorina, Abrams, and Pope 2011), or within much broader sections of the electorate because there has been a 'dramatic increase' in the number of people engaged in political activities and all of these politically active people are increasingly polarised (Abramowitz 2006; see also Abramowitz 2010a, 2010b).[5] Despite this, there is broad agreement on the – increasingly undeniable and destructive – fact of growing polarisation (Jacobson 2012; Pew Research Center 2014a). Additionally, rather than being enthusiastically supportive of their party of choice, voters' party preference is often a matter of identity politics (Green, Palmquist, and Schickler 2004; Groenendyk 2013). Although people are frequently dissatisfied with how their chosen party represents them, this results in more, not less, partisanship, as people feel greater hostility towards the opposite party than they do positive identification with their chosen party (Abramowitz and Webster 2018; Groenendyk 2018). The American public is sharply polarised, and not just through positive identification with one of the two major parties, but primarily through negative partisanship towards the party they oppose. This indicates that people's experience of politics is often less about being comfortable with or represented by a political representative and more about feeling hostility towards the opposite party and preventing them from accomplishing what they set out to do. Even if the president still 'lives' in people's living rooms, as a Republican speechwriter put it, the basic sense of cohesiveness and uniformity of feeling towards the president that speechwriters tend to ascribe to 'the public' has, similarly to the image of the national community united through daily newspaper consumption, moved far away from reality.

The 'public', as presidential speechwriters think of it for the purposes of their work, should thus likewise be understood to be a theatrical construct: an abstract, fictionalised entity that represents a specific ideal of political spectatorship. More so than with documented political reality, this fictionalised entity seems to accord with Anderson's idea of the nation as an imagined community, which 'regardless of the actual inequality or exploitation that may prevail . . . is always conceived as a deep, horizontal comradeship' ([1983] 2006, 7). This is significant in light of this book's argument that politicians' performances are of functional importance in representative democracy. In the case of the US presidency, one function of performances by the president, who is uniquely tasked with representing the whole of the nation, is to address a public evoked theatrically as an imagined community. In speechwriters' vision of national consensus around a president who has been entrusted with the country by its sovereign people, television and new media take on the role Anderson ([1983] 2006) postulates for print capitalism and the national newspaper in uniting a nation into an imagined community. *Imagined Communities* vividly evokes the 'extraordinary mass ceremony: the almost precisely simultaneous consumption ("imagining") of the newspaper-as-fiction' (35) that enabled the collective creation of an idea of national unity that cut across party affiliation and partisanship:

> It is performed in silent privacy, in the lair of the skull. Yet each communicant is well aware that the ceremony he performs is being replicated simultaneously by thousands (or millions) of others of whose existence he is confident, yet of whose identity he has not the slightest notion. Furthermore, this ceremony is incessantly repeated at daily or half-daily intervals throughout the calendar. What more vivid figure for the secular, historically clocked, imagined community can be envisioned? (35)

The idea that the president appears to the people every night on their television screens evokes a similar mass ceremony, one that assigns to the national public more explicitly the role of an audience in a series of presidential performances of a kind of 'banal nationalism' (Billig 1995), a succession of commonplace, reassuring reminders of national belonging. We might think of these presidential performances as part of what Saward calls 'sovereign grammars' (or structural features) of politics and performance. In contrast to critical grammars, which aim to show up particularised interests and emphasise distinctions between different political agents, sovereign grammars 'seek[] to constitute the citizen body as one' and to craft 'an audience out of citizen subjects-objects' (Saward 2015, 218, 219).

In sum, while there were a variety of nuances in the ways in which speech-writers evoked audiences in their work, primarily audiences were either thought of in widely homogeneous, national terms that implied that there was one ideal way of experiencing a speech or they were thought of in a way of folding audiences' concerns back into a national agenda. Additionally, since they work in a highly mediatised political landscape, presidential speechwriters were aware that they had to speak to multiple, always potentially national and international audiences, in a way that led to a very broad construction of the overall audience. Anderson argues that the emergence of print media was essential in fostering the idea of the nation as an imagined community ([1983] 2006, 45). Despite the fragmented media environment of the late twentieth and early twenty-first centuries, the broad, national exposure of contemporary presidents has meant that their public appearances attempt to perpetuate this imagination, as the singularly intense exposure of the president in the media leads speechwriters to imagine audiences as multiple yet also always at least potentially national.

Presidential Performance in the US

Performances by US presidents have traditionally been constrained by the presidential role as the supreme national representative of the entire American electorate. They aim to craft an audience out of the spectators present. In line with the president's representative task, though, no matter who is actually in the room to hear the president's speech in person, the president's audience is ultimately a national one conceived around an idea of broad national consensus. Norms for how presidents perform in public and for the national public and how they can appropriately convey the abstract quality of presidentiality have shifted through time. Early presidential oratory sought to decouple legitimacy from the president's personal qualities and to focus his public speech not on the details of policy but on the virtues of the Constitution. As early twentieth-century presidents sought to make greater use of the bully pulpit and as media technologies began to facilitate more immediate access to the president's words, a stronger focus on the president's personal relationship with the electorate emerged, alongside the idea that presidential legitimacy derived directly from the people. Nevertheless, presidential performances have typically aimed to strike a number of balances, between presidentiality and personality, revelation and detachment, self-possession and spontaneity. To achieve this, these performances rely on the quasi-fictional (because highly selective and goal-oriented) construction of the president's public persona and a similarly abstracted and fictionalised construction of the US electorate as the sort of homogeneous entity that can be addressed and engaged as one. These constructions, this chapter has argued, should be understood as being the result of the distinctly theatrical work of presidents and their speechwriting and communications teams.

The construction of the US public around an idea of national consensus and community clashes with empirical evidence of significant partisan polarisation and negative partisanship in ways that, I have suggested, leave mainstream presidential performances attempting to hold together a system through fictionalised constructions in which members of the polarised, distrusting public are less and less willing to suspend their disbelief. Alongside the prevailing view among the speechwriters interviewed that presidents would do well to balance their authentic-seeming displays of personality with the dignity and restraint of the presidential office, which results in well-considered, professionalised, and more or less (depending on the president and his ability to perform) rehearsed speeches, a different, indeed opposed, idea of what constitutes authenticity in politics has taken hold. That conception of authenticity rejects professionalisation and the careful crafting of public performances around an idea of national consensus, inviting instead off-the-cuff performance styles, improvisation, unscripted performances, and, as the following chapters will explore in detail, a much stronger positioning of the president as a lone outside infiltrator of the Washington political establishment. The performance styles of some of the five presidents before Trump were already personality-focused, playful, targeted at discussing policy, and so on, but these performance of presidential legitimacy still relied on a high degree of presidential restraint.

NOTES

1. Ted Sorensen was John F. Kennedy's most well-known speechwriter, reportedly referred to by Kennedy as 'my intellectual blood bank' (qtd in Schlesinger 2008, 104).

2. Andrew M. Schocket explains the political, racial, gendered, and cultural connotations of the common term 'Founding Fathers', which is used more frequently by Republicans than Democrats and has been employed to highlight the Whiteness and masculinity of the leaders of the American Revolution – and, by extension, the implicit Whiteness and masculinity still ascribed to legitimate US political leadership (2015, 28–32). To sidestep at least some of these connotations, this book usually refers to the 'framers' instead; issues of gender and race that come into play in performing the US presidency are examined in Chapter 3.

3. Wilson's use of the majestic plural throughout the inaugural address also has the effect of eliding the distinction between president and people. Wilson appears to speak on behalf of the people when he argues that '*we* too long delayed to look into' the corruptions of government. Later in the speech, as Wilson lays out his role as president, 'we' comes to refer more specifically to Wilson himself: 'We know our task to be no mere task of politics but a task which shall search us through and through, whether we be able to understand our time and the need of our people, whether we be indeed their spokesmen and interpreters, whether we have the pure heart to comprehend and the rectified will to choose our high course of action' (1913b).

4. A *Washington Post*/ABC poll in April 2010 likewise found that 20 per cent of Americans believed that Obama had been born in a foreign country, though a May 2011 *Washington Post* poll found that number to be only 10 per cent (Cohen 2011).

5. Alan I. Abramowitz argues that there has been a significant increase in political engagement based on a substantial rise, since the early 1990s, in the number of people who engaged in one political activity beyond voting ('active citizens') and the number of people who engaged in two political activities beyond voting ('campaign activists') (2006, 74). Against this, Morris Fiorina and Matthew Levendusky argue that calling people who engaged in one or two political activities beyond voting 'active citizens' and 'campaign activists', respectively, is misleading, because 'the record increase in the active public arose nearly entirely from talk', that is, from family members discussing politics, rather than more time-consuming and effortful political campaign activities (2006b, 100–2). However, Abramowitz contends that his argument is sound because Fiorina and Levendusky's claim that the American public is non-ideological only applies to nonvoters, that is, those who do not even engage in voting, let alone one or two political activities beyond (2006, 77).

CHAPTER 3

CULTIVATING LEGITIMACY THROUGH PERFORMANCE

In lieu of the traditional extensive medical record, Donald Trump produced a short physician's note during the 2016 US presidential election campaign. The note, which is dated from 4 December 2015, was remarkable for its brevity, but also because it did not merely attest to the candidate's good health, instead going so far as to boast, 'If elected, Mr Trump, I can state unequivocally, will be the healthiest individual ever elected to the presidency' (Bornstein 2015). Trump's physician, Dr Harold Bornstein, subsequently explained that he only spent five minutes writing the note before revising that statement again two years later to admit that '[Trump] dictated that whole letter. I didn't write that letter' (Neuman 2018).

The health of presidential candidates continued to be major topic throughout the 2016 campaign. At an event commemorating the 11 September attacks on the World Trade Center, Hillary Clinton was led away and appeared to stumble as Secret Service agents helped her into a van. The Clinton campaign later disclosed that their candidate had been diagnosed with pneumonia and dehydration, and had been advised to rest and revise her schedule. A few days later, Donald Trump appeared on the television show of the controversial TV doctor Mehmet Oz, who has been accused of promoting the work of 'psychics, homeopaths, and purveyors of improbable diet plans and dietary supplements' (Specter 2013), to discuss his health and exercise habits further. Though Trump initially agreed on the programme to stay away from the topic of Clinton's health, he answered a series of questions Dr Oz asked about his health ('OZ: Lung complaints, asthma, wheezing? TRUMP: No, nothing. Really nothing.

It's been – people are amazed because I don't get much with the colds.') and Oz himself continued to bring up Trump's opponent, noting that he was 'hoping to go over these exact same questions with Secretary Clinton' (Cillizza and Blake 2016). In the first presidential debate of the 2016 campaign, which was scheduled nine days after Trump's appearance on *The Dr. Oz Show*, the topic of Clinton's health and ability to perform as president came up again. Trump responded to a question about why he had previously asserted that Clinton did not have a 'presidential look', by insisting that 'She doesn't have the look. She doesn't have the stamina. I said she doesn't have the stamina, and I don't believe she does have the stamina. To be president of this country, you need tremendous stamina' (Politico Staff 2016). In the context of Clinton's recent pneumonia, this was an effective argument, one on which Trump doubled down after being prompted to elaborate on his point about Clinton's lack of 'presidential look' by insisting that she lacked the ability to negotiate trade deals with countries like Japan and Saudi Arabia as well as the ability and stamina do to the 'many different things' a president has to be able to do. The debate moderator, NBC journalist Lester Holt, suggested letting Clinton respond, which prompted Clinton to expound on her experience as secretary of state and to reference the Benghazi hearings she was subjected to after her tenure by noting that Trump 'can talk to me about stamina' after he had spent eleven hours testifying before a congressional committee. Trump countered this by insisting several times that though Clinton had experience as a politician, it was 'bad experience' that had resulted in many a 'bad deal' for the American people.

Trump's performance during these debate questions aimed to delegitimate Clinton as a potential future US president in several ways. In the first instance, his attack on Clinton's lack of presidential look and lack of stamina both referenced her recent, and widely reported, medical episode. But the argument about Clinton's lack of presidential physicality also had a much broader resonance, because Clinton was the first female presidential candidate of a major party and thus could not fit into the physical mould presented by forty-four male past presidents. In this sense, Clinton literally did not have a presidential look and could not embody the physicality typically associated with political power and the presidency. The first half of this chapter investigates the matter of presidential physicality in depth. It is devoted to the question of how presidential bodies convey the president's legitimacy by projecting power, authority, and the capacity to represent others through displays of youth, virility, health, and able-bodiedness. This half of the chapter also explores embodiment conceptually, asking what it means to embody a public role like the US presidency and how we might distinguish embodied performances in contemporary politics, where leaders emerge out of the collective social body of the people, from premodern ideas which understood monarchs to be a literal embodiment of their nation and to be in sole possession and/or control of the body politic.

After attacking Clinton for supposedly lacking both a presidential look and an appropriately presidential amount of stamina during the 2016 debate, Trump changed his approach to attack her based on her previous experience as a politician, as First Lady, Senator from New York, and, above all, Secretary of State, dismissing this as 'bad experience'. Clinton's previously held offices, which provide the foundation for her political expertise and as such would in traditional rhetorical theory be regarded as a significant source of ethos, or credibility, for her as a public speaker, were thus turned into the opposite: a reason to dismiss Clinton as an unqualified, unpromising, and ultimately untrustworthy candidate for the presidency. This attack was especially well placed because Trump was an outsider to politics, having never held any public office before the presidency. He was able to attack Clinton for being part of a political establishment the public had already come to distrust. The second half of the chapter engages with the effectiveness of outsider positioning and anti-establishment rhetoric in US presidential politics, focusing particularly on how rhetoric by presidents and presidential candidates that attacks other politicians and political institutions performatively restructures the terms of legitimacy through which institutions of the federal government are perceived.

Taken together, the two halves of this chapter examine how politicians' performances cultivate legitimacy through a variety of metalingual, rhetorical, affective, and gestural repertoires of engagement. Homing in on two central aspects of these repertoires, embodiment and rhetoric, the chapter examines these in the current climate of widespread political distrust within which presidential performances have increasingly called the legitimacy of political institutions into question. Drawing on theories of performativity and legitimacy, the chapter explores how anti-establishment performances use rhetoric and weaponise norms of embodiment to break with accepted norms of discourse and restructure the terms of legitimacy through which institutions of the federal government are perceived.

EMBODIMENT AND LEGITIMACY – OR, DIFFERENT KINDS OF MAGIC

It is tempting to interpret political leaders' bodies as synecdochally standing in for the entirety of their nation or constituency, such that a leader's health becomes a barometer for the prosperity, might, and/or international standing of the nation. Reading a leader's body as synecdoche seems to explain something about why leaders' bodies are so frequently the subject of media attention, why it appears, in fact, that bodies 'never enter the political arena simply as biological organs' (Coole 2007, 413). The idea of seeing leaders as literal embodiments of their nations/constituencies also has the advantage of being able to draw on a long history of political thought: Ernst Kantorowicz (1957) traces to the Middle Ages the concept of the king's two bodies, wherein the king is assumed to be in possession of both a mortal body natural and an immortal body politic, through which he embodies the state and passes on the legitimacy of his rule to his successor. Likewise, the frontispiece of Thomas Hobbes's *Leviathan* ([1651] 1985) offers a widely reproduced and memorable image of the sovereign literally containing his subjects; it visualises both the move away from divine right and towards the human-made creation of the leviathan that Hobbes's contractual theory of sovereignty accomplishes and the Hobbesian idea of authorisation, which equates the sovereign's actions with the people's, putting the sovereign's legitimacy above questioning and his actions above criticism. The idea of a leader literally embodying their nation is typically one that describes absolutist rather than democratic power, as it presumes the exclusion of people from political agency. The image therefore most readily reappears in scholarship whenever scholars seek to account for political circumstances that seem to move from the democratic and towards the unsettlingly authoritarian.

In Western political thought, democracy is usually assumed to have moved away from the literal embodiment of the body politic in a single leader and towards the abstract representation of the people's collective body politic through elected representatives. Scholars of fascism, on the other hand, have long used premodern corporeal tropes of the body politic to describe fascism as a step backwards and away from democratic forms of representation (cf. Critchley 1993; Lefort 1986; Neocleous 2003, 21–3). Research into twenty-first-century populism makes a similar conceptual move to these fascism scholars when populism scholars make claims about the renewed relevance of the corporeal, literal body politic. Benjamin Moffitt writes, for instance, that while 'talk of the body has largely disappeared from our political vocabulary following the rise of liberal democratic politics', populism (not unlike fascism) 'can be read as an attempt to re-embody the body politic', so that 'in populism, the leader does not simply represent "the people," but is actually seen as embodying "the people"'(2016, 64). This sort of embodiment is proposed to be qualitatively different from representation, and it is explicitly linked to Kantorowicz's theory of the king's two bodies and/or to Hobbes's *Leviathan*. Moffitt posits, for instance, that contemporary populist leaders' bodies should be interpreted through Kantorowicz's (1957) analysis of the concept of the king's two bodies (2016, 68), whilst Benjamin Arditi similarly argues that that the connection between people and the leader in populism entails 'the re-entry of a Hobbesian authorization of sorts into politics' (2007, 66). The issue with this characterisation of populist representation as a sort of atavistic throwback to premodern, literal ideas of political embodiment is that scholars like Moffitt and Arditi seem to disregard the gulf between premodern ideas of political embodiment and modern, abstract ideas of political representation.

Jeffrey Alexander's work, which distinguishes more broadly between premodern 'ritual' and modern 'performance', presents a similar argument. Alexander argues astutely that '[m]odernity . . . invents the very idea of performance', but he also contends that modern political performances are successful to the extent that they approach a ritual-like character (2011, 4, 27). This approach does not quite capture the contingent, provisional quality of 'performance' and tends to assume that the inherent potential for distrust in political performance, which arises from the demand to the audience to suspend disbelief, could somehow be excised, if only the performances became more like premodern forms of ritualised spectacle in less complexly differentiated societies (see Chapter 1). Timothy Raphael similarly evokes images of the literal body politic and the idea of transubstantiation in *The President Electric* (2009, passim), where these images sit uncomfortably alongside an otherwise insightful exploration of the importance of performance to the Reagan presidency which lands on the conclusion that '[i]n the postmodern state, the final arbiter of legitimacy for the statesman is television, and the critical standard for leadership is not veracity but belief' (222). This chapter engages with the degree to which premodern ideas of representation as embodiment are, in their literal-mindedness, alien to modern ways of thinking. I propose that it is precisely because literal, organological political embodiment was replaced by a concept of abstract representation that invokes the audience as an active agent that ideas about acting and performance, including ideas of embodiment as they were developed in theatre and performance studies, can now be meaningfully applied to the study of politics. Embodied performances of the US presidency by presidents as diverse as Donald Trump, Franklin Delano Roosevelt, John F. Kennedy, and Ronald Reagan will be drawn on to illustrate this.

Arguments that posit contemporary populism as a throwback to premodern literal ideas of embodiment either imply or state outright that the connection drawn between a populist speaker and their audience is qualitatively different from the representative connection as theorised in Michael Saward's model. They argue that something more intensely resonant than the connection forged by making a representative claim, the crowd's acceptance of that claim, and the accompanying elevation of the speaker into the representative of the people (or the populist movement) must be at work in populism. Moffitt explicitly refers to this more intensely resonant connection as 'embodiment'. He argues, for instance, that 'in populism, the leader does not simply represent "the people", but is actually seen as *embodying* "the people"' (Moffitt 2016, 64, emphasis in original). Claiming that 'talk of the body has largely disappeared from our political vocabulary following the rise of liberal democratic politics', Moffitt then posits that populism 'can be read as an attempt to re-embody the body politic' (64). Moffitt interprets a re-emerging focus on the bodies of politicians, especially populist ones, explicitly through Kantorowicz's work, arguing that 'the contemporary populist leader's body is stuck with a modern, secularised version of Kantorowicz's (1957) characterisation of the king's two bodies' (68). This means that 'the body politic and the leader's body [are tied together] in an existential bond' in a way that necessitates performances that emphasise the health and virility of the populist leader because 'a sagging, ill body is not a sign of a tough, united people' (65). Arditi writes in a similar vein:

> Like Rousseau, populists distrust representation as a corruption of the general will and see themselves less as representatives than as simple placeholders or spokespeople for the 'common man', but unlike Rousseau, they also distrust autonomous initiatives that empower citizens and encourage them to act by themselves. (2007, 65)

Because he sees populists as suspicious both of representation and of citizen empowerment, Arditi concludes that, moving beyond even Rousseauian anti-theatricality, the connection between people and leader in populism entails 'the re-entry of a Hobbesian authorization of sorts into politics under the guise of the personalization of political options and the *trust* for the leader' (66, emphasis in original). In other words, because populists express a distaste for representation, preferring instead to identify themselves with the people by claiming to erase the gap between representatives and represented (Sorensen 2021, 147), scholarship returns to Hobbesian theory to describe the connections populists seek to forge with their followers.

In Hobbes, 'to get themselves out from the miserable condition of Warre' which is the state of nature, wherein life is famously conceived of as 'solitary, poore, nasty, brutish, and short', the people are presupposed to have given up their right to govern themselves to the sovereign, thereby authorising his absolutist power over them ([1651] 1985, 168, 223, 227). A consequence of this authorisation is that the people are in no position to criticise the sovereign, because the sovereign's actions are their own. As the political philosopher Al P. Martinich puts it, Hobbesian authorisation means that, '[i]f they don't like the behavior of the sovereign, they should criticize themselves', because '[i]n the political case of *Leviathan*, the words and actions of the sovereign get attributed to his subjects' (2016, 318, 328). This configuration is memorably portrayed in the frontispiece of *Leviathan*, wherein the towering leviathan's torso and arms are a mosaic made up of the bodies of his subjects. The Hobbesian sovereign can be said to directly 'embody' the people, as in the frontispiece of *Leviathan*, because there is no sense that his actions are somehow in the spirit of the people's will; instead, '[t]he literal truth is that the individual subjects are the authors of what the sovereign does, and they own those actions' (Martinich 2016, 333). Martinich's use of the word 'literal' is significant here: it highlights the significance of the distinction between this direct representative relationship and the modern, more abstract concept of representation. I will expand upon this point shortly.

The idea of the king's two bodies, as explored in Kantorowicz's seminal study, bears a strong resemblance to the Hobbesian image of political embodiment. *The King's Two Bodies* (1957) traces to the Middle Ages the Tudor-era idea that the king has, in addition to his body natural (in which he resembles any other human being) also a body politic, the members of which are his subjects. The king can be said to 'embody' the state, insofar as he is figured as its head and his subjects are the members of the same holistically conceived state-organism. The idea of the king's two bodies has notable religious connotations, particularly in the designation of the state as a *corpus mysticum*, a term that can be traced to the Catholic Church, which over the course of the twelfth century started to refer to the corporate, collective body of the church as the *corpus mysticum* (as opposed to the *corpus verum*, the Eucharist) (Kantorowicz 1957, 194–8). Paul Friedland explains that the conception of the state as an organism meant that 'for medieval and early modern political theorists, monarchies were considered to be a form of representative government in which the political body was composed of one individual' (1995, 29). For present purposes, however, the crucial point about political embodiment in the king's two bodies is that, although this may have been considered a form of 'representative' government, it remains incommensurable to modern ideas of 'political representation' and can be more accurately delineated by referring to it as 'political embodiment', as distinct from modern 'political representation'. Kantorowicz warns of attempts at 'lightheartedly discarding the old organic oneness of head and limbs in the body politic and . . . rashly replacing it by the abstraction of a personified state' when discussing Tudor and pre-Tudor ideas of the king's two bodies, emphasising that in these conceptions the state was decidedly not an 'abstract personification beyond its members' but an 'organic or organological whole' (1957, 270–1). This already indicates the necessity to prevent the all-too-easy slippage between the very concrete, literal-minded, and holistic concept that is the subject of Kantorowicz's historical investigation and modern ideas of representation that rely on greater levels of abstraction. However, it is Friedland's work (1995, 2002), which expands on Kantorowicz geographically, temporally, and conceptually to trace the emergence of abstract ideas of representation during the French Revolution, that is particularly useful here.

Friedland helpfully sets premodern 're-presentation' apart from forms of 'representation' as they developed later on to indicate the literalness of the former and the abstraction the latter implies. To clarify this, Friedland explains that in the premodern conceptualisation of political embodiment, 'the entire mystical body of the French nation could be made visible, could be literally re-represented, in a tangible, visible form' (2002, 32). For instance, the presentation to the king of the laboriously collated *cahiers de doléances*, which were supposed to contain the views of each of the three estates (the nobility, the clergy, and the common people), was accompanied by a procession. This

procession was, in Friedland's words, a 'full-blown spectacle of political incarnation' that re-presented 'in the literal sense . . . the various parts and members
of the mystical body' and in this resembled the Catholic dogma of transubstantiation more closely than modern ideas about the abstract representation
of the people's will (2002, 38, 42). This was a symbiotic arrangement, wherein
'each political body depended on the others for verification of its legitimacy'
(Friedland 1995, 114). The point here is that the *corpus mysticum* of the state
became literally visible and literally embodied in the coming together of the
king and Estates General, which could claim to re-present the entire holistically
conceived state-organism. In the convocation of the Estates General, the king,
as head, and the nation, as members, came together as one state-organism that
was – albeit temporarily – made concretely visible. As the centuries went on
and royal power was consolidated in the king (and the Estates General ceased,
for the most part, to be convocated), Friedland writes, political re-presentation
was gradually transferred entirely to the king, so that 'the entire mystical body
of the nation was held to be permanently re-presented in the king alone', leading to pronouncements such as Louis XIV's '*l'État, c'est moi*' (2002, 50). In
line with Kantorowicz's investigation of the monarchy, the king thus came to
fully embody the nation as its body politic. While the outward form of political
embodiment evolved (at least in France) from the inclusion of an institutional
structure into a more purely absolutist monarchical form, this did not fundamentally change the way in which political re-presentation as embodiment was
understood to function: 'the form of re-presentation was still embodied and
concrete' (Friedland 1995, 51). The absolutist idea of the kingship Friedland
describes is also very much in line with the Hobbesian theory, in which the
people are assumed to have authorised the sovereign so that his actions are
understood to literally be the actions of the people.

The crucial distinction is between the premodern idea of 'political embodiment' (or 're-presentation') and the more abstract concept of 'political representation' that evolved throughout the eighteenth century. In the former case, the
political audience was essentially irrelevant, at least as an agency-exerting actor
within the theatre of politics. Friedland argues that 'legitimacy rested upon the
king's conviction in the truth of his re-presentation', in his conviction that he
was the body politic (with or without the inclusion of some kind of institutional
structure, as in the Estates General) (2002, 62). This meant that political rituals were not carried out primarily with their audiences in mind. Instead, royal
processions and the like were distinctly inward-focused, essentially designed to
allow political actors to get into character (Friedland 2002, 41). Significantly,
for the connection between performance and politics, this was dependent on
and in line with an idea of acting that entailed the literal metamorphosis of
an actor into their character. In other words, antitheatrical arguments at the
time tended to condemn acting not for being deceitful, ineffective, and not

genuinely transformative, but for being only too truly transformative and therefore a 'profanation of the incarnation of Christ' (Friedland 1995, 66). All of this is profoundly alien to modern ideas of both representation specifically and performance more broadly, which tend to be understood not to lead to profound, quasi-transubstantiating metamorphoses, but to rely on the one hand on the abstract representation of the will of constituents and, on the other, on the audience's temporary suspension of disbelief.

Of course, the focus on the people's authorisation of their sovereign in *Leviathan* might seem to contradict the inward focus just described. Kantorowicz likewise cites the fifteenth-century jurist John Fortescue envisioning the connection between 'the people' and the state: 'Just as the physical body grows out of the embryo, regulated by one head, so does there issue from the people the kingdom, which exists as a *corpus mysticum* governed by one man as head' (qtd in Kantorowicz 1957, 224). With respect to this apparent consideration of 'the people', it is important to stress that Hobbes's and Fortescue's focus remains inward: there was no more a concrete historical moment at which the people escaped from the state of nature by authorising the leviathan than there was a public opinion polling about the perceived legitimacy of the monarchy in sixteenth-century England. The focus on the people serves simply to legitimate the monarch's power over them by positing a theoretical authorisation event that incorporates them, as subjects, into the body politic. As Martinich writes, '[a]uthorization is supposed to immunize the sovereign from criticism' (2016, 318). The most significant difference between premodern political embodiment and modern political representation refers to the status of the political audience: in the former, 'the people' serve as a theoretical construct to consolidate and legitimate the king's power. In the latter, 'the people' actually, and at historically specific moments of, for instance, voting, polling, or public protest, allow political candidates to function as their representatives. In this sense, *Leviathan*'s frontispiece is misleading: although the people are depicted as gazing upon their leader, the Hobbesian perspective does not cast them in the role of the political audience. But how 'the people' perceive the legitimacy of politicians and political institutions today matters, as does the erosion of trust in the same. With the advent of liberal democracies in the West, sovereignty came to reside in the people rather than any individual king. Alongside this, the image of the body politic also moved from its focus on a sovereign monarch or head to the collective body of the people. Even if leaders occasionally continue to draw figurative analogies between their own bodies' capacities and the strength of their nation, the more persistent image has become that of the social body of the people (Neocleous 2003, 21–8; see also Santner 2011), itself immortal because each individual member of the body politic makes up but a minuscule part of the whole. The sovereign people are still at times imagined as a 'body', as is apparent whenever reference is made to a nation's 'orifices' (borders), which tend to be posited as being in need of protection from outsiders, or when the national body is deemed to be vulnerable to 'infections' spread by unde-sirables, as in descriptions of Jewish people under Nazism or in descriptions of undocumented immigrations as 'infestations' by Donald Trump (Neocleous 2003, 29–30; Simon 2018).

Along with the passing of sovereignty from the individual body politic of the king to that of the people, there was a shift from concrete embodiment (which privileges the perspective of those in power) to abstract representation (which shifts the focus to the political audience's reception of power's perfor-mances). This emergent outward focus on the people's perspective depended upon a parallel and simultaneous shift in ideas about acting and performance (Friedland 2002). Evolving away from the literal-minded notion that actors metamorphosed into their characters, theorists instead began to stress that act-ing was about rendering outwardly, and for the benefit of an external audience, the features of a character without undergoing a fundamental inner transfor-mation. Denis Diderot's (1883) *Paradox of Acting* most famously propounded this stance, while in the prerevolutionary United States an audience-focused ideal of rhetorical persuasion became increasingly influential (Fliegelman 1993). With the new, outward focus of performance, it became important whether a political actor's performance was bought into and trusted by the audience. In other words, rather than literally embodying, or metamorphos-ing into, a holistic state-as-living-organism, political performances of would-be representatives were now subjected to the judgements of audiences. While premodern political embodiment was literal, holistic, organismic, and focused on those in power, modern political representation emerged as fundamentally audience-focused and concerned with forging an abstract connection, through a perceived affinity of their views and aspirations, between constituents and performing politicians.

To illustrate this further, recall that the significance of the split between the body natural and the body politic as Kantorowicz explores it lies, to a signifi-cant extent, in the depersonalisation of the kingship. Unavoidably, the bodies natural of kings and queens died and were replaced by successors. These suc-cessors derived their legitimacy, at least in part, through the concept of the immortal body politic. The split between the king's bodies natural and politic thus served to assuage and negotiate anxieties over the continuation of the royal line and the political order more broadly, which makes the king's two bodies a concept that depersonalises the kingship by making it transferrable to a successor. This explains the difference between the king's wooden effigy and the king's actual corpse in the royal funeral that Joseph Roach describes (1996, 36–8): it was the king's effigy, rather than the deceased body itself, that sym-bolised the immutability of the social order. Today's equivalent is the people's collective and depersonalised body, which remains (relatively) unchanged and thus inherits the continual and perpetual character of the premodern body politic (Neocleous 2003, 17).

Contemporary populist leaders are faced with a succession problem precisely because the body politic is no longer seen to be literally embodied in the leader and regarded as transferable to a rightful successor. In the modern configuration, political leaders' bodies no longer occupy a hallowed category of their own; instead, political representatives emerge out of whilst also remaining part of the people they represent. Such representatives have to rely on their connection to political audiences – a connection forged very much in terms of Saward's representative claim: through the politician's performance and the audience's reception thereof. While populists may seek to identify themselves with or at least emulate their constituents through performances of their own ordinariness, they also tend to rely on their charisma. This mysterious quality might be seen to be based on a performer's ability to evoke such difficult-to-define properties as 'public intimacy (the illusion of availability), synthetic experience (vicariousness), and the It-Effect (personality-driven mass attraction)' (Roach 2007, 3) and it brings the problem of succession into better focus: to pass the torch successfully, any potential successor would need to be counted on not merely to pursue a specific party platform, but to somehow replicate or forge anew his predecessor's personal connection with the audience. In other words, contemporary populists use their bodies to perform an intensely personalised, but abstractly conceived, association of physical strength with strong leadership.

Whereas the concept of the king's two bodies relies on a kind of magical thinking that posits literal metamorphoses of actors into characters and of kings into body politics, the more abstract concept of political representation relies on a different kind of magic entirely: that of make-believe. The political performer's skill must be such that audiences come to suspend their disbelief in them as an authentic representative of their interests, enabling a performative operation that elevates the politician into the position of a representative that is perceived to be legitimate. While Moffitt contends that contemporary populism entails a secularised version of Kantorowicz's concept, the concept of the king's two bodies is fundamentally about the introduction of 'a whiff of incense from another world' into the sphere of secular politics (Kantorowicz 1957, 210). The idea of the king's two bodies infuses religious thinking and ceremony into the sphere of the secular, and as such is accompanied by a corresponding quasi-religious belief in miraculous metamorphoses. The concept cannot be divorced from the realm of the miraculous. Political embodiment, at least as understood by premodern theory and as explored by Kantorowicz, cannot straightforwardly be refigured as a more intense kind of representative connection. Precisely because literal embodiment was replaced by abstract representation, as the both performative and theatrical enactment of the representative relationship between performing politicians and their audiences, performance has come to be of functional importance in representative democracy.

The discussion in the previous section has left open the question of what role, if any, is played by the bodies of politicians in general, and those of populist politicians in particular, in contemporary politics. In other words, how can we grasp the significance of politicians' bodies in their public performances, given that twenty-first-century audience democracy frequently puts an increased personalised focus on politicians and their physical bodies? Moffitt's observation that many populists 'draw attention to their bodies to prove or demonstrate potency and strength' (2016, 65) is astute in this regard, especially concerning right-wing populists. But thinking through the importance of embodiment in contemporary politics and performance does not require us to posit a throwback to premodern magical thinking. Additionally, assuming that such a throwback would be possible risks blinding us to the importance of embodiment as one of the repertoires of affective, metalingual engagement through which performances in contemporary politics act upon political audiences and in which social relations are 'embedded' (Rai 2015, 1183). In the case of the US presidency there is a normative requirement for performances of able-bodied masculinity, but this requirement is based on an abstractly conceived metaphorical association between a 'strong' body and an ideal of strong leadership. It is difficult to see what the 'existential bond' Moffitt posits would consist of in the absence of a literalised idea of political embodiment in which the sovereign's body is accepted as being literally fused with the body politic.

The representative relationship between contemporary politicians – populist or otherwise – and their constituents is established and negotiated through public performances directed at audiences. To a large extent the focus on politicians' bodies in these performances is an extension of the personalised attention paid to individual politicians rather than broad party platforms in what Bernard Manin (1997) aptly calls 'audience democracy'. As audience democracy tends to divert attention away from the substance of policy towards politicians' performances in the public sphere, questions about the body that might be posed in other performance settings naturally become relevant. Elin Diamond observes that 'as soon as performativity comes to rest on *a* performance, questions of embodiment . . . become discussable' (1996, 5, emphasis in original). Building on Judith Butler's argument that performativity is 'not . . . the act by which a subject brings into being what she/he names, but, rather, . . . that reiterative power of discourse to produce the phenomena that it regulates and constrains' ([1993] 2011, xii), Diamond defines the task of performance analysis as investigating the norms and conventions that each performance reiterates. She argues:

> When performativity materializes as performance in that risky and dangerous negotiation between a doing (a reiteration of norms) and a thing done (discursive conventions that frame our interpretations), between someone's body and the conventions of embodiment, we have access to cultural meanings and critique. (1996, 5)

If we accept that the representative relationship between politicians and constituents is forged through performance, then questions of embodiment should be put to the individual performances that forge this relationship. These are questions about harnessing the perception of legitimacy by mobilising cultural associations of certain bodies with concepts of power, authority, and representative capacity.

The remainder of this section explores how theorisations of 'the body' and 'embodiment' developed in performance theory apply to embodied performances of the US presidency. Though a populist like Trump might perform his physical strength more starkly and forthrightly than a more mainstream president would, performances of populism differ in tone and inflection more so than in the actual quality of the representative relationship they aim to forge. All US presidential performances emphasise embodied masculinity, and most particularly presidential health and virility. George Washington, for instance, was, in addition to being a general, also an accomplished athlete and farmer who stood six feet two inches tall. He set what appears an at times almost comically formidable precedent of able-bodied male virility for the US presidency; in a 1789 letter, for instance, Washington requested a horse whose 'Size & strength must be equal to my weight'. Theodore Roosevelt, famously an outdoorsman who enjoyed boxing, hunting, and camping, is another prominent exponent of presidential manliness (Testi 1995; Wilson 1994). Trump's claims during the 2016 campaign that Hillary Clinton had neither the look nor the stamina for the presidency were much more crudely explicit than most other politicians would have been in asserting his own physical strength and his opponent's supposed weakness. Yet this performance relied on an underlying set of conventions that associate power and authority with able-bodied masculinity as well as on a long line of presidential precedents.

While opposition to the idea of a female US president has been falling (Burden, Ono, and Yamada 2017) and discussions of women's roles in politics are now widespread, residues of a general tendency in Western culture to normatively ascribe power and strength to healthy, able-bodied masculinity persist (Puwar 2021). According to this way of thinking, 'masculinity is defined as able-bodied and active'; therefore 'traditional notions of woman and disability converge, reflected in the ascription of characteristics such as innocence, vulnerability, sexual passivity or asexuality, dependency, and objectification [to women]' (Manderson and Peake 2005, 233–4). The classicist Mary Beard has popularised a similar reading of the cultural association of male physicality with power and authority, noting that 'the exclusion of women from power is culturally embedded' in the Western tradition going back to antiquity (2017, 79).

In performance theory as in politics, the bodies of performers frequently figure as distractions, drawing an audience's attention away from more abstract content that a performance might be attempting to convey. For Colette Conroy, for instance, '[b]odies are distractions' in the theatre, because the physical presence of the actors can become such an 'overwhelming reality' for spectators that it jeopardises their investment in the fictional world portrayed on stage (2010, 37–8). Marvin Carlson expands this basic idea beyond the specific case of stage acting, arguing that, whether on stage or screen, an actor's body, acting as a vehicle for the audience's memory of his or her past roles, can come to 'dominate the reception process', taking attention away from the immediate content of the play or film and casting its reception in light of previous roles the actor's body has inhabited (2003, 8). Because politicians' public performances are a dominant mode through which politics is staged and received in the contemporary moment, a focus on politicians' bodies is likewise inevitable. In audience democracy, politics is personalised, conveyed through public performances, and transmitted by media technologies, which enable vast audiences not merely to know the president's words, but to see his performance, potentially, as in the case of big speeches like the State of the Union address, even in live broadcast.

The embodied performance of the US presidency follows specific cultural conventions that are retained in the collective memory of its audiences. Carlson's engagement with embodied performance and collective memory, touched on in the previous chapter, carries analytical force here. For Carlson, 'ghosting' consists of presenting to the audience 'the identical things they have encountered before, although now in a somewhat different context', which means that the present experience of a play or a character in the theatre is 'always ghosted by previous experiences' of the same play, the same actor, the same character, and so on (2003, 4, 2). For an iconic role such as Shakespeare's Hamlet, audience expectations and judgements are thus shaped by the memory of previous performers.

Performances of the US presidency are likewise ghosted by the memory of previous presidents. Given the uniqueness of the presidential office and its prodigious representative task as well as ideals of self-sufficiency derived from the American founding myth of settling in the wilderness of an 'empty' continent (Jaffe 1997, 64–70), audiences are also more likely to perceive presidential candidates as competent and credible representatives of the nation if they meet norms of perceived masculinity and attendant standards of physical strength and virility. In their relation to the performer's body, these performances thus tend to foreground the physical strength associated with active, able-bodied masculinity, since power and representative capacity are normatively ascribed to bodies that can perform these qualities convincingly. This is akin to what Butler refers to as 'the acquisition of being through the citing of power' ([1993] 2011, xxiii), in that bodies need to conform to, or 'cite', a standard of perceived physical strength that is associated with power in order to become legible as potentially powerful. If, in modern societies, 'the body comes to be seen as an arrangement of meanings that is produced by social knowledges, by a system that aligns bodies and meanings in a grid of "biopower"' (Kuppers 2003, 5), then the representational power of the US presidency is resolutely aligned with the strength and virility associated with healthy, able-bodied masculinity.

Although a record number of women were elected to Congress in the 2018 midterm elections and a woman, Kamala Harris, has since become vice president, the question of whether a woman can win the presidency became a major topic of discussion during the 2020 Democratic primary: according to a much-publicised poll, a clear majority of Democratic and independent voters (74 per cent) said they would be comfortable with a female president, but only 33 per cent of these voters believed their neighbours would also be comfortable with this (Ipsos 2019). Bias against women in US presidential politics and awareness of such bias persist. In this context, the public performances of a populist like Trump reaffirm and weaponise ingrained cultural meanings embodied by masculine performers rather than attempting to reduce their influence.

One might think here also of the 2008 presidential campaign, during which John McCain's advanced age of seventy-two years and his history of melanoma were turned into a significant issue. The anxiety about the possibility of McCain not surviving his potential presidency was particularly acute because his prospective vice president, Sarah Palin, had been poorly vetted and was widely judged as too inexperienced to replace him (see Heilemann and Halperin 2010, 282, 396–416). Additionally, Palin was a woman faced with the possibility of being cast in a role that had only ever been filled by men and that seems to necessitate performances of specifically male virility. As Sophie Nield notes, nations are sometimes emblematised as female, but female emblems tend to be abstract allegories of virtues like liberty or justice which 'cannot be read as empowerment of actual women' and instead 'serve to reinforce and reiterate already existing tropes of male agency and female passivity'. In contrast to this, Nield observes that 'the associations of nations with male figures often incorporate real male rulers' (2000, 103), such as Lenin, Stalin, Hitler – or the succession of forty-five male US presidents.

It may be objected here that although all past presidents have been male, not all were able-bodied or healthy. Franklin Delano Roosevelt, for instance, is now well known to have contracted poliomyelitis in 1921. For the rest of his life, Roosevelt was unable to walk without assistance. John F. Kennedy, too, has been described as a publicly 'dynamic man full of vigor and youthful energy', but one whose 'aura of vitality belied the fact that he was patently unhealthy from an early age' (Pait and Dowdy 2017, 247). Kennedy had a long history of back pain, because of which he occasionally walked with crutches and for which he wore a back brace and was treated with injections. However, contemporary audiences were largely kept in the dark about these medical facts. FDR, and the national press with him, sought to give the impression that Roosevelt had overcome his illness and remained 'an uncommonly strong, vigorous man' (Pressman 2013, 333).[1] Kennedy's medical history, too, remained unknown to the general public (Pait and Dowdy 2017, 253). FDR, Kennedy, and their semi-secret medical conditions speak to the extent to which the US presidency as a political role is ghosted by performers who sought to conform to stringent norms of masculinity and able-bodiedness associated with the power and authority necessary to represent the nation to itself. The focus on presidents' bodies has, if anything, intensified since FDR's and JFK's days, as media technology has facilitated greater access to the images – moving and otherwise – of US presidents. In recent decades, there have been no more cases like Roosevelt's or Kennedy's, in which presidents required assistance with walking or standing, but there has long been speculation that Ronald Reagan might have suffered from Alzheimer's disease during his second term (see Berisha et al. 2015 for an investigation of this issue). Despite this, in Reagan's case, too, the impression that persists is of a strong, tall, perennially dark-haired man. Reagan's embodied performance – and the physicality demanded of US presidents more generally – is best summarised, perhaps, in Tony Kushner's *Angels in America*, where the character of Roy Cohn contrasts his own declining health with Reagan's enduring physical prowess:

> Look at Reagan: He's so healthy, he's hardly human, he's a hundred if he's a day, he takes a slug in his chest and two days later he's out west riding ponies in his PJ's. I mean who does that? That's America. It's just no country for the infirm. (2007, 192)

Of course, Trump's embodied performance in 2016, exemplified by his doctor's note and by assertions made in the first presidential debate that Hillary Clinton did not have the 'look' or the 'stamina' for the presidency (see Politico Staff 2016), was much more crudely explicit than that of most other politicians would have been. It is also significant that his White supremacist dogwhistles gained traction after, and as backlash to, the first Black president as well as in performances of 'birtherism' that sought to discredit Obama's legitimacy throughout his time in office. While asserting his own physical strength and, elsewhere and even more frequently, his Whiteness (see Peetz 2021 for a more in-depth analysis of Trump's performance of Whiteness), Trump exploited Clinton's gender and Obama's race explicitly. Clinton was the first woman who had ever become the presidential candidate of a major party and thus could not fit into a physical mould of past presidents emphasising virile masculinity, while Obama could not echo into the association of the presidency with Whiteness. In Clinton's case, concerns around her health had arisen two weeks previously, when Clinton was also reported to have contracted pneumonia and nearly collapsed on the campaign trail (Martin and Chozick 2016). Yet Trump's performance relied on an underlying set of conventions that regulate and constrain the public performances of all US presidents and that align attempts to generate democratic legitimacy with a set of physical, embodied norms that candidates strive to fulfil.

Crucially, this is a point that can be made by focusing on norms and conventions of embodiment underlying the performance of the US presidency, for instance by focusing on how these norms are perpetuated in the public imagination by successive presidential performers. Most political audiences are likely to expect presidential performers to conform to a standard of able-bodied masculinity, and such conformity contributes to those audiences' readiness to place their trust in a presidential candidate and to perceive them as a potentially legitimate representative of the nation. Populists might indeed seek to draw explicit attention to their own physical strength to play into this set of expectations of embodied performance. However, positing a populist break with previous convention forecloses the view of how populist performances actually draw on and reiterate well-established norms of embodiment. While seeking to conform to norms of embodiment that associate able-bodied, white, cisgender masculinity with power, authority, and the capacity to represent the nation, populists like Trump generate legitimacy in peculiarly conservative ways by reiterating, sharply, rudely, and with bad manners, existing norms and constraints. The striking nature of Trump's embodied performance lies not in that he forges a radically new connection with constituents but in his ability to weaponise the ways in which traditional associations of certain bodies with power, authority, and representative capacity contribute to perceptions of legitimacy.

Shifting Legitimacy and Outsider Rhetoric

By asserting that Hillary Clinton's experience was 'bad experience' in the first 2016 presidential debate, Trump was staking the claim that being an outsider to Washington politics was an asset in a presidential hopeful. Whilst Trump's use of and references to his body during this debate weaponised established norms around gender, race, health, and virility, his anti-establishment rhetoric sought to generate legitimacy not through weaponising conformity but by mobilising distrust and gesturing towards disruption. However, attempting to disavow one's own insider position vis-à-vis the political establishment is itself a well-worn pattern of US presidential rhetoric and had been pervasive prior to the election of Trump. Bonikowski and Gidron (2016, 1604) argue in a quantitative study of speeches using populist language that the campaigns of Dwight Eisenhower in 1952, Bob Dole in 1996, and Richard Nixon in 1968 'represent peaks in Republican populism', whereas those of Michael Dukakis in 1988, George McGovern in 1972, and Bill Clinton in 1992 mark highpoints of Democratic populism. As noted in the Introduction, before declaring the launch of his 2008 presidential campaign, Barack Obama was pointedly advised that he could still run as an outsider to the Washington establishment and thus continue in this populist tradition. Because Obama had not yet completed his first term in the US Senate, both Harry Reid, then Senate Majority Leader, and former Senate Minority Leader Tom Daschle identified Obama's appeal as a relative Washington outsider (Heilemann and Halperin 2010, 33–4, 70). This calculation was reflected in Obama's campaign rhetoric, which stressed the motifs of 'hope' and 'change', and it was made explicit in his campaign launch announcement, wherein Obama stated, 'I know that I haven't spent a lot of time learning the ways of Washington. But I've been there long enough to know that the ways of Washington must change' (2007). John McCain, the Republican candidate, likewise tried to pursue this message in presenting Senator McCain as a long-time maverick within the Republican Party, initially going so far as to consider Joe Lieberman, nominally a Democrat,[2] as McCain's running mate (Heilemann and Halperin 2010, 353). Of course, the eventual choice of Sarah Palin, a woman and markedly plainspoken Washington outsider from Alaska, as McCain's vice presidential candidate, was no less of a statement for change than the choice of Lieberman would have been. However, in a highly diverse and fragmented media environment, in which a politician's every utterance is refracted in innumerable different ways, it is increasingly difficult even for presidents and presidential candidates to get their messages across. As a speechwriter connected with the McCain–Palin campaign told me in our interview, the campaign's perception was that McCain's maverick message failed because 'Obama owned the change message [for] a host of reasons' and had become 'the living embodiment of change'.

The tradition of US presidents distancing themselves from Congress can arguably be traced, in broad strokes, to a shift towards popular address and away from speeches addressed exclusively to Congress that occurred at the beginning of the twentieth century (see Chapter 2). However, despite its commonness, this kind of populist presidential performance achieves a noteworthy performative gesture, especially as it relates to the cultivation of legitimacy. While some scholars of performativity, notably J. L. Austin and Pierre Bourdieu, highlight the importance of a speaker's authority to the felicitousness of their utterance, the performativity of presidential anti-Congress rhetoric operates in the opposite direction, not through the enforcement but through the disavowal of the kind of authoritative backing with which one might assume such speakers would be seen, and would wish to be seen, to be invested. Here, I build on theorisations of legitimacy and of populism to explore how performances of populism can enact performative shifts in the perception of legitimacy. Because these performances discourage the perception of the federal government as a unified whole, they rhetorically configure legitimacy in terms of a strictly competitive or zero-sum game. In this, audiences are encouraged to perceive different political players, notably the US president, who acts on behalf of the people, and Congress, which is painted as corrupt, to have diametrically opposed interests. In the zero-sum game that is rhetorically evoked to exist between these players, one player, the self-styled outsider, is able to benefit directly at the expense of the other, the political establishment. The impression is created that legitimacy is a finite resource that is contested between different institutions. As legitimacy is whittled away from established institutions and their officeholders, it is thus conferred upon the populist politician themself instead. This has important ramifications for presidential politics as contrasting requirements for effective campaigning and effective governing emerge. Furthermore, zero-sum rhetoric might bring about a state of affairs in which increasingly legitimacy is legible for political audiences only if claims to it are accompanied by the disavowal of previous institutional affiliation.

In *On Being Included*, Sara Ahmed argues that institutional speech acts, here those made within universities, tend to name commitments without enacting the named effects and therefore tend towards being 'non-performative' (2012, 56). Ahmed contrasts 'non-performatives' with infelicitous performatives, positing that in the case of the non-performative, 'the failure of the speech act to do what it says is not a failure of intent or even circumstance, *but it is actually what the speech act is doing*' (117, emphasis in original). While non-performatives are read as if they brought into effect that which they name, they are an institutional way of appearing to do something (combat institutional racism and sexism, for instance) without actually bringing that which is named into effect. Crucially, these speech acts appear to be performative and in so appearing mask their non-performative character. In sharp contrast to the performative ineffectiveness of the institutions Ahmed explores, I am concerned here with what appears to be the high performative effectiveness of the institutional outsider. While the possibility for a speech act to be felicitous would typically be seen to be tied to a number of conditions, including the institutional standing and authority of the speaker, it appears, paradoxically, that the disavowal of such standing and authority and the assertion of outsider status can be, and frequently is, performatively effective. In other words, presidential populism appears to be effective as a performative speech act not because the appropriate conditions for its felicity are in place, but because a key condition – the institutional standing and authority of the speaker – is either missing or actively disavowed. What is it about the disavowal of institutional authority that makes presidential performances of outsiderness an apparently compelling strategy, and how might disavowals of institutional authority affect perceptions of the legitimacy of the political system more broadly? Why is this kind of rhetoric, having been in the background of the self-presentation of many presidents, especially foregrounded and successful now?

Conceptualisations of legitimacy are typically sorted into normative, legal, and descriptive variants (Levitov 2016; Peter 2017), but this neat separation risks obscuring the intriguing tension between objective and subjective dimensions of legitimacy. This tension is evident, for instance, in Bush-era War on Terror policy. Bush was (at least barring disagreement with the outcome of the Bush v. Gore Supreme Court case) elected according to the rules governing US elections and therefore held his position as US president legitimately. However, some of the Bush administration's policy actions, particularly those taken in the context of the so-called War on Terror, were not subjected to established legitimation procedures. Bush's anti-terror actions were nonetheless able to garner 'vast popular legitimacy' because the War on Terror rhetoric used by Bush administration officials exerted a significant affective impact on a large part of the American electorate (Anker 2014, 110–11). As such, the subjective, emotive, and perceptual dimension of legitimacy was able to overrule its formal and objective dimension.

Typically, scholarship that explores how legitimacy can exist outside of or alongside the formal rules that govern state actions perceived as legitimate builds on Max Weber's (1978) ideas about the belief-based nature of legitimacy in order to bring into focus the malleability of how the terms of legitimacy are perceived within a political system. According to Weber, legitimacy is now most readily thought of as a set of established democratic norms and formal legal procedures that authorise the use of state power (1978, 37). In other words, by following certain formally prescribed rules (laws), state actions come to be seen as legitimate, and there exists a staff that is formally authorised 'to bring about compliance or avenge violation' of the law (34). Thus, legitimacy, as legality, depends on the existence of people upon whom the formal authority to carry out specific coercive actions has been conferred and on the existence of 'formally correct' procedures, which tend to be carried out in an 'accustomed manner' (37). However, Weber reminds us that, ultimately, this common proceduralist understanding of legitimacy – which may be seen as more complex than traditional or purely faith-based forms of legitimacy insofar as its prerequisite is the existence of a formal code of law and relatively complex rules by which laws are enacted and enforced – is ultimately based on the 'belief in the existence of a legitimate order' (31). '[B]elief in legality' (37) obviously entails that all those who are part of a social order believe that its legal norms are binding and that the enforcement of those norms is legitimate. In other words, while the subjective nature of the legitimacy of a social order might be hidden behind objective-seeming codifications, the order still depends, in the last instance, on subjective belief in legitimacy.

Saward's theory of the representative claim leans on Weber's thinking, and Rodney Barker's (2001) elaboration thereof, as Saward argues that to garner legitimacy, a political representative must make 'provisionally acceptable claims to democratic legitimacy across society . . . for which there is evidence of sufficient acceptance . . . by appropriate constituencies under reasonable conditions of judgment' (2010, 145). While 'appropriate constituencies' and 'reasonable conditions of judgment' are undoubtedly desirable, they are difficult to judge objectively. Saward's definition of democratic legitimacy brackets the possibility of unreasonable conditions of judgement, under which constituencies would presumably be manipulated by the social and/or institutional power of representative claim-makers and accept as legitimate representatives whom they would not be inclined to accept under more reasonable conditions. While Saward is right in focusing on the agency of political audiences in receiving claims to representation, it nevertheless seems worthwhile to incorporate the force of discourse – as the possibility for less than reasonable conditions of judgement – more directly into the conceptualisation of perceived and shifting legitimacy. After all, Weber considered plebiscitary leadership derived from charisma as an 'independent source of legitimacy', essentially authoritarian, but capable, by undergoing a process of 'progressive rationalization' to be transformed into the kind of 'democratic legitimacy' that Saward cites (Weber 1978, 266–7).

In contrast to Saward, *Orgies of Feeling* (2014), in which Elisabeth Anker argues that melodramatic political discourse served to justify state actions taken by the United States in the course of the so-called War on Terror, puts forth a concept of 'felt legitimacy' that posits that perceptions of legitimacy can be shaped by political discourse. Anker argues that War on Terror actions were able to garner 'vast popular legitimacy' despite the fact that they were not subjected to 'typical institutional or deliberative channels for authorizing power' (2014, 110). A large proportion of the American electorate came to perceive state actions taken in the War on Terror as legitimate in spite of the fact that these actions did not follow the established legal procedures that are typically understood to confer legitimacy. Anker's conceptualisation of 'felt legitimacy' explicitly considers the force of discourse as mobilised by political actors seeking to influence political audiences; this is why her thinking around legitimacy is so valuable here. 'Felt legitimacy' brings together Weber's focus on legitimacy as perception with Michel Foucault's critique of legitimacy, expressed in 'Society Must Be Defended' (2003), as the cultivation of a specific subjectivity that is desired by political power and that both produces and is foisted upon political subjects, but the idea of 'felt legitimacy' does not imply that subjects are wholly subjugated under an absolute power that nullifies their agency. Instead, Anker makes the more nuanced proposition to combine 'Weber's claim that belief in legitimacy can be created by affective states mobilized by social forces' with 'Foucault's claim that power and discourse produce legitimacy', and thereby open up 'a new claim that the affective states conditioning belief in legitimacy are shaped in part by political discourse' (2014, 117–18). This nuanced view, I posit, needs to be taken into account not just when studying policy like Bush's anti-terror actions, or when felt legitimacy provides 'an affective experience that authorizes state power' (111), but also when looking at electoral politics and how politicians' performances shape the perception of democratic institutions.

Felt legitimacy relates in this case to the perception of specific political actors and institutions as legitimate. Because political discourse can create perceptions of legitimacy, it is reasonable to assume that it also has the power to shift how legitimacy is perceived within an institutional system. Perceptions of legitimacy are created in the interplay of politicians' performances, audiences' reception, and the force of discourse; therefore specific performative interventions should be seen as having the power to shift how legitimacy is perceived within an institutional system. When seen through this lens, Barack Obama's transformation, in 2008, from little known first-term senator into the 'collective representation' that most credibly expressed the electorate's hope and hunger for change (Alexander 2010, 40–2), can be read as a function of a shift in the public perception of legitimacy, rather than as a miraculous event. This shift had, if anything, intensified in 2016, when the electorate elevated an even more unlikely outsider, Donald Trump, from reality TV personality and nonserious challenger to the Republican presidential nominee and subsequent winner of the US presidential election. If successful (or 'felicitous'), populist rhetoric used by presidential candidates who can credibly present themselves as political outsiders entails a performative shift of legitimacy away from established institutions and their officeholders and onto the populist politician themself. The felicity of this move would then seem to depend not on the politician's pre-existing authority, but precisely on their (actual or successfully performed) lack of prior authorisation. In other words, while, as Weber explains, state actions perceived as legitimate tend to be executed by formally authorised staff, the theatre of politics has the power to rearrange perceptions of legitimacy in such a way that such staff are no longer perceived as fully legitimate. Instead, outsiders with no prior authorisation might become privileged in the public perception as more legitimate than the functionaries of an institutional system perceived as corrupt. The remainder of this section draws on Judith Butler's theorisation of the capacity of performative utterances to enact shifts of legitimacy in order to link the concept of felt legitimacy more directly to this study's focus on populist presidential performances.

Butler sketches the possibility of shifting legitimacy in a brief passage in *Excitable Speech* (1997, 146–50), arguing against the idea that institutional authority is essentially static and has the prerogative of felicitously enacting performative speech acts. Instead, Butler carves out the possibility that performative speech acts not underpinned by institutional authority can have the effect of bringing about shifts of legitimacy. This hypothesis on performance's capacity to enact shifts in how legitimacy is perceived is crucial to the analysis of how (actual or self-fashioned) political outsiders who employ populist anti-establishment rhetoric might succeed in taking legitimacy away from established institutions and conferring it upon themselves, thereby rhetorically structuring the terms of legitimacy as a directly competitive or zero-sum game.

J. L. Austin, on whom both Butler and Pierre Bourdieu rely in describing the connection between performativity and authority, describes that the felicitousness of a performative utterance depends on 'some previous procedure, tacit or verbal', which must 'have first constituted the person who is to do the ordering an authority' (1962, 29). When this is not the case, then, in all likelihood, the utterance will be 'classed as a misfire', because 'the procedure invoked is not accepted' or because certain performatives, such as commands, are 'in order only when the subject of the verb is "a commander" or "an authority"' (27–8). Thus, for Austin, the felicitousness of a performative utterance depends on pre-established conventions and the acceptance by all parties of the authority of the speaker. In a move that separates the felicitousness of a performative utterance even more definitively from the speech act itself, Bourdieu places additional emphasis on the speaker's authority. For Bourdieu, language cannot precede authority; it merely expresses it. 'Language at most *represents* this authority, manifests and symbolizes it', Bourdieu argues, stressing that an authorised spokesperson depends on his 'accumulated symbolic capital' – that is, his prior legitimacy – rather than anything inherent in the speech act itself (1991, 109, emphasis in original). Bourdieu also makes explicit that any such authority depends on its institutional backing, as this is 'an authority whose limits are identical with the extent of delegation by the institution' (109). I cite Bourdieu's argument here both because Butler, who is keen to introduce an element of dynamism into the performative operation, explicitly positions themself in opposition to it and because it serves to highlight the remarkable performative operation involved in populist rhetoric. As will become clear, such rhetoric depends for its felicity not on the speaker's institutional backing but on the social power conferred at least in part by their (actual or successfully performed) lack of delegated institutional authority.

In countering Bourdieu's view, Butler draws on Jacques Derrida's (1988) reading of Austin, which stresses the importance of each performative iteration's break with previous context, to put forth a theory that sees performative utterances as dynamic vis-à-vis established power structures. Butler thus seeks to overturn Bourdieu's emphasis on the primacy of social power backed by institutional authority and the consequent delegation of the performative utterance to an epiphenomenal status. They posit that utterances themselves can, through 'the rehearsal of the conventional formulae in non-conventional ways', force a shift in the terms of legitimacy so that 'an invocation that has no prior legitimacy can have the effect of challenging existing forms of legitimacy, breaking open the possibility of future [social institutional] forms' (1997, 147). In doing so, Butler charges Bourdieu with failing to 'theorize the particular force of the utterance as it breaks with prior context' and failing 'to take account of the way in which a performative can break with existing context and assume new contexts, refiguring the terms of legitimate utterance themselves' (148, 150). While Butler does not offer a theory of legitimacy itself in *Excitable Speech*, it is nevertheless clear that they are referring to shifts in the perception of legitimacy. Specifically, Butler's focus on challenging existing forms of legitimacy and the reference to the future possibility of new social institutional forms seem to indicate that Butler is examining the perception of legitimacy first of all, with a legal and procedural framework of legitimacy existing perhaps on a secondary level that could be subject to change after an initial change in how legitimacy is perceived.

If we accept both the importance of subjective perceptions of legitimacy and the possibility of performative speech acts enacting shifts in how legitimacy is perceived, then it becomes possible to argue that specific patterns of political discourse might shift how audiences perceive legitimacy within a political system. In this, the success or failure of performative claims to legitimacy still depends on the investment of trust by political audiences. It was, for instance, up to political audiences to make the judgement that the first-term senator Barack Obama performed the change message more persuasively than the long-time maverick John McCain did in 2008. While the cards were arguably stacked against McCain, because it is always difficult for a presidential candidate to follow an incumbent of the same party to electoral success,[3] this perception was not inevitable. It would have been within the realm of possibility, for instance, for the electorate to instead perceive Obama as an overly ambitious career politician and McCain as a tried and tested war hero. While audiences thus do retain a measure of agency, this chapter posits that shifts in legitimacy enacted by populist rhetoric can configure legitimacy in terms of a zero-sum game: in this, a dominant strain of anti-establishmentarian discourse continuously subtracts legitimacy from established political institutions and incumbent officeholders and instead confers it upon a specific political outsider. While democratic audiences have agency in their judgement of individual political actors, it might therefore become increasingly difficult to perceive legitimacy as inhering within government institutions, to the point that the disavowal of affiliation with such institutions might, in the perception of audiences, become a prerequisite for the successful performance of claims to legitimacy. In other words, while performative utterances, specifically as they occur in political discourse, have the power to reorganise the terms of legitimacy, audiences might ultimately become predisposed to following a particular, dominant pattern of perceiving legitimacy, especially when populist rhetoric is pervasive.

POPULIST CLAIMS TO REPRESENT AND
LEGITIMACY AS A ZERO-SUM GAME

Mainstreamed populism is a strategy that cultivates legitimation through outsider rhetoric and anti-establishment discourse. To explain how ideas about performative shifts in the perception of legitimacy can be connected to political rhetoric, it is useful to refer back to Saward's theorisation of political representation as performative. Saward argues that political representation should be thought of not as a kind of formal authorisation, but as a more dynamic operation (2014, 725). According to Saward, politicians, as makers of representative claims, performatively constitute, or evoke, their audiences by ascribing certain characteristics to them. The politician simultaneously constitutes themself as the ideal representative of the audience possessing the named characteristics. This mutual constitution of the speaker and their audience on the basis of specific, usually shared, characteristics is the representative claim; it is performative because it interpellates both the constituent-audience and the politician-speaker (2006, 301–6). It is then up to the audience to suspend their disbelief in the speaker's performance and its evocation of the audience as a group sharing certain characteristics and of which the claim-maker becomes a representative accepted to be credibly authentic and legitimate. Besides the necessity of projecting personal authenticity, it follows from Saward's theorisation that, in order to make a felicitous representative claim, the claim-maker needs to evoke the audience in a way that resonates with the audience's sensibilities. It is therefore imperative that the politician is able to tap into the audience's prevailing political concerns and reflect these back to them in a way that offers a productive way forward to the audience. If a politician employs populist rhetoric at this stage, we can presume that they tap into an anti-establishment sensibility that they suppose exists among their audience. If such rhetoric is successful, then the claim-maker might come to be seen as the representative of a particular audience and be felt to be legitimate in that role. In other words, politicians claiming to represent the people will be felt to be more or less legitimate depending on how well their claims to represent resonate with the people. At this point it becomes possible to connect representative claim-making and the possibility of shifting legitimacy to populism.

Most definitions of populism agree that its most essential feature is antagonistic binary division between the people and their enemy, the establishment (Moffitt 2020, 10; Mudde and Kaltwasser 2017). According to Ernesto Laclau, for instance, such division occurs when there exists among the electorate a variety of unmet demands that come to be seen as equivalent to each other, in a process by which they 'constitute a broader social subjectivity', which creates 'a widening chasm separating the institutional system from the people' (2005a, 74). Populism thus consists of 'the unification of a plurality of demands in an equivalential chain', the consolidation of this chain 'through the construction of a popular identity', and 'the constitution of an internal frontier dividing society into two camps' (77). Lone Sorensen has more recently argued similarly that populists' appeal depends not on their policies or opinions, but on their mimetic imitation of their constituents, their claim to be of the people as well as standing up for them (2020, 148). The stress these theorists place on populist identity formation at the expense of individual policy issues or matters of political ideology is particularly useful in thinking about Obama–Trump voters (that is, people who voted for Obama in 2012 and for Trump in 2016), who, due to close margins in key swing states, 'played a crucial role in handing over the White House to the GOP' (Skelley 2017; see also Cohn 2017).

Like Saward's theory of representation, Laclau's and Sorensen's approaches to populism embed elements of performativity in the collective constitution of the people as a unified entity defined by its opposition to the establishment. Laclau asserts that 'the symbolic unification of the group around an individuality [a leader] . . . is inherent to the formation of a "people"', but he does not specify how this leader is chosen or how one among many potential leaders might make effective use of rhetoric to be elevated into the 'singularity' that is capable of representing the unified identity of the group (2005a, 100). However, using Saward's theory of representative claim-making, it is possible to shed light on the performative act that elevates a politician into a figure of identification for a populist movement. In using populist rhetoric, the politician taps into existing anti-establishment sentiment and both feeds and draws on the suspicion with which the institutional structure has already come to be viewed. The politician mobilises the existing populist division of society into two camps, the dissatisfied people and the unsatisfactory establishment, for their own political gain. By presenting themself to the electorate as an outsider determined to infiltrate the tainted system with the intent of purifying it, the politician performatively constitutes themself as a credible representative of 'the people', as defined by their disillusionment with the political establishment. Additionally, through the rejection of political institutions a sense of felt legitimacy is created, as the politician encourages the perception of themself not as part of a maligned institutional structure, but as someone in possession of personal authenticity. Sorensen describes this authenticity as emerging from populists' disruption of the distrusted politics as usual and from populists' practice of drawing on '[culturally resonant] background symbols to constitute identity through implicit contrast to the elite' (2020, 149). If a populist representative claim is successful, then the politician making that claim is able to persuade their audience to suspend their disbelief in their performance and, hence, trust them as the spokesperson for the populist movement. The development of the populist movement is thus aided by, but it also, crucially, precedes and is not wholly dependent on, the politician's intervention in it via the representative claim.

It is worth dwelling here on the empirical case for why anti-establishmentarian representative claims are compelling in the United States in the contemporary moment. Rather than simply asserting that presidential populism seems to be a successful strategy that increasingly works to rearrange how governmental legitimacy is perceived, we should ask what makes this an especially compelling strategy in the first place. How might the upsurge of presidential populism be seen to be playing into and adding fuel to an already extant tendency at work in US politics? And why might current political conditions in the United States increasingly privilege anti-institutional and anti-Washington performances by presidents and presidential candidates and encourage voters' perception of such anti-institutional claim-makers as more legitimate and authentic than institutional insiders?

Most conspicuously, presidential populism promises to reassert the voice of 'the people' within the political sphere. Obama's 2008 campaign rhetoric against the 'ways of Washington' as well as his later claims about the corruption of Congress by the gun lobby and Donald Trump's 2016 promise to 'drain the swamp' were all expressed on behalf of the people against a tainted political establishment that is perceived as having ceased to work on the people's behalf. As such, these performances purport to re-democratise a previously de-democratised political sphere. A wealth of scholarship has addressed the increasing de-democratisation of the United States in recent decades, focusing particularly on the effects of neoliberalism on democratic politics.[4] While it is beyond the scope of this book to offer a detailed exploration of neoliberalism's logic, causes, and consequences, the following brief sketch of the effects of neoliberalism on democratic politics should suffice to give an impression of the de-democratised political landscape within which recent presidential populism has flourished.

The effects of neoliberal economisation on political subjects and institutions have been described as 'difficult to overstate' in their significance for democracy since neoliberalism engages in the 'remaking[] of the purpose of both states and citizens' insofar as it entails 'the dramatic curtailment of popular participation in political life' (Brown 2015, 42). Wendy Brown argues further that neoliberalism brings about the 'destruction of public life and especially educated public life' as well as the 'marketization of the political sphere' such that 'it dramatically thins public life without killing politics', though politics is rendered 'unappealing and toxic' (39).

Sheldon Wolin has focused his observations on neoliberalism more specifically around the expansion of presidential power since 11 September 2001, arguing that 9/11 quickly became the 'principal reference point by which the nation's body politic was to be governed' (2008, 6). Wolin argues that, following 9/11, though presidential power was expanded and dissenting political views became increasingly difficult to articulate, these changes appeared largely to be governed by 'abstract totalizing power' rather than by the vision of strong political leaders such that, by obscuring its true, totalising character, 'significant change appears as modest attenuation of previous tendencies' (42, 44). For Wolin, this meant that 'democratic myths . . . have become detached from democratic practice' as the political disengagement of citizens has been increasingly encouraged and the United States has been turned into a 'managed democracy' (287), where

> the political role of corporate power, the corruption of political and representative processes by the lobbying industry, the expansion of executive power at the expense of constitutional limitations, and the degradation of political dialogue promoted by the media are the basics of the system, not excrescences upon it. (287)

These scholars are in broad agreement that neoliberalism entails the de-democratisation of political life, and in this sense constitutes a 'narrowing of public life' so that, when 'combined with the strong emphasis of governance on consensus, a hostility to politics becomes palpable' (Brown 2015, 127). In the US, de-democratisation has been accompanied by a decline of trust in politicians and political institutions, as well as by the mainstreaming of a kind of conspiracy culture that, stimulated by the rise of the security state after the Second World War and political events and scandals like the Kennedy assassination and Watergate, 'has permeated American culture' as a 'default suspicion towards the authorities' (Knight 2000, 31; see also Pew Research Center 2015; Twenge, Campbell, and Carter 2014; van der Meer 2017). Voter disaffection and disenfranchisement have been linked to effects of neoliberalisation like the influence of corporate lobbyists and the increasingly managerial, dissent-averse, and – at worst – creepingly totalitarian mode of politics. At the same time, trust in institutions – particularly, but not limited to, government institutions – has eroded while negative partisanship has risen dramatically (Abramowitz and Webster 2018). All of this is evidence for the widespread disillusionment of voters with the possibility of effecting positive change through democratic institutions.

The currency of presidential performances of outsider status must be read in this context of de-democratisation. As neoliberal managerialism has sought to limit or eradicate dissensual and agonistic political expression (Brown 2015, 127), the appeal of presidential populism in the Obama years might be seen as indicative of an aspiration to reinsert dissenting expression and to re-democratise a political system whose democratic character is now perceived as being primarily mythical rather than actively practised. As such, we might understand the appeal of presidential populism in the terms of Chantal Mouffe's work (2005a, 2005b, 2013), which has influentially postulated that the forceful reinsertion of conflict through more radicalised forms of antagonism will follow the emptying out of political life's essential agonism. Following Saward, the people are in a position to make a judgement about whether or not a representative claim-maker might credibly represent them. After the political sphere's discreditation of itself through voter disenfranchisement, managerialism, lobbyist influence, a seemingly interminable succession of scandals, and so on, performances of unauthorised anti-institutional outsiderness should be seen as particularly compelling and desirable to voters. Of course, this does not mean that populist claim-makers, once elected to the presidency, succeed or even work towards actually re-democratising the de-democratised political sphere, as certainly Trump did not and is not working towards now that he has been voted out of power.

Because anti-establishment sentiment precedes any particular representative claim made by a single politician, the populist discourse employed by this politician will be more powerfully resonant than discourse generated by any single individual in isolation could possibly be. This is where the Foucauldian perspective on the pervasive influence of discourse becomes relevant: the subjectivity of political audiences will already have been conditioned by a persistent anti-establishmentarian political discourse that more and more predisposes audiences towards suspending their disbelief in self-styled outsiders who make populist representative claims. Obama, as a junior senator who had yet to complete his first term, as the first Black US president, and as a candidate who built his campaign around the concepts of 'hope' and 'change', then channelled the simmering populist division of society in his 2008 election campaign. While running with a radically different policy agenda, Donald Trump arguably rode this same wave of disenchantment in his 2016 campaign and thus connected with key demographics even in previously tendentially Democratic states, such as Wisconsin, Pennsylvania, and Michigan, which proved decisive in the election and had previously been won by Obama.[5] It appears, then, that any policy content of the political positions expressed mattered less than the societal division itself, which is consistent with Laclau's theorisation of the logic by which populism operates, as the divisive function 'can be performed by signifiers of an entirely opposite political sign' (2005a, 87), and also is consistent with Sorensen's claim that populists 'identify with the people by virtue of "showing being ordinary" rather than through shared opinions' (2021, 148). In effect, as people's dissatisfaction with the political establishment has whittled away at the perceived legitimacy of political institutions, the populist politician's representative claim, which further denies those institutions legitimacy and seeks to confer it instead upon the politician as an outsider to or maverick infiltrator of those institutions, then enacts a further shift in legitimacy, turning presidential rhetoric into a kind of 'populist slope' as ever more anti-establishmentarian and populist-style performances are privileged and incentivised. Even as democratic procedures and legal norms remain in place, the risk is that, if a populist paradigm of political rhetoric persists, legitimacy might increasingly become legible through the disavowal of affiliation with democratic institutions, rather than through the affirmation of these institutions' value for the people.

To get back to the overall point about shifting legitimacy, it is important to stress that the kind of anti-establishmentarian rhetoric I have described works only when the populist politician in question can convince audiences to perceive them as an authentic outsider to or at least a maverick within the political system. If the politician can credibly perform their outsider persona and outsider position vis-à-vis the establishment and portray themself as part of, and willing to take action for, the people, they can then channel the prevalent anti-establishment sentiment to benefit their campaign or political status. Thus, the felicitousness of the anti-establishmentarian shift of legitimacy away from the established institutions (whose perceived legitimacy has already been worn away) and onto the populist politician as a representative of the people's movement depends not on the politician's pre-existing authority, but partly on their lack of prior authorisation. *Pace* Bourdieu, it seems to be the outsider position – in combination with the theatrical skill with which it is performed – that confers to the speaker the credibility and social power necessary to assume the position of legitimate leader of the people against the establishment.

Furthermore, with populist representative claims, legitimacy is rhetorically configured in terms of a strictly competitive or zero-sum game. The comparison between current and earlier patterns of presidential rhetoric in the US serves to illustrate this. Thomas Jefferson's 1801 inaugural address provided an early model for presidential oratory, and stressed the interdependence of the institutions of the constitutional order (see Chapter 2). This indicates that, prior to the turn of the nineteenth century and the presidencies of Theodore Roosevelt and Woodrow Wilson, the US president was felt to be legitimate because he functioned as one cog in the state machine and performed this role in public by presenting himself as the chief explicator the US Constitution (which, as a suprapolitical focal point, lent legitimacy to the institutional order as a unified whole). If one imagines Congress and the president as players in a political game, this game is here configured as a cooperative one. The president needs the other political institutions to govern and the other institutions, in turn, need the president. Their interests align towards a common goal. While the president may belong to a different political party than the House and Senate majorities, in his public performances (which are kept to a minimum), he is expected to rise above partisanship and to stress instead the cooperation between political institutions as well as the unity of a holistically conceived constitutional order.

During the course of the twentieth century, by contrast, and particularly in the contemporary moment, US presidential candidates and presidents have tended to solicit the people's acceptance by maligning other institutions, especially Congress, and presenting themselves as a contrast to these institutions and as possessing a more direct connection, however virtual and/or illusory, to the people. In other words, they attempt to manipulate perceptions of legitimacy by rhetorically working to take legitimacy away from Congress and conferring it upon themselves. The perception that is created in such performances is that the tainted Congress and the president, who is figured as its purifier, have diametrically opposed interests, so that one of the players may benefit directly at the other's expense while both players cannot benefit at once: Congress is figured as wanting to go on in its present corrupt state, while the president/presidential candidate wants to cleanse it of its corruption. It is evident that both strategies cannot be successfully pursued at once. Diametrically opposed interests, one player benefiting at the expense of the other, and the impossibility of both players gaining if they are deprived of some of their strategies are properties of strictly competitive and, more specifically, zero-sum games (Encyclopaedia Britannica 2015; Kolokoltsov and Malafeyev 2010, 5–6). In populist presidential performance, legitimacy is configured in terms of the zero-sum game: the institutions of the political order are pitted against each other and the perception of the constitutional order as a unified whole is discouraged.

Of course, voting itself, at least in a two-party system, can present itself as a binary choice in any case, and election outcomes might then be seen to come down to clear winners and losers, especially if negative partisanship predominates and election coverage focuses on campaign strategy above all else (Abramowitz and Webster 2018). However, while election outcomes in a majority voting system might also be seen as a kind of zero-sum game that plays itself out between two major parties and the preferences of many voters (Frieze 2015, 224; Niou and Ordeshook 2015, 139), these inter-party struggles are built into the system. In contrast to this, presidential rhetoric that denigrates Congress opens up a different kind of zero-sum game entirely. In this game, the people are invited by the presidential performer to align themselves with the president as a political outsider against the political system more broadly conceived. This kind of inter-institutional zero-sum game, far from being built into it, actually undermines the legitimacy of the political system.

It should be noted here that most games that arise in practice are not zero-sum games, as it is far more common for players to 'have both common and opposed interests' (Brams and Davis 2017). For instance,

> a buyer and a seller are engaged in a variable-sum game (the buyer wants a low price and the seller a high one, but both want to make a deal), as are two hostile nations (they may disagree about numerous issues, but both gain if they avoid going to war). (Brams and Davis 2017)

Similarly, in US federal politics, if effective governing is the goal, the president and Congress have to work together, as Congress wants to avoid presidential vetoes and the president ideally needs the legislature to pass legislation in line with his policy preferences. While the players may not agree on all or even most policies they want to pursue, it is nevertheless clear that their actual situation is far from the diametric opposition of the zero-sum game. This is especially the case because the configuration of the zero-sum game is incompatible with the idea of compromise, which would rather require the thinking underlying the positive-sum game ('win–win' situation) or, perhaps more likely, the negative-sum game ('lose–lose' situation).

What this discussion of basic game theory points to, then, is the contrast between starkly divisive public performances and the requirements for effective governing: populist rhetoric evokes a picture in which it looks like the positions on either side of the central binary divide have opposed interests. In other words, if the 'people plus president' win, then the corrupt establishment loses (or is replaced), and vice versa. In performances of presidential populism, one player's successful strategy is figured as their opponent's loss, and this configuration serves to shore up presidential legitimacy against an increasingly maligned Congress, which appears more and more illegitimate precisely as a result of the strategy by which the presidential player seeks to gain legitimacy through rhetoric that deprives Congress of it. Of course, in practice, once in power even a populist president in the United States relies on his party's support in Congress, and vice versa, as was evident in Senate Majority Leader Mitch McConnell's alliance with President Trump and Trump's reciprocal support of McConnell, though Trumpism certainly began to exceed Trump and is now seen as pervasive in the Republican Party. Much like the melodramatic political discourse employed during the War on Terror, performances of populism serve to radically simplify the political space in a way that may be performatively effective in a political environment perceived to have been de-democratised. Ultimately, however, these performances paint a more starkly divisive picture than is compatible with the system's institutional set-up.

PERFORMANCE AND THE CULTIVATION OF LEGITIMACY

This chapter has explored two major aspects of the performative cultivation of legitimacy in US presidential performances: embodiment and anti-establishment rhetoric. Insofar as they cultivate legitimacy performatively, presidential performances negotiate between breaking with previous context and conforming to established norms and ideals. Butler's work in particular emphasises the tension inherent in performative acts by insisting that discourse works through a 'reiterative power' that regulates and constrains but by simultaneously claiming that breaks with previous context, and new ways of cultivating legitimacy, are nevertheless possible (cf. [1993] 2011, xii; 1997, 148–50). Trump's populism relies on the embodiment of a conservative masculinity and a weaponisation of culturally ingrained norms that associate power, authority, and representative capacity with virile, able-bodied masculinity. Insofar as Trump's performances during the 2016 presidential campaign sought to embody such norms explicitly whilst rudely denigrating Hillary Clinton's physicality, his performances broke with the accepted manners of political discourse in the United States whilst at the same time conforming to conservative expectations about what presidential bodies look like.

The anti-establishment rhetoric Trump employed during his 2016 campaign, exemplified for instance by his insistence during the first debate that Clinton had merely 'bad experience', similarly sought to perform disruption by breaking with the denigrated political establishment. But this assertion of outsiderness simultaneously built on a deeply ingrained antipolitical and anti-establishment tradition in US presidential rhetoric, the beginnings of which can be traced to the turn of the twentieth century. Far from merely taking its place within the already existing anti-establishment discourse, however, presidential anti-establishmentarianism like Trump's has significant consequences as it performatively shapes perceptions of legitimacy and increasingly encourages the public to perceive legitimacy as a zero-sum game that plays itself out between different political institutions. Through the use of broadly populist rhetoric, presidents and presidential candidates emphasise their outsider status vis-à-vis the other, maligned institutions, seeking to undermine the legitimacy of those institutions whilst conferring legitimacy upon themselves. Like Sara Ahmed's seminal study of institutional performativity (2012), I argued that the institutions I examine, those of the US federal government, do not appear to function with particular performative effectiveness. Unlike Ahmed, I have focused on how the US presidency in particular favours performances by self-styled outsiders, who position themselves as as-yet unauthorised interlopers capable of infiltrating the tainted institutional system on behalf of the people with the intention of purifying it.

While discussing presidential populism and shifting legitimacy, I have several times alluded to the possibility that legitimacy might, where a populist paradigm of presidential rhetoric persists, increasingly become legible only through the disavowal of previous affiliation with established institutions rather than through the affirmation of institutional legitimacy. In the case of the United States, while the presidency has arguably had a distinctly American antipolitical bent to it for a long time (Jaffe 1997), the imperative for presidential candidates to perform their own outsiderness appears to have intensified in recent years whilst sections of the public increasingly see the federal government as entirely untrustworthy, a culmination of which is the Capitol Riot of 6 January 2021.

NOTES

1. Despite the fact that, as president, Roosevelt became 'the most frequently photographed person in America', of the approximately 35,000 photographs of FDR archived in his presidential library in New York, only two show FDR in a wheelchair, neither of which was published while Roosevelt was alive (Pressman 2013, 337). If there is any doubt about the persistence of the norms of able-bodied, masculine embodiment that apply to the US presidency, one might consider the controversy aroused by the proposal to include a statue of Roosevelt in a wheelchair in the Franklin Delano Roosevelt Memorial in Washington, DC; this statue was not added until 2001, four years after President Bill Clinton had dedicated the original memorial (Montgomery 2001; Olin 2012; Stout 1997).

2. Lieberman was defeated by the more liberal Ned Lamont in the 2006 Democratic primary in Connecticut and subsequently won re-election to the Senate as an independent, though he continued to caucus with the Senate Democrats.

3. For instance, the National Constitution Center notes that 'in seven of the last nine elections, voters have decided to switch the party controlling the White House when a candidate (or his successor) had won two prior elections' (NCC Staff 2013).

4. By neoliberalism I mean here 'a theory of political economic practices that proposes human well-being can best be advanced by liberating individual entrepreneurial freedoms and skills within an institutional framework characterized by strong private property rights, free markets, and free trade' and which understands the role of the state as limited to 'creat[ing] and preserv[ing] an institutional framework appropriate to such practices' (Harvey 2005, 2).

5. For a quantitative view of the decisive role played by Michigan, Wisconsin, and Pennsylvania in the 2016 election, see Meko, Lu, and Gamio (2017).

CHAPTER 4

THE CURRENCY OF DISTRUST IN PRESIDENTIAL PERFORMANCES SINCE WATERGATE

On 8 April 1913, just over a month after his inauguration, Woodrow Wilson chose to deliver an address in person before a joint session of Congress. Since Jefferson's time, such communications by presidents to Congress had been presented in written form. 'Washington is amazed', reported the *Washington Post* on 7 April after Wilson's decision to appear in person had been announced (1913a). On 8 April, the front page of the *Washington Post* reported on a few senators' objections to 'the precedent-breaking event today' (1913b), but on 9 April a front-page headline declared, 'Wilson Wins Congress in His Epochal Speech from House Rostrum' (1913c). Wilson's unusual step was, arguably, part of his project of putting into practice his vision of the US presidency as a role that exercised strong executive leadership, the legitimacy of which Wilson saw as rooted in the president's direct connection to the people. While Wilson was operating within a rapidly evolving media environment that was on the verge of making radio accessible to the masses, his predilection for direct rhetorical intervention as US president cannot be ascribed entirely to technological changes that transformed the media environment. To make that argument would be to disregard the influence of Wilson's well-defined ideas about what constitutes effective presidential leadership. Wilson's biographer Robert Kraig notes that Wilson was keenly aware of the increasing mediation of mass communication and had drawn the conclusion that democratic leaders had to become 'inordinately skilled rhetors' to cut through to the public in a 'highly mediated communication environment in which a message was diffused in various ways' (2004, 74–5). It is significant, however, that Wilson's observations about rhetorical skill asserted the strength of oratorical leadership necessary to cut through in an environment that was – somewhat paradoxically, from today's perspective – still dominated by print media. Radio broadcasting did not become widespread in the United States until the 1920s, and Wilson did not speak on the radio until 1923, two years after his presidency ended. Wilson's speech before Congress in 1913 was thus not broadcast to the public, though his ground-breaking decision to deliver it in person was reported on in print. On 9 April 1913, the *Washington Post* proclaimed on its front page that Wilson's visit to Congress, which had lasted only fifteen minutes, had served to humanise the president, as it had been 'Woodrow Wilson, the man, who won the hearts of his fellow men as he stood face to face before them' (1913c), and been met with applause by the assembled congressmen:

> Senators and representatives, who had come to scoff at this return, after more than a century of disuse, to the custom of Washington and Adams, yielded to the spell of the spoken words that fell from the lips of the President, who dared to brush aside precedents and demand the performance of a great public duty in the very presence of the legislative body itself. (1913c)

Moreover, the *Post* went into detail on the president's performance itself, reporting that Wilson had spoken 'in a low, well-modulated tone, easily heard in every part of the big House chamber' (1913c), and it ran two pictures of Wilson speaking in the House chamber on page 2. As such, though Wilson's address was not heard by the general public, his decision to deliver it in person still had the potential to influence public opinion. However, while subsequent presidents, among them Warren Harding in 1922 and Calvin Coolidge in 1923, were able to make use of the new medium of radio to have their voices broadcast, Wilson's ideas about strong oratorical leadership might be said to anticipate, rather than actually exploit, the revolution in media technology that privileged the spoken over the written word.

Changes in patterns of presidential oratory that took hold at the beginning of the twentieth century were driven by personal preferences of individual presidents and constitute an adaptation to a changing media environment within which the electorate consumed political coverage. Even though radio broadcasts did not become common until the 1920s, Nikola Tesla had given a public demonstration of radio broadcasting in St. Louis in 1893. This technology was very much in development before and during Wilson's presidency and an inseparable part of the environment in which Wilson's ideas developed and his convictions took hold. Wilson's view that presidential legitimacy derived directly from the president's connection with the electorate manifested itself in his predilection for performing in public settings much more frequently than had been the norm. It is not fully determinable to what degree Wilson's ideas about strong oratorical leadership developed in prescient anticipation of a media landscape that would allow presidents to be heard much more directly by the public. The evolution of presidential performances was influenced both by decisive individual actors like Wilson and by a changing media and political environment that made the Wilsonian model of presidential performance more effective. This chapter focuses on the contemporary moment and on late twentieth- and early twenty-first-century presidents, but it similarly traces both personal and environmental factors that are currently privileging presidential performances that emphasise outsiderness and controversy, demonstrating that the populist style is increasingly incentivised whilst the conventional theatricality of US presidential performance, which emphasised presidential restraint and the striking of a balance between presidentiality and personality, is increasingly less effective. Since they are not fully determined by technological developments but also shaped by the choices individuals make to exploit these developments, the rise of mainstreamed populism and the currency of distrust should not be seen as inevitable or as dead-ends; they are the result of how particular actors have shaped the culture of political performance by exploiting particular technological affordances.

The chapter initially focuses on developments in the mediatised political environment that are making the consensus-based thinking explored in Chapter 2 more difficult to translate into practice. To note briefly how this chapter fits within the overall context of the book, recall that Chapters 1 and 2 argued that distrust is an inherent feature of representative democracy due to the theatrical nature of the performances that establish representative relationships, the success of which relies on political audiences' willingness to suspend disbelief. Chapter 3 theorised how, why, and with what consequences distrust has become an explicit focal point around which the theatre of politics revolves in the contemporary moment. This chapter expands on Chapter 3 by fleshing out the conditions under which distrust has become a focal point for presidential performances and by elucidating the ways in which populist-style performances are increasingly incentivised and dominant in the contemporary US political landscape. Initially, it draws on interviews with political speechwriters to discuss the changing media environment within which speeches are performed and how political speeches as a communicative medium fit within this environment, before broadening out to examine speechwriters' views of how the media environment is evolving and the consequences of this evolution for their work. A range of case studies going back to Jimmy Carter's presidential run after the Watergate scandal and the related sharp decline of public trust in government then explore the increasing effectiveness of presidential performances of outsiderness and anti-establishmentarianism. While distrust is an inherent feature of representative democracy and was mobilised to some extent by presidents as far back as Wilson and beyond, in a more recent major shift distrust and populism have become dominant themes of US presidential performance, threatening to erode the very system of national representative politics that these performances are tasked with sustaining.

'WE WORK BETTER WITH STORIES':
SPEECHWRITING IN THE TWENTY-FIRST CENTURY

Speeches are but one part of a complex mix of communications strategies employed by contemporary politicians. The reception of speeches by political audiences in the contemporary moment is also no straightforward matter, as most audiences do not experience speeches live and in person and are instead exposed to them through the digital or print news media or via social media platforms – both settings that frame, interpret, and often break down speeches into short sound bites. Most audiences' experience of political speeches is partial, in both senses of the word: speeches tend not to be experienced in their entirety and they are usually framed by evaluative commentary. The partiality of audiences' experience of speeches begs the question of whether and how speeches can still be significant tools of effective communication within the fragmented and highly polarised media ecology of the twenty-first century. One Republican speechwriter outlined how they perceived the significance of speeches – or, rather, their insignificance – as follows in our interview:

> we still have speeches as a vehicle, but . . . they don't really reach a lot of people. . . . [W]e saw Barack Obama exploring this: going on talk shows, going on variety shows to convey his message, but I think some of that was just reinforcing support for his brand, . . . letting people get to know him as a person, versus, 'here I am, here are the things I have to tell you in this speech that I'm giving'. And so, yes, within that vehicle there are ways you can approach that, but I'm not sure that that's really gonna be the case for a whole lot longer. As much as I enjoyed writing them. . . . I think we have to approach people in shorter ways that intersect with their daily lives. So, at this point, if you give a speech, you hope that it's newsworthy enough that, you know, someone sees it in their Facebook feed. But often what pierces that bubble is something controversial.

This quote is indicative of one of three distinct lines of thought represented in the interview corpus: some speechwriters felt that the importance of speeches was diminishing because they reached fewer and fewer people in ways that were perceived as being effective. Others felt that some speeches, notably set speeches like State of the Union addresses that tend rigidly to adhere to specific norms and traditions, were becoming less important, but that speeches overall were still significant. Still others felt that speeches were now just as or even more important than they had ever been, because they allowed for extended, affectively charged engagement through storytelling. These three lines of thought were present across party lines; there was no significant division between Republican and Democratic speechwriters, suggesting that these views are broadly applicable to the profession of federal political speechwriting, rather than being determined by political affiliation or ideology.

Similarly to the Republican speechwriter quoted above, others stated that they felt the importance of speeches had diminished compared with the past, as speeches had to compete with a greater number of other communication strategies and in a much more varied media environment. A Democratic senatorial speechwriter, for instance, argued that 'digital communications, social media, and the ability to connect directly to people in real time has affected and, to some degree, limited the importance of public speaking and speechgiving'. Changes in the media ecology, especially the diversification of ways in which politicians can address political audiences, meant that in their view speeches as a communications strategy were becoming relatively less important. The above-quoted Republican speechwriter alluded to other significant changes that accompany the diversification of communications strategies, namely audiences' shorter attention spans and the blending of politics with other forms of entertainment, such as television talk and variety shows. This speechwriter also characterised the situation of giving a speech as an artificial one, as an intentionally created platform for politicians to say, 'here I am, here are the things I have to tell you in this speech that I'm giving'. A Democratic presidential speechwriter likewise chose to explore the artificiality of the speechgiving situation, making the point that 'when you get behind a podium, you lose the personal interaction of a one-on-one conversation' so that 'we lose the natural tones in our voice about how you actually communicate' and tend to sound artificial. However, for this speechwriter, this did not mean that speeches themselves were becoming less significant, merely that speechwriters and speech coaches had to be mindful of the necessity of not setting speakers up to sound artificial. The speechwriter argued that the impression of artificiality could be countered by conscious efforts of making the language of speeches resemble everyday speech:

> And I think [the speechgiving situation] sets people up . . . [I]f I just said, 'how was your day?' and you said, [speaking slowly] 'this day has been a wonderful day'– but that's how you talk in a speech, it's ridiculous. But if I said, [speaking conversationally] 'this has been a great day', you go, 'yeah, that's how humans talk'.

For this group of speechwriters, because there is something distinctly non-conversational and overtly theatrical about the speechgiving situation, speeches were either becoming less important as a communications strategy or were in danger of failing to connect with audiences if orators were not properly prepared to navigate the artificiality of the setting.

Other speechwriters argued that though individual speeches were becoming less important, speeches as a medium were still significant. These speechwriters noted that big presidential speeches still draw huge audiences and that significant speeches can be defining events for politicians and political moments. A Republican presidential speechwriter, for instance, made the point that 'the ability for a president to get his message out through that medium I don't think has diminished at all, but the value of . . . each individual speech . . . has probably diminished'. This argument was made in the context of the speechwriter's observation that 'modern presidents actually talk too much' and 'everything the president says is amplified . . . many times over', so that each individual speech matters relatively less as any impact made is quickly superseded by the next speech. Two Democratic speechwriters likewise reflected on the importance of speeches in the contemporary media landscape; one of them stated:

> when . . . there were three daily newspapers in town and three TV stations and no social media and the president spoke twice a week at most, they probably, among the noise of the system, they probably stood out to the country more. But did that make them more important? . . . I don't know that in those days presidents had any more or less luck with their programs, because they could get the bully pulpit more clearly listened to.

This way of thinking connects to the overexposure of presidents as well as the oversaturation of the political landscape with coverage by a large variety of media outlets. In this environment, some speechwriters observed, significant presidential speeches still cut through to large audiences. The majority of speeches, however, receive far less attention, and speeches also have to compete with presidential performances in other media, for instance as guests on television talk shows or in content generated in their name on social media. In fact, by way of stressing the extent to which speeches interact with and are influenced by other communication strategies, another Democratic speechwriter explained that speechwriting work itself had changed in three ways with the advent of social media: some writing was now done purely for social media; social media provided the means to evaluate speech reception more quickly and broadly as communications teams could 'measure analytically what's being picked up and from where'; and social media itself could generate issues that might be addressed in speeches, meaning that 'sometimes you give speeches in response to what's going on both in social media and in the alternative press', as has been most notably the case during the Trump presidency.

In contrast to this reasoning, which highlights the interconnectedness of speeches with other communication strategies, those speechwriters who affirmed that speeches were just as or even more important now than they had ever been tended to emphasise the unique role speeches played in an overall communications strategy. A Democratic speechwriter explained:

> the role speeches play in the broader communications ecosystem – there's social media, earned media, . . . white papers for people who want to dig into the policy, all these other methods for getting your message out. And speeches are really the place where stories are told, which is how our brains work, right? I can list for you ten reasons why a policy is good, but if I tell you a story about a human whose life has . . . been affected [by the policy], it's just how we're gonna remember things, how we're gonna [be] convinced of things. It's just – we work better with stories, right? And because speeches are the one place in our communications mix where stories are best told, if they're not told there, they're not told anywhere.

Another Democratic speechwriter made a similar point, arguing that speeches were especially important in the contemporary moment because they allowed the speaker to organise their thoughts in a structured way to present a sustained argument. The speechwriter contended that short-form communication on social media is ill-suited to this as 'it's just chaff everywhere' so that 'people can't remember what we were fighting about just a few days ago'. In their view social media did not provide 'a good place for debate or laying out any sort of comprehensive thought', as a speech would ideally do. Both of these statements allude to the way in which presidential speeches tend to address a broad national public (see Chapter 2) as well as offering perspectives on why speeches as a medium might be particularly suited to building unity. The first speechwriter posits storytelling, for which speeches are assumed to be a privileged medium, as a human universal. The second more explicitly contrasts the unifying quality of speeches with the fragmenting quality of social media and argues that speeches, as a unifying medium, are particularly needed in a moment defined by fragmentation and discord. This speechwriter saw the contemporary media landscape as at odds with the goals and purposes of speeches, but in a way that, instead of making speeches obsolete, turns them into a potential remedy. Of course, this begs the question of how writers can expect non-sympathetic audiences to listen to the comprehensive laying out of political thoughts by the side they consider their opponent or enemy. There are no easy answers to this.

A Republican speechwriter argued that speeches might become more important now than they had ever been, if those speeches gave insight into the politician as a person, rather than regurgitating carefully poll-tested sound bites.

This speechwriter asserted that 'Trump has . . . sort of smashed the credibility of the industry . . . called political consultancy' as people do not really respond to risk-averse, poll-tested language and instead 'just wanna see that you're an actual human being'. As a reaction to a politics that, the speechwriter said, has become 'almost nothing but . . . duelling TV ads', people now seem to privilege performances that come across as not overly professionalised and not designed by consultants:

> if you really want to win people's affections, then you just need to find a way to get in front of them, physically or in some other way, and just be yourself and try to persuade them with the language that you yourself fashioned.

In this view, far from being artificially stilted, speeches, at their best, are vehicles for conveying and generating affective connection through engaging storytelling. They are also posited as ideally revelatory about the speaker in a way that allows audiences to feel they are able to connect with them on an affective level, although the notion that presidential speeches contain only language that the speaker themself fashioned is a fantasy, as is the idea that politicians ever are 'just being themselves' in their public appearances. Nevertheless, speeches are seen to provide a potential antidote both to the formal language found in white papers and to poll-tested, 'politician-like' language. At their best, they can imbue politics with a connection that is both affective and charismatic, in Joseph Roach's (2007) sense. What is being criticised in the last quote is an overly self-conscious and, as a consequence, professionalised engagement with the theatrical setting in which politicians' performances take place. Bill Clinton's careful parsing of language in the wake of the Lewinsky scandal is a salient example of this. Particularly in the second quote, by the Republican speechwriter, a looser, more charismatic performance style – that is, a style of performance that drives towards projecting self-confidence and evoking a sense of public intimacy – is propounded as a potential remedy. While it is an illusion to think that a charismatic performance can give wholly authentic access to the speaker's true self, the speechwriter seems to demand a performance style that pays greater attention to the need to appear authentic (rather than necessarily being authentic) in order to foster and sustain the audience's willingness to suspend disbelief. In other words, if speechwriters proceed as if their work was not to construct a presidential persona for public performance but merely to convey their principal's essential self, then the resulting style of performance is assumed to allow audiences more readily to suspend disbelief. In addition to this, the above quotes reinforce the impression that authenticity is increasingly seen to entail off-the-cuff delivery rather than carefully rehearsed, smoothly delivered performance. The performance of presidentiality, of holding back from being too personal in public performance to convey the dignity of the presidential office, is deemed less important.

Whatever their views on the changing significance of speeches more broadly, several speechwriters noted that certain traditions of presidential oratory were out-dated and in need of reform. In particular, speechwriters stated that they thought State of the Union addresses tended to work against the best purposes of speeches (creating emotional connections, telling stories, and conveying a sense of the speaker on a human level). One Democratic speechwriter gave the State of the Union address as an example of a speech that tends to 'feel rote' and has 'no energy in it'. They went on to say that 'year after year everyone says it's gonna be different . . . and then they go out and they give a State of the Union address that's utterly conventional', which, to their own detriment, showed 'the power or the inertia of these conventions of presidential speech'. A second Democratic speechwriter called the State of the Union address 'the worst speech we have to write all year', because it 'doesn't sound like [the principal]' as 'it has 70 different policy proposals in it'. A Republican speechwriter likewise referred to the State of the Union address as 'a legislative laundry list' and contended that 'it's in danger of becoming irrelevant', as television audience numbers for it are dwindling. This speechwriter made the point that 'we've got to fix it', and indicated that it should be shortened as well as be written to be funnier and to contain more stories. These observations about the State of the Union address make clear that, while speeches in general were perceived by some to have a role among other communications strategies, in the particular case of presidential oratory the force of tradition can work against their continuing relevance amongst other political communication strategies.

Despite speechwriters' different opinions on the ongoing relevance of speeches, there was broad agreement that it was important for presidential performances to offer an emotionally resonant connection to audiences. Those speechwriters who spoke about speeches as still important tended to focus on those speeches that were successful in offering specific emotional and charismatic engagement as well as appearing to give insight into the speaker on a human level. Speechwriters who tended to see the role of speeches as diminishing in the contemporary moment valued those same functions, but saw them as being better fulfilled through other means, like social media or appearances on television talk shows. As such, there is a debate over the best medium through which the representative connection between politicians and audiences might be forged in the contemporary moment and an appreciation of the fact that forging effective connections with audiences no longer happens through time-honoured traditions of presidential speech, but in speeches that deviate from the norm and avoid the careful parsing of language that is perceived to be 'politician-like'.

Speechwriters who worked for presidential administrations from Reagan to Obama mostly conceived of their work as being involved in the construction of a vision of national unity, in which the electorate figures as a largely homogeneous imagined community. This vision is increasingly out of step with the documented rise of polarisation, political distrust, conspiracy culture, and negative partisanship within the US electorate. Speechwriters' observations on the changing media environment within which presidential performances are produced and received and their thoughts on how they perceive this environment as disincentivising performances that stress national unity and presidentiality while instead encouraging division and controversy give insight into how the mismatch between the aspirations of presidential speech and the contemporary media ecology affect the production of speeches. Throughout the interviews I conducted, speechwriters brought up the following changes in the media ecology as significant: the fragmentation of the media environment and rise of social media; the oversaturation of the media landscape and the resulting difficulty of catching the attention of audiences in the crowded media environment; concerns about antagonistic media coverage; and, in some speechwriters' views, the incentivisation and intensification of controversial and antagonistic coverage.

Fragmentation, Oversaturation, and Antagonism

[T]he odds of you actually coming into contact with the candidate themselves [sic] and having any kind of meaningful exchange [are extremely long]: they're looking at you, and they're saying, 'you're concerned about education, let me tell you what I'm gonna do on education'. In an . . . environment where that is so rare and it's much more common that the experience that you have is gonna be mediated through – mediated or constructed, right? Mediated through the press and how they interpret it or constructed by the campaign.

These words, by a Republican speechwriter, illustrate the impact they perceived the media environment to have on the production, dissemination, and reception of speechwriting work. Typically, almost everything presidents and presidential candidates say in public will be consciously constructed by them and/or their staff and reach the public after being framed by the media. Donald Trump's use of Twitter and, to a lesser degree, Sarah Palin's decision to 'go rogue' on the campaign trail (which, while not campaign-approved, was still a consciously theatrical performance) might be seen as exceptions to this rule. Speechwriting work, however, is inextricably linked to the media environment within which speeches are produced, disseminated, and received. A second Republican speechwriter observed that presidential campaigns had to be in tune with rapid changes in media technology, arguing that, in 2008, 'Barack Obama was the first candidate to really understand cable television', as 'the networks [had] started covering speeches live'. Television networks were showing the first ten minutes of the candidates' speeches, and, the speechwriter observed, 'Obama tailored his remarks to that. And [Hillary Clinton] did not'. In 2016, the media environment had already changed so that 'eight years later, [the] new technology is not cable'; instead it was social media and online advertising, which Donald Trump managed to use to his advantage: '[Trump] comes on with Twitter, with a tremendous amount of online advertising and . . . as of August 1st, I believe, [Clinton] had spent 130 million dollars on television advertising . . . [Trump had] spent zero dollars'. In fact, the Trump–Pence campaign's online advertising involved the harvesting of private information from over fifty million Facebook users by the company Cambridge Analytica, a strategy that was legally and morally dubious at best (Rosenberg, Confessore, and Cadwalladr 2018). This speechwriter was thus speaking in a highly partisan vein to explicate what were in their view Clinton's 'deficiencies as a candidate', one of which they perceived to be that neither Clinton's 2008 campaign nor her 2016 campaign catered to the dominant media effectively. Despite their partisan colouring, the statements serve to illustrate how rapidly the media environment within which campaigns are fought changes, with marked impacts on speechwriting work (for example, choosing to begin a speech with the most important campaign messages if the first ten minutes will be covered on television, rather than building up to these messages).

Within the corpus of interviews I conducted, among the most frequently mentioned developments that impact upon speechwriting work were the fragmentation of the media environment and the concomitant rise of social media. Although speechwriters disagreed on the relative significance of speeches within twenty-first-century political communications, they tended to agree on how the trend towards media fragmentation and oversaturation was affecting their work. One Democratic presidential speechwriter referred to the fragmented media landscape as one that encouraged more and more speeches by presidents directed at a variety of different media platforms: 'In a fragmented media environment . . . you wind up giving multiple speeches touching multiple audiences and multiple issues even just in a given day'. In this speechwriter's view, the fragmentation of the media environment led presidents to speak in public more frequently, contributing to the oversaturation of the media environment with political coverage, which, in turn, contributed to audiences paying less and less attention to coverage of individual presidential speeches, because 'your words don't generally carry the same weight that they do when you come out of your shell a couple times a month to give a major address'. But the speechwriter also averred that 'we're not in that historical moment any more' where it would be possible to speak only a few times a month, so that now 'the struggle for presidents is, how do we break through?' Bill Clinton White House speechwriter Michael Waldman's book *POTUS Speaks* ascribes the increase in the number of speeches presidents give to the struggle 'to connect with the public amid the clamor of four competing twenty-four-hour cable networks, a bitterly partisan Congress, and seemingly permanent investigations' (2000, 16). Somewhat paradoxically, presidents feel compelled to give many more speeches, but, as the speechwriter quoted above noted, they are less able to 'drive the news cycle' and exert their authority over how the news of the day is framed. In other words, presidents' frequent use of the bully pulpit in the contemporary moment is in fact a response to the bully pulpit's diminishing power. As the above speechwriter observed, 'the cacophony is that much greater now and the news choices are that much greater and . . . there are more filters, and [speechwriters in recent White House staffs] would often feel like, you know, "we're giving speeches and nobody's listening"'. A Republican speechwriter likewise linked fragmentation, oversaturation, and audience fatigue with presidential politics, stating, 'with so many platforms and so many outlets . . . you just run the risk of fatiguing too quickly' so that 'it really takes a big, momentous occasion for people to be interested' and for presidential speeches not just to amount to 'white noise' for the general public.

Alongside the difficulty of breaking through and presidents' increasingly diminished ability to steer the national political conversation, with a multiplicity of performances directed at diverse media platforms it becomes harder to sustain the impression of consistency. Consistency in the presidential persona presented to the public is key to communicating a sense that the persona is a 'true self' (see Chapter 2), but consistency is difficult to sustain over a lengthy career. Saward challenges the premium placed on politicians' consistency, observing that '[p]olitical representatives often need to be, or at least to appear to be, different things to different people', which is why the 'shape-shifting representative', defined as one who 'claims (or is claimed) to represent by shaping (or having shaped) strategically his persona and policy positions for certain constituencies and audiences', should not necessarily be seen as an ethically questionable figure (2014, 723). Indeed, Saward's work on 'shape-shifting representation' casts shape-shifting by political representatives in a notably positive light. He argues, for instance, that one might consider replacing the concept of the role with that of the 'subject position', because

> the concept of role ultimately fails to capture the full importance *of the very attribute* which placed it above those alternatives; it can capture active practice of representation *within* the bounds of particular roles, but not for example when the performance of representative claims *breaks* those bounds, as a regular if not routine political phenomenon . . . Shape-shifting may be a phenomenon born of political freedom and its exercise, and genuine efforts to knit together compromises between opposing interests; further, an absence of shape-shifting may in some

circumstances represent a form of politics that is static and overly predictable. (2014, 726–7, 735, emphasis in original)

One problem with Saward's championing of shape-shifting representation is that it seems to conflate the idea of being open to and inviting of compromise with the strategic and frequent changing of one's public persona. The speechwriters interviewed presented a more nuanced view: they overwhelmingly stated that they believed it either did not or should not cause a problem for a politician to change their mind on something. However, in quite a few interviews it became clear that speechwriters saw this in contrast to the act of changing one's public persona, which they saw as far more problematic. Saward's judgement that shape-shifting behaviour can be a positive force in politics expresses a normative stance about how politics should ideally function rather than an empirical consideration of the essentialist paradigm within which the theatre of politics currently operates. Saward's argument in favour of shape-shifting chimes with broader critiques of the ethics of theatre and performance; Nicholas Ridout asserts, for instance, that 'a theatre which appeals to the emotions alone – to sympathy and identification, for example – lacks ethical value' (2009, 21–2). Saward and Ridout both seek to establish ways of performing and of evaluating performance that would be more normatively and ethically defensible, and both posit that this could be achieved by encouraging a sense of distance rather than insisting on the knowability of and emotional identification with the other. Instead of being accepting of variations in politicians' performances and moving away from an emphasis on emotional identification that may very well be ethically questionable, however, a fragmented media environment drives and intensifies the demand to perform in ways that conform to an essentialist paradigm and makes emotional identification all the more important. It is also the expectation of both audiences and of speechwriters that politicians have a true self that can and should be revealed through their public performances, making them knowable to the public at a distance.

Many of the speechwriters I interviewed referred to the challenge of working with and around antagonistic media coverage, and some observed that they perceived the media landscape as increasingly incentivised towards antagonistic coverage. Naturally, speechwriters, whose role makes them part of the political establishment and whose job it is to endeavour to present their principals in the best possible light, characterised this perceived antagonism as a hindrance to their task. A Republican speechwriter, for instance, explained their ambiguous feelings about the importance of the press and the coverage they perceived as at times too antagonistic, arguing, for instance, that they were 'all for' the press reporting on Trump being 'transparently unheroic, selfish', but that, in their experience, the press also sometimes 'go overboard, sometimes they get it wrong, sometimes they don't give you a break that you should have gotten'.

The speechwriter contended that while '[y]ou can punch a hole in anybody's image . . . you should tolerate normal variations in a human being's life' and not 'punch a hole in every little myth a politician tries to convey', because '[you] should save the real scorn and the sarcasm for when there's a great discrepancy between the message and image and the reality of both'. As such, the speechwriter perceived the press as having 'sort of unwritten responsibilities to be reasonable about stuff', which were frequently neglected. A second Republican speechwriter observed similarly that 'in this highly partisan environment, [the press] love to call everybody a flip-flopping hypocrite'. A third Republican speechwriter, albeit one who no longer currently works as a speechwriter (and therefore does not have to contend with negative media reactions to their principal), expressed their thoughts about media antagonism more neutrally. They acknowledged that 'the number one complaint actually from the candidates usually is that their message doesn't get through because of the media', but also accepted that not receiving favourable coverage is 'just sort of a . . . function of the . . . system, in a democratic system you always . . . run this risk'.

Democratic speechwriters likewise argued that the media were incentivised towards antagonistic coverage. In the words of one speechwriter, 'you're more likely to hear stories of conflict as covered by a media that's rewarded by sharing stories of conflict than you are good things'. Another Democratic speechwriter characterised the increasing incentivisation of antagonistic coverage as a relatively recent evolution in the media landscape, observing that while 'we used to rely on [the news media] to resist the lowest common denominator [of] our basest instincts and to elevate public discourse and to present information to people', the current 'corporatisation of . . . American news media, the pre-eminence of ratings and eyeballs and clicks has warped our journalism so that it's . . . no different than a drug dealer', providing people with the kind of controversial, but damaging, political coverage they seem to want. This speechwriter further argued that today's intense media scrutiny 'has driven out of politics a lot of good people because they don't want their life to be lived under a microscope'. In this view, the predominance of antagonistic coverage in the present political environment was liable to lead to a situation in which people who might be effective public servants would avoid entering politics.

A Republican speechwriter put the argument that media coverage might drive good people out of politics in more general terms, arguing that running for office in contemporary democratic society was something sought by people who had certain negative traits, which meant specifically that politicians usually desired 'some combination of power and fame':

> when a person in a democratic society wants to run for office, the nature
> of that desire and the nature of that activity is . . . not something that a
> completely honest and good person will do. A good person would need

to be asked to exercise power over other people. . . . I would say, by all means, admire a politician when he or she does something that's admirable, but . . . even the ones that you regard as truly good people . . ., they'll have an amazing way of disappointing you. . . . [T]he nature of . . . being a politician in a democratic society is that you have to be a certain kind of person. Brave, maybe in some ways, and intelligent . . . and motivated, ambitious, but also somewhat untrustworthy.

The conclusion to this statement directly echoes a central argument this book makes: that distrust is an inherent feature of representative democracy. Because of the foundational position of theatrical performance within representative democracy, a level of scepticism about the purity of representatives' motives will always remain. A Democratic speechwriter brought up the fact that it used to be considered 'very uncouth' to declare one's own candidacy and that 'it's not like Abe Lincoln went, like, on campaign', because 'it was not the custom to campaign for yourself until the last hundred years'. In this perspective, politicians' declared motive to act as public servants will always be somewhat suspect, but particularly so in the contemporary moment as national political office now comes with considerable fame through public (over)exposure. The perception that politicians are courting fame as highly visible performers in public life further serves to undermine audiences' potential to place their trust in them, in this speechwriter's view.

The antagonistic nature of media coverage, the overexposure of politicians in a plethora of media outlets, and the perception that political candidates must, due to the prevalence of the first two, be hungry for fame are all factors impacting speechwriting by undermining the perceived authenticity of politicians whilst at the same time creating a situation that demands ever more stringently conceived avowals of personal authenticity that conform to an essentialist paradigm. Politicians, especially at the presidential level, are always at risk of being exposed as hypocrites, because they are constantly under a scrutiny that often appears malevolent or at least anything but generous. In this environment, it is difficult to see how, empirically, a more positive view of shape-shifting might be instilled in already distrustful political audiences fed a steady diet of antagonistic political media coverage informing them of any change in their elected representatives' behaviour. While Saward's idea that shape-shifting should be more positively evaluated has merit as a normative stance that posits how democratic politics should ideally work, empirically this idea is directly opposed to the incentives speechwriters found in a political environment marked by antagonistic and all-encompassing media coverage, which instead made it more important to anticipate media hostility and to stress politicians' consistency in performance. A Democratic speechwriter observed, somewhat pessimistically, that political scandals from the Kennedy assassination to lies about the Vietnam War and Watergate meant that 'we are mostly past the days when people are willing to invest an enormous degree of hope and trust in politicians' and that 'we'll never get back to a place where, you know, collectively, people are willing to suspend disbelief in a politician for very long'. Even if it might be beneficial for audiences not to seek emotional identification with the public personas of performing politicians that are made to stand in for their 'essential selves', any moves towards this are perceived to be foreclosed in light of the profound and pervasive distrust of politicians in the current political and media environment.

Some speechwriters perceived overexposure to have a less extreme consequence than potentially effective politicians choosing to stay out of politics altogether. They argued that overexposure produced risk-averse performances. A Democratic speechwriter, for instance, observed that the media's appetite for antagonism has had the effect 'to sanitise political speeches', as conventional politicians 'know that they're videotaped all the time and they stick to very banal language and banal ideas and very orthodox statements' in order not to give the media anything to use against them. Because of this, the speechwriter continued, many politicians tended to see speeches not as 'the main game for communicating with people', but, rather, in terms of the risk that 'someone could cut out a slice of this and put it in a TV ad and use it against me'. A Republican speechwriter likewise observed that in the White House they had had to contend with 'the risk aversion of the communications staff', which 'sometimes would . . . lead to things . . . being left on the cutting room floor', although the speechwriter also noted that, with Donald Trump, 'we're sort of off the map in terms of political rhetoric' in the opposite direction.

Another Republican speechwriter linked the 'highly partisan environment' to the lack of appetite for compromise:

> it goes back to President Reagan saying, I forget how he worded it, 'someone who agrees with me 80 percent of the time does not mean he's 20 percent my enemy'. . . . Like President Bush [41] had one line where he was talking about the 1990 budget deal and he said, 'Do I think this is the best budget deal we could get? No, I don't, but this is the best budget deal I will get from this Congress of Democrats.' And he was aware that they're not gonna get everything they want but they're gonna get the best they can. . . . [T]hat seems like ancient history now. Like, nobody talks that way now. They're all ideologically pure, you have to get 100 percent of what you want.

A Democratic speechwriter likewise identified incentives towards ideological purity as a major problem, arguing that '[i]f you are punished and beat up and your claim on power is threatened constantly if you deviate five percent from party orthodoxy, . . . and . . . your seat is safe if you are . . . a hundred percent pure, you're gonna stay a hundred percent pure'. Again, this stresses a perceived need for a specific kind of consistency in public performance, here one that closely toes the party line and discourages compromise. The Democratic speechwriter quoted immediately above linked ideological purity to the issue of gerrymandered House districts, which are not competitive for both major parties and in which incumbents might be primaried if they do not stick to orthodox positions. The perceived non-viability of compromise as a political strategy also links up with the issues of negative partisanship and polarisation: polarisation undermines the possibility for what is perceived to be comparatively risky bipartisan debate on issues, and instead extends the calcified political deadlock between the two major parties, while negative partisans are more interested in the opposing party's loss than they are in using compromise to reach any specific political goal.

In sum, because there are so many different media outlets (media fragmentation), politicians are driven to give many different public performances (overexposure); and because the different media are in competition with one another, they tend to look for conflict and controversy and to favour antagonistic coverage, especially if media outlets themselves lean either left or right (media antagonism). Speechwriters argued that, for performing politicians, media fragmentation, overexposure, and media antagonism make it more difficult to sustain a cohesive persona in public performance, which, in turn, makes speechwriting work more responsive to short-term social media distractions and potentially detracts from the usefulness of speeches as a medium altogether. Performing cohesion is especially difficult in political careers that span many years or decades, so that political outsiders, who newly enter the pressure cooker of national politics, might be seen to have an even greater competitive advantage than they already do because of how much the electorate tend to distrust established politicians and political institutions.

Antagonistic coverage also leads to the favouring of essentialist constructions of politicians as public personas without much variation between different performances, because it attempts, in the words of the speechwriters quoted above, 'to call everybody a flip-flopping hypocrite' and to 'punch a hole in every little myth a politician tries to convey'. As such, the evolution of the media environment towards fragmentation, oversaturation, and media antagonism in personalised coverage incentivises avowals of politicians' personal authenticity whilst at the same time undermining many politicians' willingness to be maximally, riskily, and antagonistically exposed. These forces stand in clear tension with each other, as politicians are more exposed but might therefore be more unwilling to open themselves up through public performance. Risk averseness leads to public performances that are formulaic and perceived to be lacking in revelatory authenticity and personal detail.

These kinds of risk-averse performances, however, are increasingly at odds with what speechwriters perceived to be the best use of speeches, which is to evoke a sense of personal, emotional, and cultural resonance between representatives and represented. It is clear, then, that the media environment in the contemporary moment favours politicians who style themselves as outsiders, whose lack of history in political office makes it more difficult to 'punch a hole' in their public persona, and who present a sharp contrast to many other politicians because their public performances deliberately stir up controversy and do not display the same risk averseness that makes others resort to carefully poll-tested, sanitised language.

Attention Spans, Entertainment, and Mainstreamed Populism

'You know, in the digital age, how many people have the attention span to sit down for an hour and a half, listen to one person talk?', one Republican speechwriter asked rhetorically in our interview. Another simply stated, 'We [Americans] . . . have very short attention spans'. A Democratic speechwriter brought up attention spans in terms of audiences being overloaded with information on social media platforms and therefore less able to focus on one issue over a period of time: 'we spend every morning fighting about Donald Trump's tweets. It's just chaff everywhere. And we accomplish nothing. And people can't remember what we were fighting about just a few days ago'. In short, speechwriters believed that the focus of political audiences was being pulled in many different directions, so that what grabs their attention tends to be coverage that frames an issue in controversial terms.

To compensate for audiences' diminishing attention spans, speechwriters noted, political media coverage was becoming more entertainment-like, as inattentive audiences are more likely to be captivated by political coverage that has high entertainment value. Speechwriters observed in particular that there was a contrast between a previous sober style and orientation towards substance and the current emphasis of entertainment, humour, and whether politicians 'look good on camera'. In this context, several speechwriters referred to the Lincoln–Douglas debates, which, in the words of one Republican speechwriter, were 'the model of . . . substantive engagement on public policy questions at the time', but 'would be stillborn these days'. Stephen A. Douglas, the incumbent, and Abraham Lincoln, the challenger, debated each other seven times during the 1858 campaign for a US Senate seat from Illinois. The debates are commonly credited with having propelled Lincoln, who was then a relative unknown, to national prominence, and are a significant touchstone in the history of US political rhetoric. In my interviews, a Democratic speechwriter averred that there was an element of performance in politics 'that was true when Lincoln/Douglas did their debates and now there's that same thing, but we also have social media and the 24-hour news cycle', which significantly changed the quality of performances given by politicians. A second Democratic speechwriter observed:

> I always say, if we held Abraham Lincoln to the standards we have today, he never would have been president. I mean, never mind that he was like a clinically depressed, probably gay Republican who looked funny and had a squeaky high voice, right? . . . Would he have been someone you wanna have a beer with?

A Republican speechwriter explicitly stated that there was 'a little bit of a reality show or beauty contest quality' to today's presidential campaigns. Another observed that 'politician-America has gone from being very sober and sombre to . . . using humour more and more . . . maybe because of the changes in our culture, I mean, we almost live in a showbiz culture'. A third Democratic speechwriter expressed frustration with the fact that campaigning and governing required different skills, but that the showier, entertainment-like campaigning skills tended to be foregrounded in the media coverage that people consumed the most:

> Why do we value the theatrics more than the content? Or why are we willing to dismiss inconsistencies or illogical arguments if [they] were delivered well? Why, when new candidates come on the scene, do people say, 'they deliver a speech really, really well', instead of, 'they make a cogent argument that no one's ever made so clearly'? It's just like, they look good on camera. That's a positive for a politician. Why does that even matter? . . . [I]n America, and I think in other countries, too, the things we judge a candidate on have nothing in most cases to do with what we judge . . . an elected representative on. So, a lot of people think Hillary Clinton would have been a great president, but just like, 'oh, she was a bad candidate'. What the fuck do the two have in common?

In partial contrast with this view, a fourth Democratic speechwriter observed that campaigning no longer stops with being elected, but that 'more and more because of the nature of the news cycle, media, fundraising, a lot of things, you're basically campaigning all the time the second you're elected anyway'. This perspective stresses the extent to which US politics demands 'permanent campaigning' (see Blumenthal 1980; Cook 2002; Elmer, Langlois, and McKelvey 2012) and sees policy as entirely displaced by a focus on campaigning which tends to emphasise personality and strategy, rather than only during election season. The qualities that make someone a good campaigner – the ability to 'look good' on camera, for instance, and being able to deliver a speech well – always predominate over the personal requirements for effective governing, like the ability to work with a variety of people and to make compromises, as well as in-depth knowledge of policy. This raises the importance of public performance in politics, as the ability to engage effectively with political audiences, even while in office, takes precedence over other skills that are not directly linked to a politician's connection with the electorate, like being able to enact substantive policy. While presidential politics did not 'become' performative and theatrical with the advent of permanent campaigning and entertainment-like coverage, these developments make the extent to which performance lies at the heart of representative democracy much more immediately apparent. Furthermore, while 'performance' can in theory take many different forms, as the contrast between the Lincoln–Douglas debates in 1858 and the Clinton–Trump debates in 2016 illustrates, shorter attention spans favour entertainment-like coverage, which, when combined with media antagonism and fragmentation, tends to be coverage that frames issues, personalities, and strategies in terms of controversy. All of these factors now benefit performers who opt for populist-style performances, as these performances tend to court controversy by setting up a simplistic binary division of the political space between 'the people' and 'the establishment', performing a sense of crisis, and displaying 'bad manners' by breaking with established norms of political performance, like what constitutes an appropriate degree of presidential dignity (Moffitt 2016, 41–5). Populist-style performances both display and seek to provoke emotion, particularly anger, which has become an increasingly dominant political emotion over the course of the widespread rise of populism in the twenty-first century (Wahl-Jorgensen 2018a, 2018b, 2018c).

The speechwriters interviewed were concerned about their ability to reach audiences in a fragmented, oversaturated media environment, which was perceived to be incentivising antagonism, spectacle, and controversy whilst discouraging potentially effective public servants from entering politics and making many politicians risk averse in their public performances. Additionally, speechwriters understood that they had to work with audiences' shortening attention spans and in an environment in which politicians' public performances are increasingly expected to function as quasi-entertainment. These last two developments incentivise the personalisation of politicians' performances and punish risk-averse performances for being carefully controlled, poll-tested, and lacking in both entertainment value and the ability to cut through the 'noise' of an already oversaturated media landscape.

Benjamin Moffitt argues that 'it is becoming *increasingly difficult* to ignore the pull of populism' (2016, 77, emphasis in original), in part because mediatisation, defined as a process by which specific spheres of life become dependent on the media, privileges populism as a political style. In making this claim Moffitt distinguishes between 'media logic' and 'political logic': the former is presumed to aim at sensationalising issues whilst the latter is geared towards finding solutions and persuading others to accept them. This stark differentiation between media and political logics resembles Schedler's (1997a) cordoning off of a 'pure' political logic from other, infecting logics, including the supposedly antipolitical logic of aesthetics (see Chapter 1). Both Schedler and Moffitt appear keen to assign 'political logic' to the 'good' side of a simplistic binary, whilst relegating other 'logics' to the bad side. However, representative politics cannot be divorced from performance, nor can it be purified from its inherent potential for distrust. The suspension of disbelief demanded of audiences is emotionally charged and requires a culturally and affectively resonant engagement with political performances, as these are received in a way that is not unlike the reception of more obviously or straightforwardly fictional constructions in theatre and film. Audiences both expect politicians to have a true self which they can access through observing their public performances and they are aware, more or less consciously, that politicians' performances are planned to pursue political agendas and strategies that lie beyond personal revelation. The interview data here presented shows that speechwriters think that market incentives are increasingly driving political coverage to be highly personalised and to resemble entertainment programming. Nevertheless, media coverage can take many different forms, and while current developments privilege the type that Moffitt identifies, it would be a mistake to equate them with 'media logic' *tout court.*

Presenting a similar line of argumentation to Moffitt's, Benjamin Arditi proposes that 'the populist mode of representation [might] become [a regular component] of liberal democratic politics' to the extent that 'populist representation has gone mainstream' (2007, 61, 68). Arditi builds on Bernard Manin's (1997) work on representation to argue that 'audience democracy intertwines with populist representation conceived as a crossover between acting for others, authorization, and the strong role of imaginary identifications and symbolic imagery', so that 'audience democracy' is here, too, seen as an ideal companion to mainstreamed populism (2007, 69). Despite my reservations about Arditi's theorisation of a 're-entry of Hobbesian authorization' into contemporary politics (see Chapter 3), Arditi is astute in observing that populists tend to rely on the 'personalization of politics and the trust for the leader' as well as the kind of 'virtual immediacy' in mediatised politics that leads people to believe that the actually present distance between them and their representatives has been closed (66). Neither personalisation nor the tension between distance and proximity is really confined to populists as issues of trust and distrust and the distance between representatives and represented are, at a fundamental level, inherent in representative democracy. However, Arditi perceptively notes, again building on Manin, that the erosion of 'mediation by party networks' in contemporary politics is a significant factor here, and one that populists, as self-styled outsiders to institutional structures, exploit particularly well (68). As such, party loyalty might be seen as an insulation of the sphere of politics from the power of performance, functioning similarly to the circumscription of presidential performances to a focus on explicating the Constitution, as preferred by the framers.[1]

Despite my criticism of Moffitt's cordoning off of 'political logic' from 'media logic' and Arditi's equation of reliance on trust with Hobbesian authorisation, the interview data largely supports Moffitt's and Arditi's view of mediatisation as a development that privileges personalisation, polarisation, negativity, simplification, and the impression of virtual immediacy (Arditi 2007, 66; Moffitt 2016, 75). Speechwriters painted a picture of the media environment as predisposed towards the kind of personalised, antagonistic coverage that is particularly at odds with attempts to minimise its impact through carefully calibrated, 'sanitising' attempts at averting the danger of negative coverage. Moffitt argues that aspects characteristic of the contemporary media (like 'sports-based dramatisation and polarisation', personalisation, and simplification) and elements of the populist style (like the 'dichotomy between "the people" and "the elite"', 'disregard for "appropriateness"', and 'distaste for complexity') correspond to each other (2016, 76). The interview corpus does confirm that speechwriters perceive similar correspondences between oversaturation, media hostility, entertainment-like coverage, and populist-style performances. However, the interview data also shows that, for many mainstream politicians, speechwriters observed these developments to have the opposite effect, making them more risk averse in their public performances rather than predisposed to give controversial performances in a more populist style. Of course, this might simply mean that populist-style performances become even more effective, as they present a sharp contrast to the risk averseness of 'politics as usual'. Populist-style representative claims have become an especially effective way of cutting through to audiences in an oversaturated, fragmented media environment that favours antagonism and demands verifications of personal authenticity conceived according to an essentialist paradigm. Populists exploit the demand for personalised avowals of a speaker's authenticity particularly well because they make little effort to balance between representing an official quality (like presidentiality) and their own public persona, which, in its unapologetic brashness might be seen as 'charismatic' in Roach's terms insofar as it projects total confidence and an apparent indifference towards the audience's judgement (see Roach 2007, 4). They also pay little attention to what are considered 'good manners' in political performance and are thus able to reiterate norms of conventions of embodiment much more explicitly, forthrightly, and combatively than others.

Additionally, populists tend to distrust speechwriters and other political professionals. A Republican speechwriter told me that they had been consulted to give advice on the writing of Donald Trump's inaugural address, but that 'they chose to go in a different direction than I advised them in some ways'. The speechwriter then explained that they 'would have handled [the inaugural address] differently' and that they did not think '[Trump is] very artful. I think his speeches are . . . heavy-handed.' Sarah Palin's decision, during the 2008 campaign, to deviate from campaign messaging and 'go rogue' is another good example. A Republican speechwriter noted that, after having been thrust into the national spotlight during the 2008 campaign, '[the Palin] family generally was much more suspicious of staff, didn't really know who they could trust'. As a consequence of their distrust of institutional structures and political insiders, the construction of the theatrical appearances of populists like Trump and Palin tends to be less professionalised. It is not that populists somehow 'embody' their constituents in more literal ways than more mainstream politicians do, although there may or may not be more intense emotional attachment (see Chapter 3), but populists do tend to eschew the professionalisation of the theatre of politics. If there is a distinctly populist mode in which these performances function, then this is specific primarily to their production and only secondarily to their dissemination and reception, particularly in the extent to which they are privileged in the current mediatised political environment. This does not make populists' success inevitable, nor does it suggest populism is the end of the road for US politics, but it does explain populists' advantages within the current media ecology.

Contradictory forces are shaping the theatre of politics in the contemporary moment: on the one hand, media antagonism, fragmentation, and overexposure foster risk-averse, carefully poll-tested, tightly circumscribed performances. On the other hand, these same developments alongside audiences' diminishing attention spans and thirst for entertainment have created a 'populist slope' in the media environment, such that a number of developments converge that increasingly incentivise populist-style public performances in presidential politics because these are seen as being particularly effective in the contrast they present to poll-tested, 'politician-like' performances. These populist-style performances contrast with the oratorical task of addressing the national public in terms that align with Benedict Anderson's idea of the imagined community as a 'deep, horizontal comradeship' ([1983] 2006, 4). Although presidential speechwriters tended to envision 'the public' as a homogeneous entity (see Chapter 2), this vision is increasingly at odds with a deeply polarised electorate which tends to see party affiliation as a matter of negative partisanship rather than positive identification. By exploring the mediatised political environment within which speechwriters work and the varied importance speechwriters ascribed to their work within this environment, this chapter provides further evidence for this argument. Anderson argues that the nation as an imagined community was made possible by the rise of print capitalism, in particular the proliferation of daily newspapers, which created an 'extraordinary mass ceremony: the almost precisely simultaneous consumption ("imagining") of the newspaper-as-fiction' (35). While Anderson's imagined community relied on a common medium (the national newspaper) for the collective creation of an idea of national unity that cut across party affiliation and partisanship, the media environment of the twenty-first century has thus far fed an opposite tendency towards division, polarisation, and negative partisanship. Mainstream presidential performances swim against the current, whilst populist-style performances swim with it: fragmentation, oversaturation, and hostility within the media landscape of the twenty-first century disrupt and frustrate attempts to evoke the nation as a deep comradeship the similarities of whose members would outweigh their differences.

The Populist Slope in Contemporary Presidential Politics

The Currency of Distrust since the Nixon Era

Thus far, this chapter has shown that presidential performances in the populist style are increasingly effective in and incentivised by the highly mediatised political environment in which they are produced, disseminated, and received. However, I posited at the beginning of the chapter that changes in the pattern of presidential oratory should be understood both as adaptations to a changing political and media environment and as driven by the personalities of individual presidential performers. While structures that used to prevent excessive personalisation and discouraged divisive performances and ad-hominem attacks against opponents, such as the primacy of party loyalty over the focus on party leaders or the circumscription in the number and style of presidential addresses, have largely been worn away, the currency of populist-style presidential performances cannot just be understood by looking at changes in the media and political environment that encourage such performances. As was the case with the changes in presidential performance inaugurated at the beginning of the twentieth century, the recent rise and intensification of populist-style presidential performances must be seen in relation to the specific individuals who have chosen to capitalise on a political and media environment in which audiences are likely to be receptive towards evocations of outsider status performed in the populist style. Performances that explicitly mobilise political distrust have gained currency since the Nixon era as Jimmy Carter, Ronald Reagan, Bill Clinton, and George W. Bush all used the trope of the outsider and elements of the populist style. This raises the question of whether outsider appeals differ between the two major parties. This question is explored first, before the chapter turns to the 2008 and 2016 presidential elections (that is, the last two elections not to feature an incumbent candidate), featuring candidates from Barack Obama, John McCain, and Sarah Palin to Donald Trump, Hillary Clinton, and Bernie Sanders to discuss how these specific performers have shaped the different ways in which presidential performances in the contemporary moment address and make use of distrust.

There is no doubt that performances of outsiderness vis-à-vis the institutions a political candidate is running for or indeed within which a politician is working have long been commonplace in US politics, especially at the presidential level. The presidency of Woodrow Wilson has been interpreted as a particular turning point in this regard, as Wilson re-envisioned presidential legitimacy as deriving directly from the president's connection to the US electorate rather than his formal constitutional position. As a consequence of Wilson's innovations, performances of presidential outsiderness, which emphasised the president's independence from other institutions of federal politics, notably Congress, gained currency. Wilson's own inaugural address referred to 'government too often debauched and made an instrument of evil' (1913b). However, in his first State of the Union address, held in-person before Congress on 2 December of the same year, Wilson proclaimed 'the very real pleasure I have experienced in co-operating with this Congress and sharing with it the labors of common service' (1913a). Wilson's anti-government positioning thus did not address itself explicitly against Congress and was significantly mellowed when he actually appeared before Congress in his role as president.

While outsiderness in presidential performance is a deeply ingrained trope that plays on the lack of trust and distrust of political audiences, its origins are difficult to pinpoint. The currency of distrust in performances of the US presidency as it presents itself in the contemporary moment is typically traced to the candidacy of Jimmy Carter (Cannon 1991, 101; Glad 1980, 366; Hess 2002; Strong, n.d.). In January 1975, in the aftermath of the Watergate scandal, trust in government had fallen to just 36 per cent, half the level at which it had been a decade earlier (Pew Research Center 2015, 18). Carter's appeal as an outsider candidate has been linked to this cataclysmic decline in political trust. According Betty Glad, a biographer of Carter, Carter's presidential campaign was well received because it was premised on the idea that '[t]o transcend and reform the government, all that was needed was a leader from the outside who was his own person and represented an idealized version of the American people – good, compassionate, moral' (1980, 367). As such, Carter's success is seen to have been down to the fact that he asked for 'an unusual kind' of trust, one that 'necessitated a leap of faith, a giving of the heart of to an unknown stranger' (367). In other words, the disillusioned electorate were ready to choose an 'unknown stranger' over the 'known' political establishment they had learned to distrust during the Nixon era, the ongoing Vietnam War, and over the course of the rise of the security state following the Second World War more generally (Knight 2000, 24–32).

Once elected, however, Carter was unable to hold on to the trust vested in him. Trust in the federal government again fell sharply, capping at 70 per cent in March 1980 (Pew Research Center 2014b). Remarkably, even though Carter as an outsider-president[2] was unsuccessful in bolstering public trust, outsider positioning and the use of rhetorical tropes that posit 'the people' against the political elite, 'Washington', or simply 'government' retained their currency. Following Carter, Ronald Reagan wanted to be seen as an 'accomplished presidential performer', but 'could not explain the simplest procedures of the federal government' (Cannon 1991, 51, 101). Lou Cannon, a Reagan biographer, explicitly links Reagan's acting ability and actorly sensibility to his 'bond with the electorate'. Indeed, Cannon goes further, positing that it was this bond and Reagan's 'experience as an actor' that 'would ultimately make it possible for him to mobilize public opinion and translate some of his "simple answers" into useful legislation' (47). Timothy Raphael similarly suggests the significance of Reagan's ability to create a bond with the electorate through mediated communication, arguing that Reagan's 'journey from culture worker to president' shows that 'the modes and methods of dramatization modelled by the movies, radio, and television have so altered our experience of both geographic space and historical time that they irreversibly diminished the dimensions of the *un*mediated world' (2009, 6, emphasis in original). Reagan's success as a politician is seen as directly linked to his ability to connect with the American public – an ability that, in turn, is linked to Reagan's acting skill rather than any policy-specific qualifications or expertise. Personalisation and distrust of experts are linked to the populist style. Furthermore, prior to becoming president, as Governor of California, Reagan is described by Cannon as '[t]he citizen-politician [who] became a citizen-governor and . . . was proud that he still referred to the government as "them"' (1991, 48). Of course, Reagan's first inaugural address (1981), following a landslide election victory in which Reagan carried forty-four out of fifty US states against the incumbent Carter, then included the indelibly antipolitical phrase, 'In this present crisis, government is not the solution to our problem; government is the problem.'

Strikingly, despite his lack of interest in the minutiae of policy and despite presenting himself as a political outsider, Reagan has remained a model Republican president, mentioned by name in every Republican presidential primary debate since (Fahey 2015). At the same time, although trust in government rose during the Reagan presidency (as it would to a more limited extent in the later years of the Clinton presidency), it has never again even come close to a pre-Nixon level and has surpassed the 50 per cent mark only once: in the aftermath of 9/11 (Pew Research Center 2014b, 2015, 2017).[3] The currency of distrust, both as a political phenomenon and as a trope of presidential performance, has not waned since Watergate. In addition to the 'neoliberal' turn during Reagan's presidency (see Harvey 2005, 9), Reagan's actorly awareness of the political audience and his ability to forge a specific, personable bond with this audience have endured. A Republican speechwriter noted in our interview that in their perception tailoring jokes to particular audiences started with Reagan. The speechwriter observed, 'President Reagan really changed an awful [lot], he was so effective at using humour that . . . most of the politicians that have followed him, it's almost incumbent upon them now to use humour at one point or another'. This shift towards more personalised, entertainment-like, and, therefore, tendentially more populist performances applies to both Democratic and Republican presidents.

Following Reagan's two terms and George H. W. Bush's one-term presidency,[4] Bill Clinton's playing of the saxophone on *The Arsenio Hall Show* during the 1992 presidential campaign marks another significant step in the history of the consumption of politics as entertainment (Clinton 1992). The 1992 campaign is also notable in the history of US populism for the independent candidacy of the businessman Ross Perot, who briefly led in the polls and won a considerable portion of the popular vote, 18.9 per cent (see Brown 1997). But the personalisation of presidential politics was driven even further during the Clinton presidency: Clinton appeared on MTV in 1994 to answer questions of a deeply personal nature, including whether he preferred boxers or briefs (Clinton 1994b). He also chose to comment on this MTV appearance again at the White House Correspondents' Dinner on 23 April 1994, making light of and drawing further attention to the fact that, as a sitting president, he had talked about his preferred type of underwear on national television (Clinton 1994a). Clinton's southern accent and, as a former Governor of Arkansas, his comparative lack of history with the Washington establishment likewise played well with political audiences. Clinton's performance style gestured towards populism without fully exploiting the populist style: performances like those on MTV and at the White House Correspondents' Dinner broke with the manners expected of the president, and some speeches, like Clinton's inaugural address, evoked the binary opposition between the people and the political establishment. Nevertheless, like Reagan (and indeed Wilson and Carter), Clinton played with these tropes occasionally, rather than fully and consistently embracing them.

Political trust was already on an upward trend and it spiked after the terrorist attack on 11 September 2001 destroyed the World Trade Center in New York. In November 2001, public trust in government reached a moving average of 54 per cent, the only time since the Nixon era that the Pew Research Center has recorded a figure for the entire US electorate that surpassed the 50 per cent mark (2014b). Following the cataclysmic 9/11 attack early in his presidency and the subsequent spike in political trust, it is perhaps unsurprising that George W. Bush spoke in a different way to the themes of populism and outsiderness than the other presidents explored here. Michael Foley (2007) has shown that, unusually, Bush's foreign policy, especially the so-called War on Terror, followed the tradition and tropes of US presidential populism. Elisabeth Anker's work (2014) argues in a similar vein that the Bush administration's War on Terror rhetoric used melodramatic political discourse that evoked a simplistic moral universe divided along a binary line into 'good Americans' and 'evil terrorists' to produce the widespread feeling that government actions taken during the War on Terror were legitimate, although these were in many cases not authorised according to accepted legitimation procedures. Rather than being directed at the Washington political elite itself, Bush's rhetoric targeted the world beyond the United States, the 'distant and disembodied entities of a multilateral international order', most notably the United Nations, which was depicted as 'literally . . . the international equivalent of Washington D.C.' (Foley 2007, 671, 673). Bush's populism, such as it was, was directed outwards rather than towards the United States federal government itself, in a way that corresponded to the political climate following 9/11. Bush's 2000 presidential campaign against Al Gore also used anti-government rhetoric to great effect; Marc J. Hetherington argues that Bush's 'tagging of Gore with the government' in the slogan 'He [Al Gore] trusts government. I trust you.' was instrumental in his campaign's success (2005, 2).

In addition to his administration's foreign policy populism, Bush's lack of polish in performance and his Texas accent had an outsider appeal of their own. In writing about Bush as an apparently awkward and unpolished political performer, performance scholar Maaike Bleeker asked, 'Why did [people] believe and support [Bush], especially if he was such a bad actor?' (2009, 255). Part of Bush's appeal was precisely that he was a bad actor, that he appeared visibly uncomfortable with big speeches and big words, and that he never lost the Texas accent that appeared out of place in Washington. Bleeker describes Bush as presenting himself on television as a 'serious and self-confident president' (251), before then doubling back on herself and describing Bush as a 'bad actor', one whose acting is liable to be exposed as acting and who might therefore, as Michael Moore's *Fahrenheit 9/11* (2004) strongly suggests, be distrusted. As quoted above, however, Bleeker also points to the support Bush was able to garner from those who elected him in the first place as a paradoxical phenomenon.

To those opposed to him, Bush might have appeared simply as a bad actor, one who appeared to invite all the criticism based in antitheatrical thinking that Bleeker's essay explores. However, there is a compelling argument to be made that to his supporters, Bush's appeal was connected to what has since Reagan been the Republican stock argument: that government is the problem. Part of Bush's personal appeal was that, regardless of his quasi-dynastic family background, he still appeared as something of an outsider, one who, much like Clinton before him, had a southern accent but who, unlike Clinton, also delivered speeches awkwardly and did not come across as a polished political actor. The idea that Bush is making faces at the camera before delivering a serious address to the American people, as Moore shows in the opening sequence of *Fahrenheit 9/11*, might appear to liberals like Moore to expose him as an inauthentic and cynical actor. To Bush's supporters, however, making faces whilst in the role of president would have read entirely differently: it signalled that Bush had not been fully absorbed by the Washington elite, did not take himself too seriously, was still a human being. In short, if there is anything compelling in Bush's populist appeal, it is the very lack of polish of his performances.

Bleeker's argument and Bush's unpolished appeal illustrate that whether or not a performance comes across as compelling or relatable in any way is very much in the eye of the beholder. It is worth dwelling here on the question of whether there is a marked difference in the Republican and Democratic use of outsider positioning and elements of the populist style. Reagan's famous statement that 'government is the problem' is inextricably linked to 'Reaganomics', marked by reductions in government spending and tax cuts, and distinctly Republican in outlook. Reagan's ongoing appeal is closely connected to his having presided over the 'neoliberal turn' which has influenced US and world politics profoundly in the four decades since. Nevertheless, both Republicans and Democrats have long mobilised political distrust as a dominant political affect effectively by presenting themselves as political outsiders.

In my interviews, several Democratic speechwriters were careful to distinguish between Republican and Democratic anti-establishment appeals. For instance, as a follow-up to their statement that 'everybody always tends to run against Washington', I asked a Democratic presidential speechwriter whether and how they perceived there to be a difference between Democrats and Republicans in making such outsider appeals. The speechwriter responded as follows:

> Yes, there's a big difference. Because Democrats actually believe in government. . . . Look at Mitch McConnell, the Senate Majority Leader. He's been in office now six terms. And all he says is that Washington is broken. Congress is broken. Everything is broken. You're in charge of it! . . . Do something to fix it. He knows . . . that [it's] against his best interests to make it work. . . . Democrats have a harder argument. Which is, government's broken because these goons keep breaking it on purpose. And government should exist for the common good . . . You know, for decades we've all said, . . . you could put [the Republican platform] on a bumper sticker: Smaller government, lower taxes, strong military. Boom, that's it. Democrats believe in everything. You can't put us on a bumper sticker. That's why 'yes, we can' worked, because it's the first thing you could. But yeah, there is a big difference.

I pressed the speechwriter to clarify whether they thought this difference came across, if, after all, 'everyone' runs against Washington. In response, the speechwriter first stated that it did not come across, then expanded on the specific issue of government shutdown, to conclude that they did think the difference between Republicans and Democrats came across after all:

> No, I – I don't. I think that the Republican argument typically wins just 'cause it's an easier, clearer argument. . . . You know, it's always funny when – again, right now, Republicans are threatening another government shutdown and they always think they won't take the blame for it. And we know we don't have to work that hard to put the blame on them because there are two parties – first of all, one, right now, controls every branch of government, so if the government shuts down it's by definition their fault. But even in mixed government, people are going to blame the Republicans for a government shutdown, because they know Republicans hate government. Why would Democrats shut down the government? We like it. We like doing things. So, yeah, . . . I think that innately comes through. That argument has always been on our side when it comes to a shutdown.

On the one hand, this speechwriter conceded that the difference between Republican and Democratic arguments did not always come across, because the Republican argument was simply against the government, whereas the Democratic argument was to say that government in general was beneficial, but that Washington, as it currently appeared, was broken and in need of reform.[5] Hence, in the speechwriter's estimation, audiences found the Republican argument generally clearer and easier to comprehend and did not see the nuanced differences from this in the Democratic argument. However, the speechwriter seemed to evade further exploration of the question, steering the conversation away from the basic distinction set up between Democrats and Republicans to argue that Democrats, because of a presumed innately more pro-government stance, are less likely to be blamed for a government shutdown.

I had a strikingly similar conversation about the distinct nature of Democratic and Republican outsider appeals with a second Democratic presidential speechwriter, one who had worked for a different president than the first. Following a portion of the interview during which the speechwriter had expounded their views on why people had distrusted politicians for a long time, I asked the speechwriter if, in their work, they would try to 'work against that kind of distrust' or if they would 'try to use that kind of distrust'. In response, the speechwriter observed that this question revolved around a partisan divide:

> Well, depends on which side of the aisle you're on. . . . I feel like the politicians I've worked for and that I wanna work for do what they can to restore people's faith in government, in collective action, in our sense of mutual obligation. . . . Because without it, it's total social decay. On the

Republican side, whether they concede it or not, they have been sowing deep distrust in the whole idea of government and not just the particular programs, but the idea of government as being inherently inimicable to liberty, to freedom, to individual rights. Going way, way back, I mean, this was the argument that was made against Roosevelt during the New Deal, this was the argument of Goldwater, this was the argument of Reagan.

I responded to what appeared to me to be a partisan view by giving the example of Obama as a Democratic politician who ran for president as a Washington outsider. The speechwriter responded by characterising this as a 'different but related thread'. It is worth quoting from their response at some length here, not just because it lays out in detail the perceived nuances between the different partisan arguments, but also and especially because the response itself strikingly illustrates the risk that these nuances are erased in the public's reception of outsider performances by different partisans:

> it is absolutely related. And that is, the outsider. I mean, people are not very open to the Hillary Clinton argument . . . 'I understand, I've been around a long time. I understand how it works, and so you need me to help sort it out.' We are much more drawn – and this has been the case for a very long time – to people coming from the outside to say, 'look, we're all looking at Washington, . . . it's a disaster, we know how fucked up it is. . . . I'm not part of the problem, but I'm going to come in and fix it because only someone from the outside can fix it.' . . . [S]o in that way, Reagan and Clinton, you know, Clinton had had political office but he was from Arkansas, he was not, you know – It always helps to run against Washington, but running against Washington is different than running against government. You can be a progressive and, like Obama, . . . say, 'Washington sucks, like everybody there is stuck in all these old ideological arguments, they're all just fighting with each other, they're dominated by the special interests, . . . we need to sort of a bring new perspective into Washington and make government work because government has to work.' We need it to work. That is a different argument than: 'I'm Trump, the whole system is rigged, you know, we're going to go in there and we're just gonna knock shit down, look out, because, you know, government is a negative force and we are gonna cripple it.' . . . [I]t's the same argument used to different ends. And that's why the outsider thread and the anti-government thread can either go together or not go together. . . . [Y]ou know, Bernie Sanders is a more extreme version of the Obama argument. . . . Obama said, 'the culture of Washington is fucked up and priorities are wrong and they're caught up in stupid arguments, we need to get in there and set things right'.

Bernie Sanders says, 'the whole system is corrupt, it's rigged', just as Trump was saying, and people are controlling it and pulling the strings to screw you and that breeds a whole other level of cynicism. It's very difficult I think to make that argument and then go in and actually make the system work and make it accountable. And so, . . . if you believe . . . in the role of government, you have to be careful about how far you go with your critique. . . . [I]t's one thing to say it's not working as it should, it's another thing to say that the whole thing is corrupt. . . . [D]on't get me wrong, there's a lot of corruption, there really is, but if you go too far in that direction then you start to suggest that it's irredeemable. And that's a dangerous place to be. Because then the only answer is to just cripple it. . . . I think that Bernie Sanders and the supporters of Bernie Sanders didn't really quite reckon with the sort of ultimate consequences of what it is was that they were out there arguing.

To unpack this line of argumentation, note how, first, the speechwriter appears to concede that both Reagan and Clinton presented similar outsider narratives in their presidential election campaigns: both had held political office only as governors, not in Washington, before running for president. Then the speechwriter goes on to contrast Obama's outsider rhetoric with Trump's, arguing, much like the first speechwriter above, that Obama made a more nuanced, less simplistic point. Then, however, the speechwriter contradicts himself, saying that Obama's and Trump's are, after all, 'the same argument' but 'used to different ends'. This shows how complex the reception work audiences are expected to do becomes, as audiences have to distinguish not just between subtly different arguments but, potentially, between arguments that are made along the very same lines but are intended to achieve different purposes. The confusion between different types of outsider appeals becomes still more complex, however: the speechwriter goes on to argue that the rhetoric presented by those in the more progressive, openly democratic socialist wing of the Democratic Party (which the speechwriter clearly did not support), such as Bernie Sanders, resembles, in its insistence that 'the whole system is corrupt', even more closely the rhetoric put forth by Republicans. They end by suggesting that the confusion between the two arguments, one of which is fundamentally more pro-government and follows a progressive agenda, whilst the other is fundamentally more anti-government and follows a hard-line conservative agenda, is in fact dangerous, precisely because the similarity of the arguments risks conditioning audiences to believe that the government, 'Washington', Congress, and so on, are 'irredeemable'. While the intent behind different kinds of outsider appeals may be different, this quote shows that the appeals themselves can still look remarkably similar, even identical.

Both of the Democratic speechwriters quoted above were confident in identifying the ideological difference behind the Republican and Democratic outsider appeals. At the same time, they also conceded that they knew this difference would get lost to political audiences, who, in addition to already being distrustful of the federal government, get to hear, over and over, that 'Washington', Congress, government, or simply, 'the system' is broken and corrupt. As the long quote above suggests, populist rhetoric using the outsider trope might over time be driven to intensify and become more extreme both in style and in the assertion of government corruption, as audiences become more and more accustomed to outsider appeals and ever more controversial performances are necessary to catch the electorate's attention in a highly fragmented and oversaturated media environment.

The 2008 and 2016 Elections

During the last few months of George W. Bush's presidency, political trust was again at a historic low, plateauing at 24 per cent from August 2007 until Bush left office (Pew Research Center 2014b). In light of this, it is unsurprising that distrust and the need to resist and reform the Washington establishment, which was painted and perceived as corrupt, were major themes for the 2008 presidential election campaign and beyond. Indeed, throughout this book, I have drawn on examples from the 2008 and 2016 presidential campaigns and the 44th and 45th presidencies to investigate the significance of outsider positioning and mainstreamed populism in performances of the US presidency. I have used performances by Barack Obama, John McCain, and Sarah Palin in 2008 and performances by Hillary Clinton and Donald Trump in 2016 to think through questions of performance, theatricality, embodiment, and legitimacy. In drawing on these examples, I have has suggested that there is a particular affinity between Obama's appeal as an outsider in 2008 and beyond and Donald Trump's appeal in 2016. This affinity is such that both of these presidents' campaigns were to a significant extent about the currency of distrust itself, both in terms of the present relevance of distrust to US federal politics and in terms of this distrust being mobilised and used in the establishment of the representative relationship between political performers and their audiences.

The 2008 and 2016 campaigns gave rise to performances that more persistently drew on the populist style, rather than intermittently using select elements of the style in performances of outsiderness, as earlier presidents and presidential candidates had done. On the Republican side, there was arguably a progression from vice presidential candidate Sarah Palin's performance in 2008 to Donald Trump's performance in 2016. As will be seen, to an extent, this populist intensification in right-wing politics must be seen as consciously identified as a potentially winning strategy in 2008 and then actively encouraged in 2016 by Stephen K. Bannon, the Trump campaign's 'chief executive officer'. Meanwhile, on the Democratic side, Obama's performance as a relative Washington outsider who promised to bring change proved successful in the race against the self-styled maverick John McCain in 2008. But Hillary Clinton, who had had a long history as part of the political establishment, was not able to present herself in a similar way either in 2008 as a primary candidate or eight years later as the Democratic presidential candidate, despite becoming the first woman ever to have been chosen as the presidential candidate of a major party in 2016. In addition to this, Clinton faced a serious left-wing populist primary challenge from Bernie Sanders in 2016, after having lost the primary to Obama, then a relatively unknown outsider, in 2008. Across the board of candidates in 2008 and 2016, the currency of distrust was a dominant theme to be reckoned with.

During the 2008 presidential campaign, Sarah Palin, the Republican vice presidential candidate, captured the attention of the American public in a unique way. As Governor of Alaska Palin was, for most, an unknown entity before John McCain, the Republican candidate, nominated her as his running mate. The nomination of Palin was intended to shake up a race in which McCain seemed, despite presenting himself as a long-time maverick in Washington politics, to be trailing behind Barack Obama, who was a relatively new face in American politics himself and captivated the public with his campaign's motifs of 'hope' and 'change' after having first made a name for himself on the national stage with his 2004 Democratic National Convention Speech in support of the Kerry–Edwards campaign. In our interview, a speechwriter associated with the McCain–Palin campaign assessed the importance of change as a theme in the 2008 campaign as follows:

> the American electorate was unhappy and determined to have change. 2008. And Obama owned the change message [for] a host of reasons. One, there had been a Republican incumbent president for eight years, the economy was in not great shape and then it tanked, you know, at the end. Stuck in Iraq, people were very unhappy with how that turned out. So they wanted change, they wanted change in a big way. And here you got a guy who had only been there for a little while, very elegant, very eloquent, you know, very good speaker, also, personally, the living embodiment of change. What do you do about that, you know? I mean, McCain was always seen as a reformer and wanted to run as one . . . 'And I'm about change, too' – and we just had a hard time putting it – I mean, it matters who you're running against. If he'd been running against Hillary, it's a different race. . . . Two experienced politicians going at each other, you know. . . . [P]eople wanted change and [Obama] was the biggest change on offer.

As this speechwriter experienced it, the electorate's 'unhappiness', as manifested in the high level of distrust of the government, meant that the candidate who could promise the greatest change was likely to be successful.

As McCain himself appeared to be spreading the change message less successfully than Obama, his vice presidential candidate, Sarah Palin, was chosen to reinvigorate the floundering campaign. Palin proved to be more than up to this task. Unlike McCain, Palin was a gifted performer who knew how to use her status as a Washington outsider for her benefit and roused the public with populist-style performances in which she presented herself as an advocate for the 'real America', evoking an image that pitted the American heartland against coastal elites. Because Palin was chosen quickly and with the rationale that McCain's vice presidential pick should shake up the race, she underwent minimal vetting before being chosen – which proved problematic as facts about her personal life, like as her teenage daughter's pregnancy, which critics presented as salacious and scandalous, were inevitably brought to light (Heilemann and Halperin 2010, 360–8). The McCain campaign also found Palin difficult to control; by October, it was reported that Palin had 'gone rogue' as she had chosen not to follow the campaign's direction and to speak her mind instead (Dickerson 2008). Palin eventually embraced the narrative of herself as a rogue politician, publishing a memoir entitled *Going Rogue: An American Life* in 2009. Palin's populist appeal as an outsider to Washington politics and a candidate who readily embraced a narrative that divided the United States into its 'real' heartlands and 'fake' coastal elites was matched by her virtuosic ability as a performer. In an interview with me, a second speechwriter affiliated with the McCain–Palin campaign characterised Palin as 'just naturally gifted as a performer'. The speechwriter went on to describe the experience of Palin speaking on the campaign trail:

> she was very cognisant of: 'if you're gonna hear what I have to say . . . I'm gonna have to give you a reason to watch me', you know. And so, and she did! She gave people lots of reasons to watch her. And she was very, you know, very entertaining, very relaxed . . . I mean, I've never seen anybody as good . . . in a stump speech environment as her. It was electric. . . . [Y]ou would walk into these rooms and . . . people would wait for four hours, five hours, eight hours in line to see her and they did not leave disappointed.

The galvanising potential inherent in Palin's blend of outspoken performance and populist message was apparently noted by Stephen Bannon, the co-founder of Breitbart News, who went on to become the chief executive officer on Donald Trump's 2016 presidential campaign. Bannon wrote and directed the 2011 documentary *The Undefeated* on Palin's life up to and including the 2008 campaign. *The Undefeated* uses audio from Palin's *Going Rogue* audio-book to trace Palin's professional journey from her election as mayor of the Alaskan city of Wasilla to her election as Governor of Alaska and her role in the 2008 presidential campaign. The documentary presents Palin as a politi-cian who has always operated in a notably populist vein and as very much in line with Reagan's famous diagnosis that 'government is the problem'. As Mayor of Wasilla, for instance, Palin is seen to give a summary of the func-tions of local government, which for her are limited to 'infrastructure develop-ment, fiscal responsibility and [pause] simply being on the side of the people'. She is portrayed as someone who succeeded in attracting big business through common-sense 'kitchen table economics'. In her campaign for governor, Palin appears to channel Reagan even more explicitly, arguing that 'more government isn't the solution'. Her reasoning that this is because Alaska is blessed with natural resources ripe for exploitation harks back to the founding myth of the United States as an 'empty' but bountiful continent and connects up neatly with Erwin Jaffe's (1997) hypothesis that this founding myth gave rise to a funda-mentally antipolitical mindset. In Bannon's documentary, Palin, as governor, is repeatedly referred to as the 'CEO of Alaska', further lending her a pro-business and antipolitics veneer. To top this off, the documentary uses stock footage of unidentifiable men smoking cigars in poorly lit rooms to evoke the Alaskan legislators whose budget proposals Palin vetoes point by point.

Bannon's involvement in the spinning of Palin's narrative and his subsequent central role in the Trump campaign strongly suggests a sense of intentional continuity between the two. Palin debuted a particular brand of conservative Republican populism, based on Reaganesque arguments about the problem-atic nature of government, but performed in a more partisan, more controver-sial, and thus even more overtly entertainment-focused style. In 2016, as trust continued to be at historic lows,[6] the Trump campaign continued to pursue and make use of this populist appeal. In this particular style of populism, the decent people of the American heartland, and their socially and economically conservative values, are pitted against coastal elites, particularly the political elites of Washington, who are framed as corrupt and out of touch with the con-cerns of 'real America'. The style is performed by apparently unselfconscious and charismatic performers and makes effective use of the fragmented media environment, where its controversially articulated messages are amplified by supporters and vilified by opponents. One of the speechwriters connected with the 2008 Republican presidential campaign explicitly identified this sense of continuity between the McCain–Palin and Trump campaigns:

> I think she paved the road for him. In the sense that, this populist stuff . . . she was the first politician to really, really hit on that populist

theme and she rode that all the way through the 2012 elections . . . She kind of crafted this spot for herself as an outsider, you know, telling everybody these elites in Washington don't know what the heck they're doing. . . . [T]his is like always the phrase people use, right: out here in 'real America' – because the Beltway is not real America – out here, outside the bubble, out here in 'real America', we know that . . . you should have control over your kids' education, that . . . you can spend your money better than Washington can . . . that rhetorical style is classic with her, and . . . she did that through Instagram and Facebook posts and, you know, she had this very robust social media platform post-the 2008 campaign. She used it, and she would use these speeches, and there was an aspect of theatre and performance to her. I think to her detriment, so a lot of us kind of cringed when she did it, but it got her a lot of attention. It's very much the showmanship of Trump. . . . [A]ll of that . . . this populist theme, the language, the vernacular, the really casual language . . . that's what makes Trump pop on the debate stage with all of the primary candidates . . . they're all, . . . 'well, I passed a bill last year', and Trump's like, 'this is garbage'. . . . [W]hereas people are used to . . . a certain decorum, and there are places you don't go, because that's a low blow . . . Trump observes none of that.

In the speechwriter's view, Palin's performance in 2008 primed the electorate for Trump's performance in 2016 and made obvious the potential of the populist style. However, the speechwriter noted that there were some areas in which Palin observed standards of decorum that Trump flaunted. For instance, the speechwriter stated that Palin would not have attacked an opposing candidate's spouse or children, while Trump went after Ted Cruz's wife (by, for example, sharing an unflattering picture of her that compared her with his wife Melania, a former model, on Twitter) during the Republican presidential primary. Although the connection between Trump and Palin may also have been brought up by this speechwriter to lend greater significance to their work on Palin's losing campaign, Bannon's connection to both campaigns makes it compelling to see the 2008 and 2016 campaigns as existing on a populist slope, such that an intensified version of the style that was debuted in 2008 was performed in 2016. This populist style was both shaped by specific individuals – that is, Palin and Trump, and their own sense of or lack of boundaries – and incentivised by a disenchanted, distrusting electorate and a media environment that courts controversy as entertainment and therefore seems to demand ever more strikingly outrageous performances.

However, in 2008, Palin's performance of folksy populism was greeted with a tremendous backlash: after initially being seen as a central asset for the campaign for her ability to inspire and generate enthusiasm, Palin eventually came to be seen as its major liability. John McCain's advanced age and questionable health were much discussed in terms of his fitness for the presidency, at least in part because his prospective vice president was widely judged to be lacking the experience and expertise to replace him. Palin, as the first female Republican vice presidential candidate, did not fit readily into the mould offered by past vice presidents, let alone the ideal of embodied masculinity that underlies performances of the presidency itself, especially at a time when no major party had ever fielded a female presidential candidate. The anxiety about the possibility of McCain not surviving his potential presidency was particularly acute, not merely because Palin was seen to be inexperienced and difficult to control by party functionaries, but also, simply, because she was a woman. A speechwriter affiliated with the McCain–Palin campaign noted that it appeared during the campaign that Palin's public self-presentation could be easily superseded in the public imagination by parodies of Palin, most notably comedian Tina Fey's impersonation of Palin on the variety television show *Saturday Night Live* (2008):

> [Palin] had made a point, which is actually true, that . . . in Alaska, . . . there is Little Diomede Island and Big Diomede Island and one is over in Russia and one is in the United States. So, if you're standing on land in Alaska, you can actually see Russia. Tina Fey was on TV and it becomes this whole, 'I can see Russia from my house'. To this day, everyone believes Sarah Palin actually said that. And that's amazing, because . . . that sketch that Tina Fey did become in a lot of ways the reality of Sarah Palin. It's a manufactured reality . . . But you can see there's like a kernel of authenticity that's sitting at the bottom of that, but it . . . has . . . consumed what people thought of her. . . . [I]t didn't become humour, in a way it stood in for people's real experience of Sarah Palin.

While Fey's portrayal of Palin might have cemented the impression, it is also plausible that Palin's populist-style performances, which relied on simplistic arguments (like the division of the US political space into the 'real America' and 'fake' coastal elites), in combination with her gender, opened her up to a level of criticism and ridicule that effectively derailed the McCain–Palin campaign to a degree never experienced by the Trump campaign. *The Undefeated* opens with a montage of the frequently below the belt, highly personal, and openly misogynistic attacks against Palin by liberals during the 2008 presidential campaign. Bannon's documentary takes an openly hagiographic stance towards Palin, and Bannon remains a hard-right political operator intent on spreading propagandistic messages that vilify the political left. Nevertheless, institutional misogyny in the United States is far from limited to the political right, and the montage demonstrates this. The above-quoted McCain–Palin campaign speechwriter put the discrepancy in the reception Palin and Trump experienced in stark terms: in the end, the speechwriter said, '[Trump] becomes President of the United States and [Palin] becomes one of the most maligned politicians in the United States'.

The progression from Palin, whose populist style came to be seen as a liability, to Trump, who managed to win the presidency with even more sharply pointed populist performances, can also be seen in terms of Palin preparing the public by moving the style of mainstream political discourse to be more colloquial, outspoken, and willing to court controversy. This reading is alluded to in the speechwriter's assertion, quoted above, that Palin 'paved the road' for Trump as well as the argument that there is a populist slope towards ever more distinctly populist-style performances. I argued in Chapter 2 that presidents tend to present contrasts to their predecessors; in that sense, Trump's off-the-cuff style contrasts with Obama's more studied, professorial approach. Nevertheless, Obama, too, ran as a Washington outsider whilst Palin's more flamboyant presentation of her own political outsiderness created a platform for Trump in 2016. In 2016, the next presidential race that did not feature an incumbent candidate, Donald Trump, with Bannon's help, pursued a populist strategy that strongly resembled Palin's but featured even more sharply pointed performances in the 'bad manners' style, such as the oft-repeated promise to 'drain the swamp' of Washington, DC, or the assertion, repeated in all three presidential debates, that Hillary Clinton had had nothing but 'bad experience' as a member of the Washington elite (Donald J. Trump for President 2016b).

On the other side of the political aisle, the prospect of following a two-term president from the same party put Hillary Clinton in a similarly difficult position in 2016 to that in which John McCain found himself eight years earlier. Clinton also faced a significant primary challenge from the previously independent senator and self-declared democratic socialist Bernie Sanders,[7] who campaigned against 'the billionaire class', highlighting issues of income and wealth inequality (Foran 2016; Friends of Bernie Sanders, n.d.; Sanders 2015). Sanders's supporters launched petitions against the use of so-called superdelegates, who do not have to vote in line with the popular vote and were seen to overwhelmingly support Hillary Clinton's presidential run (Strauss 2016; see also Wolf 2017). Meanwhile, in contrast to Sanders's populist style, the Clinton campaign appeared to struggle with Clinton's status as a long-time member of the political establishment. Leaked emails of Clinton's campaign manager John Podesta illustrate the Clinton campaign's struggle with her status as 'part of the system', stressing the need to show that Clinton knows 'how much has to change' (Greenberg 2016; see also Schwerin 2015).[8] As such, it is clear that Clinton's insider status as a former First Lady, Senator, and Secretary of State was, far from being straightforwardly seen as providing her with valuable experience and expertise, instead interpreted as a potential liability. Furthermore, the press reported that Clinton's policy platform was being dragged to the left owing to the popular groundswell behind the Sanders campaign (Beinart 2016; Stein 2016), but despite this apparent leftward drag, between 6 and 12 per cent of people who voted for Sanders in the 2016 Democratic primary then chose to vote for Donald Trump in the general election (Sides 2017). Democratic turnout in 2016 was a also significant problem: 7 per cent of people who voted for Obama in 2012 did not vote at all in 2016 whilst a further 3 per cent voted for a third-party candidate (McElwee et al. 2018). Like the existence of so-called Obama–Trump voters, the data showing that 6–12 per cent of Sanders primary voters ended up voting for Trump in the general election speaks to the appeal of populism as a marker of identification along a simple line of binary division.

Focusing on political distrust and on the ways in which populism speaks to and makes use of widespread distrust cannot explain the 2008 and 2016 elections in their entirety. For instance, the currency of distrust in elites alone does not explain the issue of institutional misogyny, as experienced by female candidates like Sarah Palin and Hillary Clinton, who were less able to cultivate the perception of legitimacy for not fitting into the association of power, authority, and representative capacity with male embodiment. It likewise does not capture the extent to which Trump's presidency presented a white supremacist backlash against Obama's eight years in office. Nevertheless, political distrust became an explicit focal point in the 2008 and 2016 election campaigns, to the extent that all candidates involved in these elections had to specify their position vis-à-vis the political establishment. Outsiders, particularly Palin and Trump, who courted controversy in visible ways, and Obama, who could credibly present himself as 'the living embodiment of change', were able to galvanise the public in ways their opponents could not. These political actors and the specific ways in which they chose to perform within a political and media environment that incentivises an entertainment-like, controversy-courting style of performance have shaped the development of US presidential performance in the early twenty-first century.

In contrast to Palin and Trump, it would be difficult to accuse Obama and Sanders of displaying the 'bad manners' Moffitt argues are a constitutive element of the populist style (2016, 57–63).[9] Obama's tearful speech in January 2016, with which this book opens, as well as his many talk show appearances throughout his presidency are striking instances of political performance. Similarly, in one of the most remarkable moments of the Democratic primary debates, Bernie Sanders was invited to comment on the controversy surrounding Hillary Clinton's use of a private email server whilst Secretary of State. Sanders declined to turn this into an issue, stating instead, 'let me say something that may not be great politics. But I think the secretary is right, and that is that the American people are sick and tired of hearing about your damn e-mails' (CNN 2015). In stepping away from the expected 'politician-like' behaviour by choosing not to attack his opponent and instead say something that was ostensibly 'not great politics', Sanders strikingly broke through. The moment was widely reported on and, to some, demonstrated that Sanders was 'no ordinary politician' (e.g. Hanley 2016). In light of these examples of Democratic politicians, 'bad manners' is too one-sidedly negative a characterisation of the populist style. Instead, in addition to the binary division of the political space into 'the people' and 'the elite' and the evocation of a sense of crisis, populists should be seen to display a tendency to surprise in public performance through striking, media-savvy displays of 'bad manners', emotional displays, or even shows of solidarity.[10] In any case, as public trust in government has remained historically low, anti-establishmentarian performances by presidents and presidential candidates have become increasingly dominant and persuasive, to the point that they were being consistently deployed in 2008 and 2016. Presidential populism thus appears as a distinct phenomenon that, in a heavily mediatised and fragmented political environment where distrust is pervasive, exerts a force independent of policy or political ideology.

Like the far-reaching changes Woodrow Wilson initiated, which continue to shape our understanding of effective oratorical leadership by US presidents, this chapter has shown that presidential populism cannot be said to be purely the result of a media and political environment that develops to incentivise certain kinds of performance over others. Changes initiated by successful individual performers should be seen to dovetail with the development of the environment that makes specific performance styles more likely to succeed. While certain kinds of performances, like shape-shifting performances that adapt not just the politician's views on policy but also their public persona to any given setting, might be deemed to be normatively or ethically desirable, they cannot take hold in an environment that tends, through highly antagonistic and polarised coverage, instead to demand performances that convey rigorous consistency along essentialist lines. In the late twentieth and early twenty-first centuries, changes in media technology like the digitalisation, multiplication, and fragmentation of media outlets, alongside other environmental factors like the de-democratisation of the United States and the increasing polarisation of political views, do not necessarily force political performers to stress the theme of outsiderness, to perform in the populist style, and to eschew shape-shifting or actively deny ever having shape-shifted. But these developments have made consistent, populist-style performances that stress a political performer's outsiderness more effective and hence more appealing to politician-performers.

Performances of outsiderness have persisted in US presidential politics and have coexisted with historically low levels of public trust in government since the Nixon era. In these circumstances, populist-style performances and performances of anti-establishmentarian outsiderness are privileged, as they play to an antagonistic, fragmented, and oversaturated media environment and speak directly to an electorate that is already distrustful towards democratic institutions and officeholders and is continually being encouraged to keep on distrusting.

1. For detailed exploration of the transition from party democracy to audience democracy, see Manin (1997, 206–36).
2. For detailed explorations of Carter's status as an outsider in the White House, see Cannon (1991, 101–2); Glad (2009); Hess (2002).
3. The percentages given in the main text refer to figures that extrapolate to the entire US electorate. Just for Republicans, trust in government during the Reagan, George W. Bush, and, briefly, the George H. W. Bush presidencies did surpass the 50 per cent mark, though still not returning to pre-Watergate levels (Pew Research Center 2014b).
4. George H. W. Bush's presidency will not be discussed at length and can instead be considered as an extension of the Reagan presidency, since Bush had served as Reagan's vice president for two terms and the two shared some speechwriting staffers. Bush's presidential campaign stressed his involvement in the Reagan White House and his commitment to continuing Reagan's legacy (Knott, n.d.). Bush's inaugural address (1989) reaffirmed this by opening with the statement that Reagan had 'earned a lasting place in our hearts and in our history'.
5. In light of the affirmation of Democrats' belief in government, it should be noted that highs in Democrats' trust in government have actually tended to be lower than highs in Republicans' trust. During the Democratic presidencies of Carter, Clinton, and Obama, Democrats' trust in government was higher than Republicans', but not as high as Republicans' trust during the Reagan, Bush 41, and Bush 43 presidencies (Pew Research Center 2017).
6. During the Obama presidency, public trust in government never exceeded 30 per cent at all, and usually hovered around the high teens and low twenties, with even figures of trust among Democrats fluctuating between the teens and thirties (Pew Research Center 2017).
7. Sanders is the longest-serving independent in the history of Congress, having served first in the House of Representatives as a Member from Vermont (1991–2007) and then as Senator from Vermont (2007–present), but he caucuses with the Democrats.
8. With due regard to research ethics, it should be noted here that the sources Greenberg 2016 and Schwerin 2015 are part of the large volume of emails stolen from the private Gmail account of John Podesta, the chairman of the Clinton–Kaine 2016 presidential campaign, by individuals with ties to Russia and the Russian government intent on interfering with the 2016 US presidential election. The emails were subsequently released by WikiLeaks in October and November 2016. On 13 July 2018, Special Counsel for the US Department of Justice Robert S. Mueller III indicted twelve Russian individuals on charges of conspiracy, aggravated identity theft, and money laundering in relation to the theft and release of these emails. In the indictment, WikiLeaks is referred to as 'Organisation 1' (Mueller 2018; Mazzetti and Benner 2018). The citing of these now publicly available emails here in no way indicates that the author condones the actions of the hackers or of WikiLeaks in releasing the illegally obtained material.
9. This is so because Obama's and Sanders's performances do not usually include swearing, over-the-top claims or political incorrectness, but Moffitt does allow that

'bad manners' could extend to 'presenting oneself in more "colourful" ways than we usually expect from politicians', which would make it a far broader category (Moffitt 2016, 59–61).

10. My point that the inclusion of 'bad manners' as a constitutive element of the populist style more accurately describes right-wing rather than left-wing populism echoes criticism that has been levelled at recent conceptualisations of populism more broadly: Bécquer Seguín shows that current theorists of populism tend to focus on populism only as a 'threat', missing nuances in different manifestations of the phenomenon (2017, 294). Seguín particularly argues that while scholars like Jan-Werner Müller (2014) and Nadia Urbanati (2014) purport to write about both left-wing and right-wing populism, their theories are in fact more applicable to instances of right-wing populism. A similar dynamic seems to me to be at work in Moffitt's definition of the populist style as including displays of 'bad manners' rather than something more encompassing, like media-savvy displays that catch the public's attention through a variety of techniques, including displays of emotion, solidarity, and controversial rhetoric.

AFTERWORD: THE PENDULUM AND THE SLOPE

This book has characterised the performances of US presidents as following two trajectories. On the one hand, there is a need for balance and contrast in how presidents perform: between each president and their predecessor, between the abstract quality of presidentiality and personal authenticity, between associations with signifiers of high and low social classes, and so on. As such, presidential performances can be said to follow the trajectory of a pendulum in presenting resonant contrasts between one president and the next in a way that serves as a corrective and, ideally, staves off the public's fatigue. In this view, Clinton's approachability served as a contrast to Bush Senior's aloofness, whereas Bush Junior's Christian morality served as a contrast to Clinton's perceived moral failings. Obama's elegant rhetoric contrasted with George W. Bush's lack of rhetorical skill, whilst Trump's rudeness and his racist emphasis on White supremacy clashed strikingly with Obama's considered and professorial style as well as forcefully speaking back against the demise of what had been a White patriarchal monopoly on the highest political office. The election of Joe Biden in 2020 can be seen as a corrective to Trump, insofar as Biden is a career politician, Obama's vice president, and a known champion of reaching across the political aisle who is elected to follow the most populist president in recent memory.

But the pendulum is not the only, nor arguably currently the most important, trajectory of presidential performance. Performances of mainstreamed populism are incentivised in a fragmented and hostile media environment and so common that audiences, fatigued and angered by politics as usual, have come to expect them. I argued in the Introduction that the Capitol Riot of 6 January 2021 epitomised the politics of distrust with which this book is concerned. The riot is perhaps the most striking consequence to date of a 'populist slope' in presidential rhetoric leading to ever more forceful renunciations of Washington's politics as usual, but not the only one. The 12th American Values Survey found that '[a]fter the violent attacks on the U.S. Capitol on January 6, 2021, the prospect of political violence threatening a peaceful transfer of power has become more than an abstract question' (PRRI 2021a, 37). It shows that nearly one in five Americans, and 30 per cent of Republicans, agree with the statement 'Because things have gotten so far off track, true American patriots may have to resort to violence in order to save our country' (37). Agreement with the statement also correlates with the consumption of right-wing news sources like Fox News. In this context, Biden's election might not spell not the demise of the populist slope so much as an interlude within it. At the time of writing this, Republican Representative Liz Cheney of Wyoming, a vocal critic of Trump and Vice Chair of and one of only two Republicans on the House Select Committee investigating the 6 January attack on the Capitol, is in the headlines for having, as expected, resoundingly lost her primary to Harriet Hageman, a candidate endorsed by Trump (Martin 2022).

President Biden avoided references to his predecessor, apparently in an effort to let his own presidency speak for itself, rather than being defined entirely in relation to Trump throughout his first year in office (Zeleny, Collins, and Liptak 2022). But on 6 January 2022, the first anniversary of the riot, Biden gave a forceful speech that broke with his previous treatment of his predecessor by reckoning directly with Trump's legacy and attacking the former president, though Biden still did not utter his name:

> My fellow Americans, in life, there's truth and, tragically, there are lies – lies conceived and spread for profit and power. We must be absolutely clear about what is true and what is a lie. And here is the truth: The former president of the United States of America has created and spread a web of lies about the 2020 election. He's done so because he values power over principle, because he sees his own interests as more important than his country's interests and America's interests, and because his bruised ego matters more to him than our democracy or our Constitution.

Biden went on to assert that Americans were living 'at an inflection point in history', where they had to decide between democracy and autocracy, and he reaffirmed the importance of the so-called Founding Fathers who had 'set in motion an experiment [in democracy] that changed the world' as well as the 'sacred' status of the Capitol and the Constitution. Clearly, Biden did not consider the threat of Donald Trump and his continued influence within the Republican Party to have been finally vanquished, nor did he any longer seek to project the impression that he did, though the equation of Trump with autocratic leadership is likely to fall on deaf ears among Trump's followers, who associate Biden and not Trump with governmental overreach.

The representative relationship between the people and their political representatives is built, particularly at the national and most acutely at the presidential level, through politicians' public performances and audiences' suspension of disbelief in these. In the Introduction I asked whether, in light of the split and sensationalised media coverage of Barack Obama's tearful speech on gun control in January 2016, it is ever possible for political audiences to really know their political representatives. In many ways this book has argued for why that is not the case: the theatrical nature of the representative relationship does not allow for the revelation of the performer's 'authentic', unselfconscious self, though audiences aspire to gain insight into this self and performers seek to project a sense of their own authenticity. The book also asked why it seems that we keep talking about the authenticity of politicians, if even the authenticity of something as wetly material as the tears on Obama's cheeks can be hotly debated in a fragmented and polarised media environment. Persistent attempts to verify or falsify politicians' authenticity are a by-product of the highly personalised nature of political media coverage in the contemporary moment and they arise from the theatrical nature of political performance itself. To suspend one's disbelief is a temporary, unstable, irresolute sort of move, but real-world consequences, not least the coming together of a nation as an imagined community that is more than the sum of its disparate parts, are at stake in vesting one's trust in a political representative. Because of this, the theatrical – and therefore abstracting and fictionalising – construction of a politician's public self is something that people, even political speechwriters whose work involves them in this construction, are simultaneously aware of and keen to disavow in favour of the assertion of a more stable, essential kind of identity. The fact that political performance, as a practice that is both performative and theatrical, sits at the heart of representative democracy means that distrust is likewise an ineradicable potential within the system.

This book's epigraph showcases Woodrow Wilson's belief that politics cannot be reduced to rational deliberation. His speech *Leaders of Men*, first held as a commencement address at the University of Tennessee in 1890, explores why '[s]ome of the gifts and qualities which most commend the literary man to success would inevitably doom the would-be leader to failure', and concludes that persuasion and information exist independently of each other (1952, 29). Twenty-three years before he was elected president himself, Wilson argued that politics has to 'ravish', to be shouted over, to speak to the sensibilities of audiences here and now. In Wilson's view, political leaders had to be persuasive actors capable of rousing their audiences. This book has endeavoured to explain why this should be so. Performance lies at the heart of representative democracy, which means that political audiences have to suspend their disbelief in the public performances of would-be political representatives to vest their trust in them. But the possibility of distrust inheres within the system as an essential accompaniment of its reliance on trust and the suspension of disbelief. Matters of trust and distrust, belief and disbelief are not detached and wholly rational. They demand an investment of something greater than mere fact – an emotionally resonant connection or the excitement Michael Tomko sees as necessary for the ongoing suspension of disbelief (2016, 4). Norms of political performance may proscribe rousing performances, but, ultimately, speeches work best when they are not mere explanations and enumerations of policy. Those speeches that are, like most State of the Union addresses, tend to be forgettable. The speechwriters interviewed for this research overwhelmingly conveyed that they felt speeches work best when they tell stories, create emotional resonances between speaker and audience(s), and communicate a clear and consistent sense of who the speaker is, their 'authentic' character and beliefs.

Representative politics relies on emotion as much as or more so than rational fact, and audiences of presidential performances have to vest their trust in performances they witness (mostly) from a distance. Distrust is the inextricable complement to, or the flipside of, the system's reliance on trust and to the suspension of disbelief asked of political audiences. Often, of course, the willingness to suspend disbelief depends on the ideological alignment between speaker and audience, particularly in a highly polarised environment like the contemporary United States. However, declining levels of trust in politics and the success of populists who purport to infiltrate institutional politics from the outside indicate that audiences across the political spectrum are increasingly distrustful of politicians and political institutions. Outsider appeals performed by politicians along populist lines harness the inherent potential for distrust within the system and amplify it. It is difficult to escape the linkage between Wilson's strong rhetorical leadership and his positioning of himself against the 'great Government' in his inauguration speech, for instance (see Chapter 2). Wilson's claim that 'the evil has come with the good' (1913b) is an assertion of the inherent goodness of democratic government as well as its present need for purification. Declarations like this make clear that distrust, once recognised as an inherent property of representative democracy, becomes a resource to be exploited.

While positing that distrust inheres within a political system whose core is performance-based, this book has moved towards an enquiry of what is at stake as this distrust has increasingly become an explicit focal point around which the theatre of politics revolves, as in performances of the US presidency in the contemporary moment. Performances of populism simplify the political space into a binary opposition between the president plus the people on the one side and the political establishment, 'Washington', Congress, or 'the system' on the other. As legitimacy takes on properties of the zero-sum game, increasingly disparate requirements emerge for effective campaigning and effective governing. While presidential rhetoric may make it look as though the people plus president and the legislature have diametrically opposed interests, in practice the president needs the legislature's support to govern effectively, and vice versa. Legitimacy is increasingly seen as lying outside of political institutions in a way that can obscure differences between political parties and encourage the view that the institutions of democratic government are beyond redemption. While politicians who paint themselves as institutional outsiders may do so for their own political gain, the pervasiveness of anti-establishment discourse may condition audiences to discount the legitimacy of the political system altogether and to disregard matters of policy, such that disruptions of the system by self-styled outsiders are perceived as the main possibility for political action that can be aspired to be enacted through the institutions of democratic government. This is the possibility that Biden's speech on the anniversary of the Capitol Riot sees realised and positions itself against.

Presidential populism is paradoxical in that it leads the only political actor cast to represent the entirety of the nation to undermine the very system they are tasked with sustaining. Performances of outsiderness by US presidents and other politicians appropriate vocabularies of more grassroots-based forms of opposition, resistance, and protest. They are strange hybrids of critical and sovereign grammars of politics and performance, for while conventional performances of the presidency are paradigmatic examples of sovereign grammars insofar as they 'seek[] to constitute the citizen body as one', populist performances at once seek to address a generalised 'people' and to undermine trust and amplify distrust in the nation's elected representatives, thus attempting to rile up the citizen body into a mode of opposition or resistance against government institutions (Saward 2015, 218). While populism addresses its audiences as 'the people', rather than addressing their more distinctive or particular capacities, it reduces 'the people's' identity to their opposition to the establishment. In a sense presidential populism does evoke 'the citizen body as one', but in doing so it empties out more particularised or distinctive views in favour of a simple binary opposition between people and establishment whilst arguing or implying that those who wield sovereign power are fatally compromised. This is problematic not because there are no legitimate grievances with the federal government – far from it – but because what is purported to be a stance of protest increasingly becomes a diffuse and default mode of mainstream politics. The expression of critical grammars is being appropriated by those seeking election and those in government, rather than used primarily by those seeking recognition for justified grievances. Protest begins to look ubiquitous.

However, presidential performances, by nature, prop up, rather than subvert, the social and political order. They may propose that the system is in need of drastic reform or that its personnel needs replacing – as in Trump's promise to 'drain the swamp'. When they are successful, they may transform political parties, as Trump's influence on the Republican Party has shown (Cobb 2021; Hopkins and Noel 2021). For all their bluster, though, presidential performances in the populist style still tend to imply the continuation of the extant system, not revolutionary change. White House Chief Strategist Stephen

Bannon, who had more serious ambitions for the 'deconstruction of the administrative state' (Rucker and Costa 2017) than Trump himself, was dismissed after a mere eight months in the White House. The Trump presidency's failure to 'drain the swamp' (Friedersdorf 2017) illustrates that the primary goal of his populism was not to subvert the system but to get elected and remain in office,[1] even by attempting to block the peaceful transfer of power. The Capitol Riot indicates that presidential populism can serve to redirect oppositional feelings towards the absolute support of a particular president or presidential candidate, particularly because its appeal depends on the vague claim of being one of the people rather than on specific policies or political programmes (Sorensen 2021, 148). More often than not it above all serves to bolster the performer's public profile while rendering compromise and collaboration increasingly unattractive and untenable.

If presidential populism works to rearrange perceptions of legitimacy and intensify audiences' distrust of government without actually working to bring about the radical change it purports to want to bring about, the danger is that it might also warp people's perceptions of what it means to materially resist, oppose, or protest against sovereign power by reducing opposition to the support of whatever populists are promising to purify the tainted system. Distrust, ultimately, is a feature of the system, an always-present potential within it. But distrust is a feature that can become a bug.

Note

1. It should be noted, however, that Trump's attempt to remain in power was opportunistic rather than premeditated, at least insofar as he had never expected to win in 2016 (Wolff 2018).

BIBLIOGRAPHY

Abbott, Lyman. 1909. 'A Review of President Roosevelt's Administration: IV – Its Influence on Patriotism and Public Service.' *The Outlook*, 27 February, 430, 433–4.

ABC News/*Washington Post*. 2010. 'ABC News/*Washington Post* Poll: Birthers.' Conducted 22–5 April 2010. https://abcnews.go.com/images/PollingUnit/Birthers_new.pdf

Abramowitz, Alan I. 2006. 'Disconnected, or Joined at the Hip?' In *Characteristics and Causes of America's Polarized Politics*, edited by Pietro S. Nivola and David W. Brady, 72–85. Baltimore: Brookings Institution Press.

Abramowitz, Alan I. 2010a. *The Disappearing Center: Engaged Citizens, Polarization, and American Democracy*. New Haven, CT: Yale University Press.

Abramowitz, Alan I. 2010b. 'Transformation and Polarization: The 2008 Presidential Election and the New American Electorate.' *Electoral Studies* 29: 594–603. https://doi.org/10.1016/j.electstud.2010.04.006

Abramowitz, Alan I., and Steven W. Webster. 2018. 'Negative Partisanship: Why Americans Dislike Parties but Behave Like Rabid Partisans.' *Advances in Political Psychology* 39 (S1): 119–35. https://doi.org/10.1111/pops.12479

Adams, John. 1797. Inaugural Address. The Avalon Project at Yale Law School. Accessed 19 July 2018. http://avalon.law.yale.edu/18th_century/adams.asp

Adiseshiah, Siân. 2016. 'Spectatorship and the New (Critical) Sincerity: The Case of Forced Entertainment's *Tomorrow's Parties*.' *Journal of Contemporary Drama in English* 4 (1): 180–95. https://doi.org/10.1515/jcde-2016-0014

Ahmed, Sara. 2012. *On Being Included: Racism and Diversity in Institutional Life*. Durham, NC: Duke University Press.

Alexander, Jeffrey C. 2006. 'Cultural Pragmatics: Social Performance between Ritual and Strategy.' In *Social Performance: Symbolic Action, Cultural Pragmatics, and Ritual*, edited by Jeffrey C. Alexander, Bernhard Giesen, and Jason L. Mast, 29–90. Cambridge: Cambridge University Press.

Alexander, Jeffrey C. 2010. *The Performance of Politics: Obama's Victory and the Democratic Struggle for Power*. Oxford: Oxford University Press.

Alexander, Jeffrey C. 2011. *Performance and Power*. Cambridge: Polity Press.

Alexander, Jeffrey C. 2016. 'Performance and Politics: President Obama's Dramatic Reelection in 2012.' *TDR: The Drama Review* 60 (4): 130–42. https://doi.org/10.1162/DRAM_a_00600

Alexander, Jeffrey C., and Bernadette N. Jaworsky. 2014. *Obama Power*. Cambridge: Polity Press.

Alston, Adam. 2016. *Beyond Immersive Theatre*. London: Palgrave Macmillan.

Anderson, Benedict. [1983] 2006. *Imagined Communities: Reflections on the Origins and Spread of Nationalism*. Rev. ed. London: Verso.

'Andrea Tantaros: Obama Used "Raw Onion" to Cry for Gun Victims.' 2016. YouTube video 3:19, posted by 'Raw Story', 5 January. https://www.youtube.com/watch?v=CIvAgKrq4tc

Anker, Elisabeth. 2014. *Orgies of Feeling: Melodrama and the Politics of Freedom*. Durham, NC: Duke University Press.

Arditi, Benjamin. 2007. *Politics on the Edges of Liberalism: Difference, Populism, Revolution, Agitation*. Edinburgh: Edinburgh University Press.

Aronowitz, Stanley. 1992. *The Politics of Identity: Class, Culture, Social Movements*. New York: Routledge.

Austin, J. L. 1962. *How to Do Things with Words: The William James Lectures Delivered at Harvard University in 1955*. Oxford: Oxford University Press.

Baldassarri, Delia, and Andrew Gelman. 2008. 'Partisans without Constraint: Political Polarization and Trends in American Public Opinion.' *American Journal of Sociology* 114 (2): 408–46. https://doi.org/10.1086/590649

Bannon, Steve, writer and director. 2011. *The Undefeated*. Los Angeles: Victory Film Group.

Barish, Jonas. 1981. *The Antitheatrical Prejudice*. Berkeley: University of California Press.

Barker, Rodney. 2001. *Legitimating Identities*. Cambridge: Cambridge University Press.

Barthes, Roland. 1977. 'The Death of the Author.' In *Image Music Text*, 142–8. London: Fontana Press.

Beard, Mary. 2017. *Women & Power*. London: Profile Books.

Beinart, Peter. 2016. 'Why America Is Moving Left.' *The Atlantic*, January/February. https://www.theatlantic.com/magazine/archive/2016/01/why-america-is-moving-left/419112/

Berisha, Visar, Shuai Wang, Amy LaCross, and Julie Liss. 2015. 'Tracking Discourse Complexity Preceding Alzheimer's Disease Diagnosis: A Case Study Comparing the Press Conferences of Presidents Ronald Reagan and George Herbert Walker Bush.' *Journal of Alzheimer's Disease* 45 (3): 959–63. https://doi.org/10.3233/JAD-142763

Bertsou, Eri. 2019. 'Rethinking Political Distrust.' *European Political Science Review* 11 (2): 213–30. https://doi.org/10.1017/S1755773919000080

Biden, Joseph R. 2022. Remarks by President Biden to Mark One Year since the January 6th Deadly Assault on the U.S. Capitol. The White House, 6 January. https://www.whitehouse.gov/briefing-room/speeches-remarks/2022/01/06/remarks-by-president-biden-to-mark-one-year-since-the-january-6th-deadly-assault-on-the-u-s-capitol/

Billig, Michael. 1995. *Banal Nationalism*. London: Sage.

Bimes, Terri. 2007. 'The Practical Origins of the Rhetorical Presidency.' *Critical Review* 19 (2/3): 241–56. https://doi.org/10.1080/08913810701766124

Bimes, Terri, and Stephen Skowronek. 1998. 'Woodrow Wilson's Critique of Popular Leadership: Reassessing the Modern–Traditional Divide in Presidential History.' In *Speaking to the People: The Rhetorical Presidency in Historical Perspective*, edited by Richard J. Ellis, 134–61. Amherst: University of Massachusetts Press.

Blake, John. 2016. 'Why Obama's Tears Are so Revolutionary.' CNN, 9 January. https://edition.cnn.com/2016/01/08/politics/obama-gun-control-tears/index.html

Bleeker, Maaike. 2009. 'Being Angela Merkel.' In *The Rhetoric of Sincerity*, edited by Ernst van Alphen, Mieke Bal, and Carel Smith, 247–62. Stanford, CA: Stanford University Press.

Blumenthal, Sidney. 1980. *The Permanent Campaign: Inside the World of Elite Political Operatives*. Boston: Beacon Press.

Bonikowski, Bart, and Noam Gidron. 2016. 'The Populist Style in American Politics: Presidential Campaign Discourse, 1952–1996.' *Social Forces* 94 (4): 1593–621. https://doi.org/10.1093/sf/sov120

Bornstein, Harold N. 2015. Letter 'To Whom My Concern' [*sic*], 4 December. https://web.archive.org/web/20160211094937/https://www.donaldjtrump.com/images/uploads/Health_Record.pdf

Bottici, Chiara. 2007. *A Philosophy of Political Myth*. Cambridge: Cambridge University Press.

Bottici, Chiara, and Benoît Challand. 2013. *Imagining Europe: Myth, Memory and Identity*. Cambridge: Cambridge University Press.

Bottoms, Stephen, and Brenda Hollweg, eds. 2015. 'Electoral Theatre.' Special issue, *Contemporary Theatre Review* 25 (2): 159–294. https://www.tandfonline.com/toc/gctr20/25/2

Bourdieu, Pierre. 1991. *Language and Symbolic Power*. Edited by John B. Thompson. Translated by Gino Raymond and Matthew Adamson. Cambridge: Polity Press.

Brams, Steven J., and Morton D. Davis. 2017. *Encyclopaedia Britannica*, s.v. 'Game Theory', 2 November. https://www.britannica.com/science/game-theory/

Brito Vieira, Monica. 2020. 'Representing Silence in Politics.' *American Political Science Review* 114 (4): 976–88. https://doi.org/10.1017/S000305542000043X

Brown, Gwen. 1997. 'Deliberation and Its Discontents: H. Ross Perot's Antipolitical Populism.' In *The End of Politics? Explorations into Modern Antipolitics*, edited by Andreas Schedler, 115–58. Basingstoke: Macmillan.

Brown, Wendy. 2015. *Undoing the Demos: Neoliberalism's Stealth Revolution.* New York: Zone Books.

Bruck, Connie. 1994. 'Hillary the Pol.' *New Yorker*, 23 May. https://www.newyorker.com/magazine/1994/05/30/hillary-the-pol

Burden, Barry C., Yoshikuni Ono, and Masahiro Yamada. 2017. 'Reassessing Public Support for a Female President.' *Journal of Politics* 79 (3): 1073–8. https://doi.org/10.1086/691799

Burns, Elizabeth. 1972. *Theatricality: A Study of Convention in the Theatre and in Social Life*. London: Longman.

Bush, George H. W. 1989. Inaugural Address. The Avalon Project at Yale Law School. Accessed 25 August 2018. http://avalon.law.yale.edu/20th_century/bush.asp

Butler, Judith. 1997. *Excitable Speech: A Politics of the Performative*. New York: Routledge.

Butler, Judith. [1993] 2011. *Bodies That Matter: On the Discursive Limits of 'Sex'*. Abingdon: Routledge.

Cannon, Lou. 1991. *President Reagan: Role of a Lifetime*. London and New York: Simon & Schuster.

Capra, Frank, director. 1939. *Mr. Smith Goes to Washington*. Los Angeles: Columbia Pictures Corporation.

Carlson, Marvin. 2002. 'The Resistance to Theatricality.' *SubStance* 31 (2/3): 238–50. https://doi.org/10.1353/sub.2002.0022

Carlson, Marvin. 2003. *The Haunted Stage: The Theatre as Memory Machine*. Ann Arbor: University of Michigan Press.

Carlyle, Thomas. 1837. *The French Revolution: A History*. London: James Frazer.

Christensen, Jen. 2016. 'Trump and the Small Hands Equals Small Manhood Myth, or Reality?' CNN, 8 March. https://edition.cnn.com/2016/03/08/health/trump-small-hands-penis/index.html

Cillizza, Chris. 2016. 'President Obama Cried in Public Today. That's a Good Thing.' *Washington Post*, 5 January. https://www.washingtonpost.com/news/the-fix/wp/2016/01/05/why-men-should-cry-more-in-public

Cillizza, Chris, and Aaron Blake. 2016. 'Donald Trump's Interview with Dr. Oz Was Just as Amazingly Strange as We Thought It Would Be.' *Washington Post*, 15 September. https://www.washingtonpost.com/news/the-fix/wp/2016/09/15/donald-trumps-visit-with-dr-oz-was-just-as-amazing-as-you-though-it-would-be/

Clinton, Hillary. 1992a. Comments on cookies and tea. YouTube video 00:15, posted by 'Gadfly Productions', 15 July 2016. https://www.youtube.com/watch?v=y_mm_OwcX8k

Clinton, Hillary. 1992b. Hillary Clinton's first *60 Minutes* interview. YouTube video 10:24, posted by '60 Minutes', 28 August 2019. https://www.youtube.com/watch?v=-UqKNgrwK8E

Clinton, William Jefferson. 1992. Clinton Appearance on Arsenio Hall Show, 3 June. C-SPAN video 4:38. Accessed 14 September 2018. https://www.c-span.org/video/?26472-1/clinton-appearance-arsenio-hall-show

Clinton, William Jefferson. 1993. Inaugural Address. YouTube video 14:37, posted by 'C-SPAN', 14 January 2009. https://www.youtube.com/watch?v=2SWjIPwm954

Clinton, William Jefferson. 1994a. Remarks at the White House Correspondents' Dinner, 23 April. The American Presidency Project. http://www.presidency.ucsb.edu/ws/index.php?pid=50040

Clinton, William Jefferson. 1994b. Interview on MTV's 'Enough is Enough' Forum, 19 April. The American Presidency Project. http://www.presidency.ucsb.edu/ws/?pid=49995

CNN. 2015. 'CNN Democratic Debate – Full Transcript.' CNN Press Room, 13 October. http://cnnpressroom.blogs.cnn.com/2015/10/13/cnn-democratic-debate-full-transcript/

CNN/ORC International. 2015. Poll conducted September 4–8, 2015. http://i2.cdn.turner.com/cnn/2015/images/09/12/iranpoll.pdf

Cobb, Jelani. 2021. 'What Is Happening to the Republicans?' *New Yorker*, 8 March. https://www.newyorker.com/magazine/2021/03/15/what-is-happening-to-the-republicans

Cohen, Jon. 2011. 'Poll: Numbers of "Birthers" Plummets.' *Washington Post*, 5 May. https://www.washingtonpost.com/blogs/behind-the-numbers/post/number-of-birthers-plummets/2011/05/04/AF3GAZxF_blog.html

Cohn, Nate. 2017. 'The Obama-Trump Voters Are Real. Here's What They Think.' *New York Times*, 15 August. https://www.nytimes.com/2017/08/15/upshot/the-obama-trump-voters-are-real-heres-what-they-think.html

Coleman, Stephen. 2013. *How Voters Feel*. Cambridge: Cambridge University Press.

Coleridge, Samuel Taylor. 1834. *Biographia Literaria or, Biographical Sketches of My Literary Life and Opinions*. New York: Leavitt, Lord.

'Congress and the Public.' n.d. Gallup. Accessed 16 July 2018. https://news.gallup.com/poll/1600/congress-public.aspx

Conroy, Colette. 2010. *Theatre & the Body*. Basingstoke: Palgrave Macmillan.

Cook, Corey. 2002. 'The Contemporary Presidency: The Permanence of the "Permanent Campaign": George W. Bush's Public Presidency.' *Presidential Studies Quarterly* 32 (4): 753–64. https://doi.org/10.1111/j.0360-4918.2002.00246.x

Coole, Diana. 2007. 'Experiencing Discourse: Corporeal Communicators and the Embodiment of Power.' *British Journal of Politics and Inter-*

national Relations 9 (3): 413–33. https://doi.org/10.1111%2Fj.1467-856x.2006.00258.x

Cooper, John Milton, Jr. 2011. *Woodrow Wilson: A Biography*. New York: Vintage.

Critchley, Simon. 1993. 'Re-tracing the Political.' In *The Political Subject of Violence*, edited by David Campbell and Michael Dillon, 73–93. Manchester: Manchester University Press.

Davis, Tracy. 2003. 'Theatricality and Civil Society.' In *Theatricality*, edited by Tracy Davis and Thomas Postlewait, 127–55. Cambridge: Cambridge University Press.

Davis, Tracy. 2005. 'Do You Believe in Fairies? The Hiss of Dramatic License.' *Theatre Journal* 57 (1): 57–81. https://doi.org/10.1353/tj.2005.0007

Derrida, Jacques. 1988. 'Signature Event Context.' In *Limited Inc*, edited by Gerald Graff. Translated by Jeffrey Mehlman and Samuel Weber, 1–23. Evanston, IL: Northwestern University Press.

de Wilde, Pieter. 2013. 'Representative Claims Analysis: Theory Meets Method.' *Journal of European Public Policy* 20 (2): 278–94. https://doi.org/10.1080/13501763.2013.746128

Diamond, Elin. 1996. 'Introduction.' In *Performance and Cultural Politics*, edited by Elin Diamond, 1–12. Abingdon: Routledge.

Dickerson, John. 2008. 'Palin's Campaign vs. McCain's.' *Slate*, 20 October. http://www.slate.com/articles/news_and_politics/politics/2008/10/palins_campaign_vs_mccains.html

Dickerson, John. 2020. *The Hardest Job in the World: The American Presidency*. New York: Random House.

Diderot, Denis. 1883. *The Paradox of Acting*. Translated by Walter Herries Pollock. London: Chatto & Windus.

DiMaggio, Paul, John Evans, and Bethany Bryson. 1996. 'Have American's [*sic*] Social Attitudes Become More Polarized?' *American Journal of Sociology* 102 (3): 690–755. https://doi.org/10.1086/230995

Disch, Lisa. 2011. 'Toward a Mobilization Conception of Democratic Representation.' *American Political Science Review* 105 (1): 100–14. https://doi.org/10.1017/S0003055410000602

Disch, Lisa. 2015. 'The "Constructivist Turn" in Democratic Representation: A Normative Dead-End?' *Constellations* 22 (4): 487–99. https://doi.org/10.1111/1467-8675.12201

Dolar, Mladen. 2006. *A Voice and Nothing More*. Cambridge, MA: MIT Press.

Donald J. Trump for President. 2016a. *Donald Trump's Contract with the American Voter*. Election campaign flyer. https://assets.donaldjtrump.com/_landings/contract/O-TRU-102316-Contractv02.pdf

Donald J. Trump for President. 2016b. 'Trump Pledges to Drain the Swamp and Impose Congressional Term Limits.' Press release, 18 October. https://

web.archive.org/web/20170429203039/https://www.donaldjtrump.com/press-releases/trump-pledges-to-drain-the-swamp

Douglass, Robin. 2013. 'Rousseau's Critique of Representative Sovereignty: Principled or Pragmatic?' *American Journal of Political Science* 57 (3): 735–47. https://doi.org/10.1111/ajps.12020

Encyclopaedia Britannica. 2015. *Encyclopaedia Britannica*, s.v. 'Positive-Sum Game', 15 December. https://www.britannica.com/topic/positive-sum-game

Edkins, Jenny, and Adrian Kear, eds. 2013. *International Politics and Performance*. Abingdon: Routledge.

Ellis, Richard J. 1998. 'Introduction.' In *Speaking to the People: The Rhetorical Presidency in Historical Perspective*, edited by Richard J. Ellis, 1–15. Amherst: University of Massachusetts Press.

Ellis, Richard J. 2008. *Presidential Travel: The Journey from George Washington to George W. Bush*. Lawrence: University of Kansas Press.

Ellis, Richard J., and Alexis Walker. 2007. 'Policy Speech in the Nineteenth Century Rhetorical Presidency: The Case of Zachary Taylor.' *Presidential Studies Quarterly* 37: 248–70. https://doi.org/10.1111/j.1741-5705.2007.02596.x

Elmer, Greg, Ganaele Langlois, and Fenwick McKelvey. 2012. *The Permanent Campaign: New Media, New Politics*. New York: Peter Lang.

Fahey, Mark. 2015. 'When Did Republicans Become Obsessed with Reagan?' CNBC, 5 October. https://www.cnbc.com/2015/10/05/when-did-republicans-become-obsessed-with-reagan.html

Farley, Robert. 2016. 'Sorting Out Obama's Gun Proposal.' FactCheck, 8 January. https://www.factcheck.org/2016/01/sorting-out-obamas-gun-proposal/

Féral, Josette. 2002. 'Theatricality: The Specificity of Theatrical Language.' *SubStance* 31 (2/3): 94–108. https://doi.org/10.1353/sub.2002.0026

Fiorina, Morris. 2017. *Unstable Majorities: Polarization, Party Sorting, and Political Stalemate*. Stanford, CA: Hoover Institution Press.

Fiorina, Morris, Samuel J. Abrams, and Jeremy Pope. 2011. *Culture War? The Myth of a Polarized America*. 3rd ed. Boston: Longman.

Fiorina, Morris, and Matthew Levendusky. 2006a. 'Disconnected: The Political Class versus the People.' In *Characteristics and Causes of America's Polarized Politics*, edited by Pietro S. Nivola and David W. Brady, 49–71. Baltimore: Brookings Institution Press.

Fiorina, Morris, and Matthew Levendusky. 2006b. 'Rejoinder.' In *Characteristics and Causes of America's Polarized Politics*, edited by Pietro S. Nivola and David W. Brady, 95–111. Baltimore: Brookings Institution Press.

Fischer-Lichte, Erika. 1998. 'Inszenierung und Theatralität.' In *Inszenierungsgesellschaft: Ein einführendes Handbuch*, edited by Herbert Willems and Martin Jurga, 81–90. Opladen: Westdeutscher Verlag.

Fischer-Lichte, Erika. 2009. 'Theatricality: A Key Concept in Theatre and Cultural Studies.' *Theatre Research International* 20 (2): 85–9. https://doi.org/10.1017/S0307883300008294

Fliegelman, Jay. 1993. *Declaring Independence: Jefferson, Natural Language, and the Culture of Performance.* Stanford, CA: Stanford University Press.

Foley, Michael. 2007. 'President Bush, the War on Terror, and the Populist Tradition.' *International Politics* 44: 666–91. https://doi.org/10.1057/palgrave.ip.8800211

Foran, Claire. 2016. 'Bernie Sanders's Big Money.' *The Atlantic*, 1 March. https://www.theatlantic.com/politics/archive/2016/03/bernie-sanders-fundraising/471648/

Foucault, Michel. 2003. *'Society Must Be Defended': Lectures at the Collège de France 1975–76.* Edited by Mauro Bertani and Alessandro Fontana. Translated by David Macey. New York: Picador.

Fralin, Richard. 1978. 'The Evolution of Rousseau's View of Representative Government.' *Political Theory* 6 (4): 517–36. https://doi.org/10.1177/009059177800600405

Fried, Michael. [1967] 1998. 'Art and Objecthood.' In *Art and Objecthood: Essays and Reviews*, 148–72. Chicago: University of Chicago Press.

Friedersdorf, Conor. 2017. 'Trump Has Filled, Not Drained, the Swamp.' *The Atlantic*, 21 September. https://www.theatlantic.com/politics/archive/2017/09/meet-the-new-swamp/540540/

Friedland, Paul Andrew. 1995. 'Representation and Revolution: The Theatricality of Politics and the Politics of Theatre in France, 1789–1794.' PhD diss., University of California at Berkeley, 1995. Microfilm.

Friedland, Paul Andrew. 2002. *Political Actors: Representative Bodies and Theatricality in the Age of the French Revolution.* Ithaca, NY: Cornell University Press.

Friends of Bernie Sanders. n.d. 'Income and Wealth Inequality.' Berniesanders.com. Accessed 18 July 2018. https://berniesanders.com/issues/income-and-wealth-inequality/

Frieze, James. 2015. 'Beyond the Zero-Sum Game: Participation and the Optics of Opting.' *Contemporary Theatre Review* 25 (2): 216–29. https://doi.org/10.1080/10486801.2015.1020714

Fuchs, Elinor. 1996. *The Death of Character: Perspectives on Theater after Modernism.* Bloomington: Indiana University Press.

'Gallup Daily: Obama Job Approval.' n.d. Gallup. Accessed 19 July 2018. https://news.gallup.com/poll/113980/gallup-daily-obama-job-approval.aspx

Gamm, Gerald, and Renée M. Smith. 1998. 'Presidents, Parties, and the Public: Evolving Patterns of Interaction, 1877–1929.' In *Speaking to the People: The Rhetorical Presidency in Historical Perspective*, edited by Richard J. Ellis, 87–111. Amherst: University of Massachusetts Press.

Glad, Betty. 1980. *Jimmy Carter: In Search of the Great White House*. New York and London: W. W. Norton.

Glad, Betty. 2009. *An Outsider in the White House: Jimmy Carter, His Advisors, and the Making of American Foreign Policy*. Ithaca, NY, and London: Cornell University Press.

Gluhovic, Milija, Silvija Jestrovic, Shirin M. Rai, and Michael Saward. 2021. 'Introduction.' In *The Oxford Handbook of Politics and Performance*, edited by Shirin M. Rai, Milija Gluhovic, Silvija Jestrovic, and Michael Saward, 1–25. Oxford: Oxford University Press.

Givens, Ann. 2017. 'Chicago's Murder Rate Is Typical for a Major Metropolis – Until Fatal Shootings Are Factored In.' *The Trace*, 4 January. https://www.thetrace.org/2017/01/chicago-murder-rate-fatal-shootings/

Goffman, Erving. [1956] 1990. *The Presentation of Self in Everyday Life*. London: Penguin.

Goktepe, Katherine. 2018. '"Sometimes I Mean Things so Much I Have to Act": Theatrical Acting and Democracy.' *Constellations* 25 (3): 373–87. https://doi.org/10.1111/1467-8675.12350

Goodman, Paul. 2002. 'Current and Future Uses of Gold in Electronics.' *Gold Bulletin* 35 (1): 21–6. https://doi.org/10.1007/BF03214833

Green, Donald, Bradley Palmquist, and Eric Schickler. 2004. *Partisan Hearts and Minds: Political Parties and the Social Identities of Voters*. New Haven, CT, and London: Yale University Press.

Greenberg, Stan. 2016. 'Money.' E-mail Message to John Podesta, sent 4 February at 20:09. WikiLeaks. https://www.wikileaks.com/podesta-emails/emailid/17478

Greenstein, Fred I. 1988. 'Nine Presidents: In Search of a Modern Presidency.' In *Leadership in the Modern Presidency*, edited by Fred I. Greenstein, 296–352. Cambridge, MA: Harvard University Press.

Groenendyk, Eric W. 2013. *Competing Motives in the Partisan Mind: How Loyalty and Responsiveness Shape Party Identification and Democracy*. Oxford: Oxford University Press.

Groenendyk, Eric W. 2018. 'Competing Motives in a Polarized Electorate: Political Responsiveness, Identity Defensiveness, and the Rise of Partisan Antipathy.' *Advances in Political Psychology* 39 (S1): 159–71. https://doi.org/10.1111/pops.12481

Habermas, Jürgen. 1989. *The Structural Transformation of the Public Sphere: An Inquiry into a Category of Bourgeois Life*. Cambridge, MA: MIT Press.

Habermas, Jürgen. [1992] 1996. *Between Facts and Norms*. Cambridge: Polity Press.

Hamilton, Alexander, James Madison, and John Jay. [1788] 2003. *The Federalist Papers*. Edited by Clinton Rossiter. Introduction and notes by Charles R. Kessler. New York: Signet Classics.

Hanley, Brian. 2016. 'Bernie Sanders Won the Debate, and Perhaps the Election, When He Defended Hillary Clinton.' *HuffPost*, 13 October 2015, updated 13 October 2016. https://www.huffingtonpost.com/brian-hanley/bernie-sanders-won-the-de_1_b_8290498.html

Harvey, David. 2005. *A Brief History of Neoliberalism*. Oxford: Oxford University Press.

Heilemann, John, and Mark Halperin. 2010. *Race of a Lifetime*. London: Penguin.

Hemberger, Suzette. 1994. Review of *Declaring Independence: Jefferson, Natural Language, and the Culture of Performance* by Jay Fliegelman. *American Political Science Review* 88 (2): 471–2. https://doi.org/10.2307/2944743

Herbert, Jon. 2016. 'The Oratory of Bill Clinton.' In *Democratic Orators from JFK to Barack Obama*, edited by Andrew Crines, David S. Moon, and Robert Lehrman, 117–47. Basingstoke: Palgrave Macmillan.

Hess, Richard. 2002. 'Jimmy Carter's "Outsider" Image: Rhetoric of the Carter Presidency.' In *The Image of the Outsider: Proceedings – 2002 Conference Society for the Interdisciplinary Study of Social Imagery*, edited by Will Wright and Steven Kaplan, 194–202. Pueblo: University of Southern Colorado.

Hetherington, Marc J. 2005. *Why Trust Matters: Declining Political Trust and the Demise of American Liberalism*. Princeton, NJ: Princeton University Press.

Hetherington, Marc J., and Thomas J. Rudolph. 2015. *Why Washington Won't Work: Polarization, Political Trust, and the Governing Crisis*. Chicago: University of Chicago Press.

Hetherington, Marc J., and Thomas J. Rudolph. 2018. 'Political Trust and Polarization'. In *The Oxford Handbook of Social and Political Trust*, edited by Eric M. Uslaner, 599–616. Oxford: Oxford University Press.

Hobbes, Thomas. [1651] 1985. *Leviathan*. Edited by C. B. Macpherson. London: Penguin Classics.

Hofstadter, Richard. [1964] 2008. 'The Paranoid Style in American Politics.' In *The Paranoid Style in American Politics and Other Essays*, 3–40. New York: Vintage.

Hooghe, Marc. 2018. 'Trust and Elections.' In *The Oxford Handbook of Social and Political Trust*, edited by Eric M. Uslaner, 617–32. Oxford: Oxford University Press.

Hopkins, Dan, and Hans Noel. 2021. 'How Trump Has Redefined Conservatism.' *FiveThirtyEight*, 24 June. https://fivethirtyeight.com/features/how-trump-has-redefined-conservatism/

Hopper, Nate. 2016. 'Why You Shouldn't Laugh at Donald Trump's Hands.' *TIME*, 20 October. http://time.com/4539487/donald-trump-small-hands/

Hughey, Matthew W. 2012. 'Show Me Your Papers! Obama's Birth and the Whiteness of Belonging.' *Qualitative Sociology* 35 (2): 163–81. https://doi.org/10.1007/s11133-012-9224-6

Inchley, Maggie. 2015. *Voice and New Writing, 1997–2007: Articulating the Demos*. Basingstoke: Palgrave Macmillan.

Intelligence Squared. 2016. 'Yes, He Can! No, He Couldn't. Obama Is a Failed President.' YouTube video 46:46, posted by 'iqsquared', 5 July. https://www.youtube.com/watch?v=i-UdS0h4-gs

Ipsos. 2019. 'Nominating Woman or Minority Come Second to Nominating Candidate Who Can Beat Trump.' Press release for poll conducted 10–11 June 2019. https://www.ipsos.com/sites/default/files/ct/news/documents/2019-06/daily-beast-gender-topline-2019-06-17-v2.pdf

Ipsos/Reuters. 2021. 'Ipsos/Reuters Poll: The Big Lie.' Poll conducted 17–19 May 2021. https://www.ipsos.com/sites/default/files/ct/news/documents/2021-05/Ipsos%20Reuters%20Topline%20Write%20up-%20The%20Big%20Lie%20-%2017%20May%20thru%2019%20May%202021.pdf

Jacobson, Gary C. 2012. 'The Electoral Origins of Polarized Politics: Evidence from the 2010 Cooperative Congressional Election Study.' *American Behavioral Scientist* 56 (12): 1612–30. https://doi.org/10.1177%2F0002764212463352

Jaffe, Erwin. 1997. 'Our Own Invisible Hand: Antipolitics as an American Given.' In *The End of Politics? Explorations into Modern Antipolitics*, edited by Andreas Schedler, 57–90. Basingstoke: Macmillan.

Jefferson, Thomas. 1801. First Inaugural Address. The Avalon Project at Yale Law School. Accessed 19 July 2018. http://avalon.law.yale.edu/19th_century/jefinau1.asp

Kalisch, Eleonore. 2000. 'Aspekte einer Begriffs- und Problemgeschichte von Authentizität und Darstellung.' In *Inszenierung von Authentizität*, edited by Erika Fischer-Lichte and Isabel Pflug, 31–44. Tübingen: Francke.

Kantorowicz, Ernst. 1957. *The King's Two Bodies: A Study in Medieval Political Theology*. Princeton, NJ: Princeton University Press.

Kennedy, John F. 1961. Inaugural Address. The Avalon Project at Yale Law School. Accessed 11 September 2018. http://avalon.law.yale.edu/20th_century/kennedy.asp

Kingston, Paul W. 2000. *The Classless Society*. Stanford, CA: Stanford University Press.

Knight, Peter. 2000. *Conspiracy Culture: From Kennedy to* The X-Files. London: Routledge.

Knott, Stephen. n.d. 'George H. W. Bush: Campaigns and Elections.' Miller Center at the University of Virginia. Accessed 14 September 2018. https://millercenter.org/president/bush/campaigns-and-elections

Kolokoltsov, Vassili N., and Oleg A. Malafeyev. 2010. *Understanding Game Theory: Introduction to the Analysis of Many Agent Systems with Competition and Cooperation.* Singapore and London: World Scientific.

Kraig, Robert Alexander. 2004. *Woodrow Wilson and the Lost World of the Oratorical Statesman.* College Station: Texas A&M University Press.

Kugler, Christine, and Ronald Kurt. 2000. 'Inszenierungsformen von Glaubwürdigkeit im Medium Fernsehen: Politiker zwischen Ästhetisierung und Alltagspragmatik.' In *Inszenierung von Authentizität*, edited by Erika Fischer-Lichte and Isabel Pflug, 149–62. Tübingen: Francke.

Kumar, Hari Stephen. 2013. '"I Was Born . . ." (No You Were Not!): Birtherism and Political Challenges to Personal Self-Authorizations.' *Qualitative Inquiry* 19 (8): 621–33. https://doi.org/10.1177%2F1077800413494351

Kuppers, Petra. 2003. *Disability and Contemporary Performance: Bodies on the Edge.* New York: Routledge.

Kushner, Tony. 2007. *Angels in America: Parts One and Two.* London: Nick Hern Books.

Laclau, Ernesto. 2005a. *On Populist Reason.* London: Verso.

Laclau, Ernesto. 2005b. 'Populism: What's in a Name?' In *Populism and the Mirror of Democracy*, edited by Francisco Panizza, 32–49. London: Verso.

Laracey, Mel. 1998. 'The Presidential Newspaper: The Forgotten Way of Going Public.' In *Speaking to the People: The Rhetorical Presidency in Historical Perspective*, edited by Richard J. Ellis, 66–86. Amherst: University of Massachusetts Press.

Lavender, Andy. 2016. *Performance in the Twenty-First Century: Theatres of Engagement.* Abingdon: Routledge.

Lefort, Claude. 1986. *The Political Forms of Modern Society: Bureaucracy, Democracy, Totalitarianism.* Edited by John B. Thompson. Cambridge, MA: MIT Press.

Lehmann, Hans-Thies. 2009. *Postdramatic Theatre.* Translated by Karen Jürs-Munby. London and New York: Routledge.

Lehrman, Robert A. 2010. *The Political Speechwriter's Companion: A Guide for Writers and Speakers.* Washington, DC: CQ Press.

Levin, Laura, and Barry Freeman. 2016. 'Performing Politicians: A CTR Wrecking Ball.' *Canadian Theatre Review* 166: 5–9. https://doi.org/10.3138/ctr.166.001

Levitov, Alex. 2016. 'Normative Legitimacy and the State.' *Oxford Handbooks Online.* https://doi.org/10.1093/oxfordhb/9780199935307.013.131

Listhaug, Ola, and Tor Georg Jakobsen. 2018. 'Foundations of Political Trust'. In *The Oxford Handbook of Social and Political Trust*, edited by Eric M. Uslaner, 559–78. Oxford: Oxford University Press.

Lutz, Tom. 1999. *Crying: The Natural and Cultural History of Tears.* New York: W. W. Norton.

McElwee, Sean, Jesse H. Rhodes, Brian F. Schaffner, and Bernard L. Fraga. 2018. 'The Missing Obama Millions.' *New York Times*, 10 March. www.nytimes.com/2018/03/10/opinion/sunday/obama-trump-voters-democrats.html

Major Cities Chiefs Association. 2018. *Violent Crime Survey – National Totals, Year End Comparison 1 January 1 to December 31, 2017 and 2016*, 28 February. https://www.majorcitieschiefs.com/pdf/news/mcca_violent_crime_report_2017_and_2016_year_end_update_copy1.pdf

Manderson, Lenore, and Susan Peake. 2005. 'Men in Motion: Disability and the Performance of Masculinity.' In *Bodies in Commotion: Disability & Performance*, edited by Carrie Sandahl and Philip Auslander, 230–42. Ann Arbor: University of Michigan Press.

Manin, Bernard. 1997. *The Principles of Representative Government*. Cambridge: Cambridge University Press.

Martin, Carol. 2013. *Theatre of the Real*. Basingstoke: Palgrave Macmillan.

Martin, Jonathan. 2022. 'Liz Cheney Is Defeated by Trump-Backed Harriet Hageman in Wyoming.' *New York Times*, 16 August. https://www.nytimes.com/2022/08/16/us/politics/harriet-hageman-liz-cheney-wyoming.html

Martin, Jonathan, and Amy Chozick. 2016. 'Hillary Clinton's Doctor Says Pneumonia Led to Abrupt Exit from 9/11 Event.' *New York Times*, 11 September. https://www.nytimes.com/2016/09/12/us/politics/hillary-clinton-campaign-pneumonia.html

Martinich, Al P. 2016. 'Authorization and Representation in Hobbes's *Leviathan*.' In *The Oxford Handbook of Hobbes*, edited by Al P. Martinich and Kinch Hoekstra, 315–38. Oxford: Oxford University Press.

Mason, Jennifer. 2002. *Qualitative Researching*. 2nd ed. London: Sage.

Mast, Jason L. 2012. *The Performative Presidency: Crisis and Resurrection during the Clinton Years*. Cambridge: Cambridge University Press.

Mazzetti, Mark, and Katie Benner. 2018. '12 Russian Agents Indicted in Mueller Investigation.' *New York Times*, 13 July. https://www.nytimes.com/2018/07/13/us/politics/mueller-indictment-russian-intelligence-hacking.html

Meko, Tim, Denise Lu, and Lazaro Gamio. 2017. 'How Trump Won the Presidency with Razor-Thin Margins in Swing States.' *Washington Post*, 11 November. https://www.washingtonpost.com/graphics/politics/2016-election/swing-state-margins/

Merida, Kevin. 1998. 'It's Come To This: A Nickname That's Proven Hard to Slip.' *Washington Post*, 20 December. https://www.washingtonpost.com/wp-srv/politics/special/clinton/stories/slick122098.htm

Milkis, Sidney M. 1998. 'Franklin D. Roosevelt, Progressivism, and the Limits of Popular Leadership.' In *Speaking to the People: The Rhetorical*

Presidency in Historical Perspective, edited by Richard J. Ellis, 182–210. Amherst: University of Massachusetts Press.

Mirabile, Francesca. 2016. 'Chicago Isn't Even Close to Being the Gun Violence Capital of the United States.' *The Trace*, 21 October. https://www.thetrace.org/2016/10/chicago-gun-violence-per-capita-rate/

Mirabile, Francesca, and Daniel Nass. 2018. 'What's the Homicide Capital of America? Murder Rates in U.S. Cities, Ranked.' *The Trace*, 28 April. https://www.thetrace.org/2018/04/highest-murder-rates-us-cities-list/

Moffitt, Benjamin. 2016. *The Global Rise of Populism: Performance, Political Style, and Representation*. Stanford, CA: Stanford University Press.

Moffitt, Benjamin. 2020. *Populism*. Cambridge: Polity Press.

Montanaro, Laura. 2012. 'The Democratic Legitimacy of Self-Appointed Representatives.' *The Journal of Politics* 74 (4): 1094–107. https://doi.org/10.1017/s0022381612000515

Montgomery, David. 2001. 'A Memorial for All of Us.' *Washington Post*, 11 January. https://www.washingtonpost.com/archive/politics/2001/01/11/a-memorial-for-all-of-us/

Moore, Michael, director and writer. 2004. *Fahrenheit 9/11*. New York: Dog Eat Dog Films.

Moore, Michael, director and writer. 2016. *Michael Moore in Trumpland*. New York: Dog Eat Dog Films.

Mouffe, Chantal. 2005a. 'The "End of Politics" and the Challenge of Right-Wing Populism.' In *Populism and the Mirror of Democracy*, edited by Francisco Panizza, 50–71. London: Verso.

Mouffe, Chantal. 2005b. *On the Political*. Abingdon: Routledge.

Mouffe, Chantal. 2013. *Agonistics: Thinking the World Politically*. London: Verso.

Mudde, Cas. 2004. 'The Populist Zeitgeist.' *Government and Opposition* 39 (3): 541–63. https://doi.org/10.1111/j.1477-7053.2004.00135.x

Mudde, Cas, and Cristóbal Rovira Kaltwasser. 2017. *Populism: A Very Short Introduction*. Oxford: Oxford University Press.

Mueller, Robert S., III. 2018. Indictment United States of America v. Netyshko et al., 13 July. https://www.justice.gov/file/1080281/download

Müller, Jan-Werner. 2014. '"The People Must Be Extracted from within the People": Reflections on Populism.' *Constellations* 21 (4): 483–93. https://doi.org/10.1111/1467-8675.12126

Murse, Tom. 2016. 'Executive Actions versus Executive Orders.' ThoughtCo, 26 March. https://www.thoughtco.com/executive-actions-versus-executive-orders-3367594

NCC Staff. 2013. 'Historic Re-election Pattern Doesn't Favor Democrats in 2016.' *Constitution Daily*, National Constitution Centre, 25 January. https://constitutioncenter.org/blog/historic-re-election-pattern-doesnt-favor-democrats-in-2016/

Neocleous, Mark. 2003. *Imagining the State*. Maidenhead: Open University Press.

Neuman, Scott. 2018. 'Doctor: Trump Dictated Letter Attesting to His "Extraordinary" Health.' NPR, 2 May. https://www.npr.org/sections/thetwo-way/2018/05/02/607638733/doctor-trump-dictated-letter-attesting-to-his-extraordinary-health

Neustadt, Richard E. [1960] 1990. *Presidential Power and the Modern Presidents: The Politics of Leadership from Roosevelt to Reagan*. New York: Free Press.

Newton, Kenneth, Dietlind Stolle, and Sonja Zmerli. 2018. 'Social and Political Trust.' In *The Oxford Handbook of Social and Political Trust*, edited by Eric M. Uslaner, 37–56. Oxford: Oxford University Press.

Nield, Sophie. 2000. 'National Identity and the Female Body.' In *Feminisms on Edge: Politics, Discourses and National Identities*, edited by Karen Atkinson, Sarah Oerton, and Gill Plain, 101–10. Cardiff: Cardiff Academic Press.

Nield, Sophie. 2006. 'On the Border as Theatrical Space: Appearance, Dislocation and the Production of the Refugee.' In *Contemporary Theatres in Europe: A Critical Companion*, edited by Joe Kelleher and Nicholas Ridout, 61–72. Abingdon: Routledge.

Nield, Sophie. 2010. 'On St Margaret Street.' *Law Text Culture* 14 (1): 3–11. https://ro.uow.edu.au/ltc/vol14/iss1/2/

Nield, Sophie. 2014. '"Speeches That Draw Tears": Theatricality, Commemoration and Social History.' *Social History* 39 (4): 547–56. https://doi.org/10.1080/03071022.2014.986293

Nield, Sophie. 2015. 'Tahrir Square EC4M: The Occupy Movement and the Dramaturgy of Public Order.' In *The Grammar of Politics and Performance*, edited by Shirin M. Rai and Janelle Reinelt, 121–33. London: Routledge.

Niou, Emerson M. S., and Peter C. Ordeshook. 2015. *Strategy and Politics: An Introduction to Game Theory*. New York: Routledge.

Not My President PAC. n.d. 'We Deserve Better.' Notmypresidentpac.com. Accessed 22 July 2018. https://notmypresidentpac.com/about-us/

Obama, Barack. 2007. 'Barack Obama's Presidential Announcement.' Speech in Springfield, Illinois, 10 February. YouTube video 22:03, uploaded by 'BarackObamadotcom', 10 December 2007. https://www.youtube.com/watch?v=gdJ7Ad15WCA

Obama, Barack. 2016. 'Remarks by the President on Common-Sense Gun Safety Reform.' The White House Office of the Press Secretary, 5 January. https://obamawhitehouse.archives.gov/the-press-office/2016/01/05/remarks-president-common-sense-gun-safety-reform. Video: 'Watch President Obama announce gun control initiatives at White House.' 2016. YouTube video

36:44, uploaded by 'PBS NewsHour', 5 January 2016. https://www.you-tube.com/watch?v=7IUVJCRfNS8

Olin, Laurie. 2012. 'The FDR Memorial Wheelchair Controversy and a "Taking Part" Workshop Experience.' *Landscape Journal* 31 (1/2): 183–97. https://www.jstor.org/stable/43332537

Olin Wright, Erik. 1985. *Classes*. London: Verso.

Pait, T. Glenn, and Justin T. Dowdy. 2017. 'John F. Kennedy's Back: Chronic Pain, Failed Surgeries, and the Story of Its Effects on His Life and Death.' *Journal of Neurosurgery: Spine* 27 (3): 247–55. http://thejns.org/doi/abs/10.3171/2017.2.SPINE17229

Palin, Sarah. 2009. *Going Rogue: An American Life*. New York: Harper-Collins.

Parry-Giles, Shawn J. 2001. 'Political Authenticity, Television News, and Hillary Rodham Clinton.' In *Politics, Discourse and American Society: New Agendas*, edited by Roderick P. Hart and Bartholomew H. Sparrow, 211–27. Lanham, MD: Rowman & Littlefield.

Parry-Giles, Shawn J. 2014. *Hillary Clinton in the News: Gender and Authenticity in American Politics*. Urbana: University of Illinois Press.

Parry-Giles, Shawn J., and Trevor Parry-Giles. 2002. *Constructing Clinton: Hyperreality & Presidential Image-Making in Postmodern Politics*. New York: Peter Lang.

Peetz, Julia. 2019. 'Semi-Structured Elite Interviews with U.S. Presidential Speechwriters in Interdisciplinary Research on Politics and Performance.' *SAGE Research Methods Cases*. https://dx.doi.org/10.4135/9781526477569

Peetz, Julia. 2021. 'The Counter-Theatricality of Right-Wing Populist Performance.' *Studies in Theatre and Performance* 41 (3): 247–62.

Peter, Fabienne. 2017. 'Political Legitimacy.' *Stanford Encyclopedia of Philosophy*, updated 24 April. https://plato.stanford.edu/entries/legitimacy/

Pew Research Center. 2014a. *Political Polarization in the American Public*, 12 June. http://assets.pewresearch.org/wp-content/uploads/sites/5/2014/06/6-12-2014-Political-Polarization-Release.pdf

Pew Research Center. 2014b. 'Public Trust in Government, 1958–2014', 13 November. http://www.people-press.org/2014/11/13/public-trust-in-government/

Pew Research Center. 2015. *Beyond Distrust: How Americans View Their Government*, 23 November. http://assets.pewresearch.org/wp-content/uploads/sites/5/2015/11/11-23-2015-Governance-release.pdf

Pew Research Center. 2017. 'Public Trust in Government, 1958–2017', 14 December. http://www.people-press.org/2017/12/14/public-trust-in-government-1958-2017/

Plato. [c. 380 BCE] 1968. *The Republic of Plato*. Translated by Allan Bloom. 2nd ed. New York: Basic Books.

Plato. 2008. *Laws*. Translated by Benjamin Jowett. Project Gutenberg, last updated 15 January 2013. https://www.gutenberg.org/files/1750/1750-h/1750-h. htm#link2H_4_0006

Politico Staff. 2016. 'Full Transcript: First 2016 Presidential Debate.' *Politico*, 27 September. https://www.politico.com/story/2016/09/full-transcript-first-2016-presidential-debate-228761

PolitiFact. n.d. 'The Obameter: Tracking Obama's Promises.' Accessed 14 September 2018. https://www.politifact.com/truth-o-meter/promises/obameter/

PRRI. 2021a. *Competing Visions of America: An Evolving Identity or a Culture Under Attack? Findings from the 2021 American Values Survey*. https:// www.prri.org/wp-content/uploads/2021/10/PRRI-Oct-2021-AVS.pdf

PRRI. 2021b. 'Dramatic Partisan Differences on Blame for January 6 Riots.' PRRI, 15 September. https://www.prri.org/research/dramatic-partisan-differences-on-blame-for-january-6-riots/

Pressman, Matthew. 2013. 'Ambivalent Accomplices: How the Press Handled FDR's Disability and How FDR Handled the Press.' *The Journal of the Historical Society* 13 (3): 325–59. https://doi.org/10.1111/jhis.12023

Puwar, Nirmal. 2021. 'The Force of the Somatic Norm: Women as Space Invaders in the UK Parliament'. In *The Oxford Handbook of Politics and Performance*, edited by Shirin M. Rai, Milija Gluhovic, Silvija Jestrovic, and Michael Saward, 251–64. Oxford: Oxford University Press.

Rai, Shirin M. 2014. 'Political Aesthetics of the Nation: Murals and Statues in the Indian Parliament.' *Interventions: International Journal of Postcolonial Studies* 16 (6): 898–915. https://doi.org/10.1080/1369801X.2014.882147

Rai, Shirin M. 2015. 'Political Performance: A Framework for Analysing Democratic Politics.' *Political Studies* 63 (5): 1179–97. https://doi. org/10.1111%2F1467-9248.12154

Rai, Shirin M., Milija Gluhovic, Silvija Jestrovic, and Michael Saward, eds. 2021. *The Oxford Handbook of Politics and Performance*. Oxford: Oxford University Press.

Rai, Shirin M., and Rachel E. Johnson, eds. 2014. *Democracy in Practice: Ceremony and Ritual in Parliament*. Basingstoke: Palgrave Macmillan.

Rai, Shirin M., and Janelle Reinelt, eds. 2015a. *The Grammar of Politics and Performance*. London: Routledge.

Rai, Shirin M., and Janelle Reinelt. 2015b. 'Introduction.' In *The Grammar of Politics and Performance*, edited by Shirin M. Rai and Janelle Reinelt, 1–18. London: Routledge.

Rai, Shirin M., and Carole Spary. 2019. *Performing Representation: Women Members in the Indian Parliament*. Oxford: Oxford University Press.

Rancière, Jacques. [2004] 2013. *The Politics of Aesthetics: The Distribution of the Sensible*. Edited and translated by Gabriel Rockhill. London and New York: Bloomsbury Academic.

Raphael, Timothy. 2009. *The President Electric: Ronald Reagan and the Politics of Performance*. Ann Arbor: University of Michigan Press.

Rawls, John. 1999. *A Theory of Justice*. Rev. ed. Cambridge, MA: The Belknap Press of Harvard University.

Reagan, Ronald. 1981. First Inaugural Address. The Avalon Project at Yale Law School. Accessed 22 July 2018. http://avalon.law.yale.edu/20th_century/reagan1.asp

Reinelt, Janelle. 2011. 'Rethinking the Public Sphere for a Global Age.' *Performance Research* 16 (2): 16–27. https:// doi.org/10.1080/13528165.2011.578724

Rhodan, Maya. 2016. 'Why Obama Cries Over Gun Control.' *TIME*, 5 January. http://time.com/4168680/barack-obama-gun-control-tears/

Ridout, Nicholas. 2008. 'Performance and Democracy.' In *The Cambridge Companion to Performance Studies*, edited by Tracy C. Davis, 11–22. Cambridge: Cambridge University Press.

Ridout, Nicholas. 2009. *Theatre & Ethics*. Basingstoke: Palgrave Macmillan.

Roach, Joseph. 1993. *The Player's Passion: Studies in the Science of Acting*. Ann Arbor: University of Michigan Press.

Roach, Joseph. 1996. *Cities of the Dead: Circum-Atlantic Performance*. New York: Columbia University Press.

Roach, Joseph. 2007. *It*. Ann Arbor: University of Michigan Press.

Rogers, Katie. 2017. 'All the President's Handshakes.' *New York Times*, 14 July. https://www.nytimes.com/2017/07/14/us/politics/president-donald-trump-handshakes.html

Rosenberg, Matthew, Nicholas Confessore, and Carole Cadwalladr. 2018. 'How Trump Consultants Exploited the Facebook Data of Millions.' *New York Times*, 17 March. https://www.nytimes.com/2018/03/17/politics/cambridge-analytica-trump-campaign.html

Ross, Lee, David Greene, and Pamela House. 1977. 'The "False Consensus Effect": An Egocentric Bias in Social Perception and Attribution Processes.' *Journal of Experimental Social Psychology* 13 (3): 279–301. https://doi.org/10.1016/0022-1031(77)90049-X

Rousseau, Jean-Jacques. [1762] 1923. *The Social Contract and Discourses*. Trans. G. D. H. Cole. London: J. M. Dent & Sons.

Rucker, Philip, and Robert Costa. 2017. 'Bannon Vows a Daily Fight for "Deconstruction of the Administrative State".' *Washington Post*, 23 February. https://www.washingtonpost.com/politics/top-wh-strategist-vows-a-daily-fight-for-deconstruction-of-the-administrative-state/2017/02/23/03f6b8da-f9ea-11e6-bf01-d47f8cf9b643_story.html

Ryan, Erica. 2013. '5 Memorable Nicknames and the Politicians They Stuck To', NPR, 20 July. http://www.npr.org/sections/itsallpolitics/2013/07/20/202961821/

Sachs, Jeffrey D. 2018. 'America's Health Crisis and the Easterlin Paradox.' In *World Happiness Report*, by John F. Helliwell, Richard Layard, and Jeffrey D. Sachs, 146–59. https://s3.amazonaws.com/happiness-report/2018/WHR_web.pdf

Sanders, Bernie. 2015. 'Democratic Socialism and Foreign Policy.' Speech at Georgetown University. YouTube video 1:07:39, uploaded by 'Bernie Sanders', 19 November 2015. https://www.youtube.com/watch?v=eQcmzGIKrzg

Santner, Eric. 2011. *The Royal Remains: The People's Two Bodies and the Endgames of Sovereignty*. Chicago: University of Chicago Press.

Saturday Night Live. 2008. 'Sarah Palin and Hillary Address the Nation.' Sketch performed by Tina Fey and Amy Poehler. Aired on NBC, 13 September. YouTube video 6:03, uploaded by 'Saturday Night Live', 23 September 2013. https://www.youtube.com/watch?v=vSOLz1YBFG0

Saward, Michael. 2006. 'The Representative Claim.' *Contemporary Political Theory* 5 (3): 297–318. https://doi.org/10.1057/palgrave.cpt.9300234

Saward, Michael. 2010. *The Representative Claim*. Oxford: Oxford University Press.

Saward, Michael. 2014. 'Shape-Shifting Representation.' *American Political Science Review* 108 (4): 723–36. https://doi.org/10.1017/S0003055414000471

Saward, Michael. 2015. 'Afterword: Sovereign and Critical Grammars.' In *The Grammar of Politics and Performance*, edited by Shirin M. Rai and Janelle Reinelt, 218–25. London: Routledge.

Schedler, Andreas, ed. 1997a. *The End of Politics? Explorations into Modern Antipolitics*. Basingstoke: Macmillan.

Schedler, Andreas. 1997b. 'Introduction: Antipolitics – Closing and Colonizing the Public Sphere.' In *The End of Politics? Explorations into Modern Antipolitics*, edited by Andreas Schedler, 1–20. Basingstoke: Macmillan.

Schlesinger, Robert. 2008. *White House Ghosts: Presidents and their Speechwriters*. New York: Simon & Schuster.

Schocket, Andrew M. 2015. *Fighting Over the Founders: How We Remember the American Revolution*. New York: New York University Press.

Schwerin, Dan. 2015. 'DRAFT: TPP Statement.' E-mail from 'speechdrafts@hillaryclinton.com' on behalf of Dan Schwerin to 'Speech Drafts', sent 6 October at 17:50. WikiLeaks. https://wikileaks.org/podesta-emails/emailid/17724

Seguín, Bécquer. 2017. 'Podemos and the Ideals of Populist Proceduralism.' *Arizona Journal of Hispanic Cultural Studies* 21: 287–309. https://doi.org/10.1353/hcs.2017.0014

Sennett, Richard. [1977] 1986. *The Fall of Public Man*. London: Faber & Faber.

Severs, Eline. 2012. 'Substantive Representation through a Claims-Making Lens: A Strategy for the Identification and Analysis of Substantive Claims.' *Representation* 48 (2): 169–81. https://doi.org/10.1080/00344893.2012.683491

Shapiro, Emily. 2016. 'The History behind the Donald Trump "Small Hands" Insult.' ABC News, 4 March. https://abcnews.go.com/Politics/history-donald-trump-small-hands-insult/story?id=37395515

Sides, John. 2017. 'Did Enough Bernie Sanders Supporters Vote for Trump to Cost Clinton the Election?' *Washington Post*, 24 August. https://www.washingtonpost.com/news/monkey-cage/wp/2017/08/24/did-enough-bernie-sanders-supporters-vote-for-trump-to-cost-clinton-the-election/

Simon, Abigail. 2018. 'People Are Angry President Trump Used This Word to Describe Undocumented Immigrants.' *Time*, 19 June. https://time.com/5316087/donald-trump-immigration-infest/

'Sister Marches.' n.d. Womensmarch.com. Accessed 22 July 2018. https://www.womensmarch.com/sisters

Skelley, Geoff. 2017. 'Just How Many Obama 2012–Trump 2016 Voters Were There?' *Rasmussen Reports*, 1 June. http://www.rasmussenreports.com/public_content/political_commentary/commentary_by_geoffrey_skelley/just_how_many_obama_2012_trump_2016_voters_were_there

Sorensen, Lone. 2021. *Populist Communication: Ideology, Performance, Mediation*. Cham: Palgrave Macmillan.

Specter, Michael. 2013. 'The Operator.' *New Yorker*, 27 January. https://www.newyorker.com/magazine/2013/02/04/the-operator

Stein, Jeff. 2016. 'Bernie Sanders Moved Democrats to the Left. The Platform Is Proof.' *Vox*, 25 July. https://www.vox.com/2016/7/25/12281022/the-democratic-party-platform

Stevenson, Peter W. 2016. 'A Brief History of the "Lock Her Up!" Chant by Trump Supporters against Clinton.' *Washington Post*, 22 November. https://www.washingtonpost.com/news/the-fix/wp/2016/11/22/a-brief-history-of-the-lock-her-up-chant-as-it-looks-like-trump-might-not-even-try/

Stid, Daniel. 1998. 'Rhetorical Leadership and "Common Counsel" in the Presidency of Woodrow Wilson.' In *Speaking to the People: The Rhetorical Presidency in Historical Perspective*, edited by Richard J. Ellis, 162–81. Amherst: University of Massachusetts Press.

Stout, David. 1997. 'Roosevelt Heirs Try to Calm Furor Over Memorial.' *The New York Times*, 12 April. https://www.nytimes.com/1997/04/12/us/roosevelt-heirs-try-to-calm-furor-over-memorial.html

Strauss, Daniel. 2016. 'Sanders Supporters Revolt against Superdelegates.' *Politico*, 14 February. https://www.politico.com/story/2016/02/bernie-sanders-superdelegates-democrats-219286

Strong, Robert A. n.d. 'Jimmy Carter: Campaigns and Elections.' Miller Center at the University of Virginia. Accessed 14 September 2018. https://miller-center.org/president/carter/campaigns-and-elections

Tabachnick, David Edgar. 2016. 'The Four Characteristics of Trumpism.' *The Hill*, 5 January. https://thehill.com/blogs/congress-blog/presidential-campaign/264746-the-four-characteristics-of-trumpism/

Testi, Arnaldo. 1995. 'The Gender of Reform Politics: Theodore Roosevelt and the Culture of Masculinity.' *The Journal of American History* 81 (4): 1509–33. https://doi.org/10.2307/2081647

Tomko, Michael. 2016. *Beyond the Willing Suspension of Disbelief: Poetic Faith from Coleridge to Tolkien*. London: Bloomsbury.

Tomlin, Liz. 2013. *Acts and Apparitions: Discourses on the Real in Performance Practice and Theory, 1990–2010*. Manchester: Manchester University Press.

Traister, Rebecca. 2016. 'Hillary Clinton vs. Herself.' *New York Magazine*, 30 May. http://nymag.com/daily/intelligencer/2016/05/hillary-clinton-candidacy.html

Trilling, Lionel. 1972. *Sincerity and Authenticity*. London: Oxford University Press.

Trump, Donald J. 2017. Inaugural Address. The White House, 20 January. https://www.whitehouse.gov/briefings-statements/the-inaugural-address/

Tulis, Jeffrey K. 1987. *The Rhetorical Presidency*. Princeton, NJ: Princeton University Press.

Tulis, Jeffrey K. 2007. 'The Rhetorical Presidency in Retrospect.' *Critical Review* 19 (2–3): 481–500. https://doi.org/10.1080/08913810701766397

Twenge, Jean M., W. Keith Campbell, and Nathan T. Carter. 2014. 'Declines in Trust in Others and Confidence in Institutions among American Adults and Late Adolescents, 1972–2012.' *Psychological Science* 25 (10): 1914–23. https://doi.org/10.1177%2F0956797614545133

Urbanati, Nadia. 2014. *Democracy Disfigured: Opinion, Truth, and the People*. Cambridge, MA: Harvard University Press.

Uslaner, Eric M. 2018. 'The Study of Trust.' In *The Oxford Handbook of Social and Political Trust*, edited by Eric M. Uslaner, 3–14. Oxford: Oxford University Press.

van Alphen, Ernst, and Mieke Bal. 2009. 'Introduction.' In *The Rhetoric of Sincerity*, edited by Ernst van Alphen, Mieke Bal, and Carel Smith, 1–16. Stanford, CA: Stanford University Press.

van der Meer, Tom W. G. 2017. 'Political Trust and the "Crisis of Democracy".' *Oxford Research Encyclopedia of Politics*. https://doi.org/10.1093/acrefore/9780190228637.013.77

Volokh, Eugene. 2017. 'Did President Trump Label the Constitution or House and Senate Rules as "Archaic"?' *Washington Post*, 1 May. https://www.washingtonpost.com/news/volokh-conspiracy/wp/2017/05/01/did-president-trump-label-the-constitution-or-house-and-senate-rules-as-archaic/

Wahl-Jorgensen, Karin. 2018a. *Emotions, Media and Politics*. Cambridge: Polity Press.

Wahl-Jorgensen, Karin. 2018b. 'Media Coverage of Shifting Emotional Regimes: Donald Trump's Angry Populism.' *Media, Culture & Society* 40 (5): 766–78. https://doi.org/10.1177%2F0163443718772190

Wahl-Jorgensen, Karin. 2018c. 'Toward a Typology of Mediated Anger: Routine Coverage of Protest and Political Emotion.' *International Journal of Communication* 12: 2071–87. http://ijoc.org/index.php/ijoc/article/view/6788/2348

Waldman, Michael. 2000. *POTUS Speaks: Finding the Words That Defined the Clinton Presidency*. New York: Simon & Schuster.

Wallace, David Foster. 2006. 'Up, Simba: Seven Days on the Trail of an Anticandidate.' In *Consider the Lobster and Other Essays*, 156–243. New York: Little, Brown.

Walton, Kendall L. 1980. 'Appreciating Fiction: Suspending Disbelief or Pretending Belief?' *Disposition* 5 (13/14): 1–18.

Warner, Michael. 1986. 'Franklin and the Letters of the Republic.' *Representations* 16: 110–30. https://doi.org/10.2307/2928515

Warner, Michael. 1990. *The Letters of the Republic: Publication and the Public Sphere in Eighteenth-Century America*. Cambridge, MA: Harvard University Press.

Warren, Mark. 2018. 'Trust and Democracy.' In *The Oxford Handbook of Social and Political Trust*, edited by Eric M. Uslaner, 75–94. Oxford: Oxford University Press.

Washington, George. 1789. First Inaugural Address. The Avalon Project at Yale Law School. Accessed 19 July 2018. http://avalon.law.yale.edu/18th_century/wash1.asp

Washington, George. 1793. Second Inaugural Address. The Avalon Project at Yale Law School. Accessed 19 July 2018. http://avalon.law.yale.edu/18th_century/wash2.asp

Washington, George. 1798. Letter from George Washington to William Fitzhugh, 5 August. Founders Online. Accessed 7 August 2018. https://founders.archives.gov/documents/Washington/06-02-02-0392

Washington Post. 1913a. 'Wilson to Read Message in House.' 7 April, 1, 4. Microfilm.

Washington Post. 1913b. 'Senators Frown on Wilson's Visit.' 8 April, 1, 3. Microfilm.

Washington Post. 1913c. 'Wilson Wins Congress in His Epochal Speech from House Rostrum.' 9 April, 1, 4. Microfilm.

Washington Post. 2011. Washington Post poll conducted 28 April–1 May. https://www.washingtonpost.com/wp-srv/politics/polls/postpoll_05052011.html

Weber, Max. 1978. *Economy and Society: An Outline of Interpretive Sociology*. Edited by Guenther Roth and Claus Wittich. Translated by Ephraim Fischoff et al. Berkeley: University of California Press.

Wilson, R. L. 1994. *Theodore Roosevelt, Outdoorsman*. Agoura, CA: Trophy Room Books.

Wilson, Woodrow. 1913a. First Annual Message. The American Presidency Project. Accessed 14 September 2018. http://www.presidency.ucsb.edu/ws/index.php?pid=29554

Wilson, Woodrow. 1913b. First Inaugural Address. The Avalon Project at Yale Law School. Accessed 19 July 2018. http://avalon.law.yale.edu/20th_century/wilson1.asp

Wilson, Woodrow. 1952. *Leaders of Men*. Edited and with introduction and notes by T. H. Vail Motter. Princeton, NJ: Princeton University Press.

Wolf, Z. Byron. 2017. 'Could Bernie Sanders Have Won a Primary That Wasn't "Rigged"? Um.' CNN, 4 November. https://edition.cnn.com/2017/11/04/politics/bernie-sanders-2016-election-donna-brazile/index.html

Wolff, Michael. 2018. *Fire and Fury: Inside the Trump White House*. New York: Henry Holt.

Wolin, Sheldon. 2008. *Democracy Incorporated: Managed Democracy and the Specter of Inverted Totalitarianism*. Princeton, NJ: Princeton University Press.

Zeleni, Jeff, Kaitlan Collins, and Kevin Liptak. 2022. 'Inside Biden's Fiery Speech and His Decision to Confront Trump's Danger Head On.' CNN, 7 January. https://edition.cnn.com/2022/01/06/politics/inside-biden-january-6-speech/index.html

INDEX

9/11, 5, 23, 93, 119, 152–4; *see also* war on terror

EU representative:
Easy Access System Europe
Mustamäe tee 50, 10621 Tallinn, Estonia
Gpsr.requests@easproject.com

www.ingramcontent.com/pod-product-compliance
Lightning Source LLC
Chambersburg PA
CBHW070845300326
41935CB00039B/1447